The Middle East from Empire to Sealed Identities

Lorenzo Kamel

EDINBURGH
University Press

Edinburgh University Press is one of the leading university presses in the UK. We publish academic books and journals in our selected subject areas across the humanities and social sciences, combining cutting-edge scholarship with high editorial and production values to produce academic works of lasting importance. For more information visit our website: edinburghuniversitypress.com

Edinburgh University Press Ltd
The Tun – Holyrood Road
12 (2f) Jackson's Entry
Edinburgh EH8 8PJ

First published in hardback by Edinburgh University Press 2019

Typeset in 11/15 Adobe Garamond Pro by
IDSUK (DataConnection) Ltd, and
printed and bound by CPI Group (UK) Ltd, Croydon, CR0 4YY

A CIP record for this book is available from the British Library

ISBN 978 1 4744 4894 9 (hardback)
ISBN 978 1 4744 4895 6 (paperback)
ISBN 978 1 4744 4896 3 (webready PDF)
ISBN 978 1 4744 4897 0 (epub)

Based on exhaustive work in numerous archives and in several languages, Lorenzo Kamel has produced what I think is one of the most definitive works on the transition from empire to nation-state. It is impressively ambitious and does what many major historians have been promising to do: to show how hard, Western conceptions of identity shaped and formed the thinking and decisions of statesmen and other political elites in the nineteenth and early twentieth centuries. It also deals with the penetration of hard national categories among the various peoples of the empire. It is an authoritative book and will be very widely consulted.

Nicholas Doumanis
Author of *Before the Nation* and Professor, School of Humanities and Languages, The University of New South Wales, Sydney

This book will make an important mark on the field. It shows the ways in which ethnic and other divisions were historically constructed in the Middle East under the influence of imperial powers. The work combines meticulous archival research in multiple languages with careful analysis of broader trends to map the transition from empire to homogenised nation-states. This ability to document with rich detail and at the same time be able to present the larger picture with great clarity is rare. The author pulls off the feat with great erudition.

Beth Baron
Distinguished Professor of History, The Graduate Center and City College, CUNY
Past President (2015–17), Middle East Studies Association
Director, Middle East and Middle Eastern American Center

In this engaging revisionary study, Lorenzo Kamel shows how modern Western-ist intellectual prejudices have distorted our understanding of identity and conflict in the modern Middle East. Based on original archival research and an exhaustive survey of secondary literature, the author reveals a world that can only be characterised as 'medieval' if one misunderstands the Middle Ages. Focusing on the long nineteenth century, the book provides a chronological continuation of much of the most interesting work being done in pre-modern Mediterranean Studies.

Brian A. Catlos
Author of *Muslims of Latin Christendom* and Professor, Faculty of Religious Studies, University of Colorado, Boulder

Lorenzo Kamel is a dedicated and meticulous scholar, extremely experienced and internationally recognised for his research methodology. His extensive archival work, which forms the basis of many of his most important publications, is impressive by any academic standard. His archival research, informed by exemplary linguistic skills, has, without question, created new understandings of the complex dynamics shaping our inquiry into modern European empires, and the history of the Middle East in the nineteenth and twentieth centuries. *The Middle East from Empire to Sealed Identities* will continue this outstanding trend.

Sara Roy
Senior Research Scholar, Harvard University's Center for Middle Eastern Studies

Contents

Figures

Abbreviations

ACAC	American Colony Archive Collections, Jerusalem
AP	Aberdeen Papers
ASDMAE	Archivio Storico-Diplomatico del Ministero degli Affari Esteri, Rome
ASV	Archivio Segreto Vaticano, Vatican City
BAP	Balfour Papers
BLMC	British Library Manuscript Collection, London
BOA	Başbakanlık Osmanli Arşivi, Istanbul
BOL	Bodleian Library, Oxford
BP	Benson Papers
CAB	Cabinet Office
CAMS	Centre for Asia Minor Studies, Athens
CDM	Centre for Documents and Manuscripts, 'Amman
CHIR	Center for Heritage and Islamic Research, Abu Dis
CP	Cecil Papers
CSA	Cyprus State Archives, Nicosia
CZA	Central Zionist Archive, Jerusalem
DP	Davidon Papers
EP	Ellis Papers
FO	Foreign Office
FP	Fulham Papers
GP	Gladstone Papers
HP	Harley Papers
ISA	Israel State Archives, Jerusalem
ITAC	[Archives of the] Israeli Trust of the Anglican Church, Jerusalem
JBGP	John Bagot Glubb Papers

JEMF	Jerusalem and the East Mission Fund
JFC	Joint Foreign Committee of the Board of Deputies and the Anglo-Jewish Association
JHSP	John Hope Simpson Report
JIA	Jabotinsky Institute Archive, Tel Aviv
JNUL	Jewish National and University Library, Jerusalem
KKL	Keren Kayemeth Lelsrael
LANT	Les Archives Nationales de Tunisie, Tunis
LJS	London Jews Society
LPL	Lambeth Palace Library, London
MDC	Moshe Dayan Center, Tel Aviv
MECA	Middle East Centre Archives, St Antony's College, Oxford
MP	Mill Papers
NARA	National Archives and Records Administration, Washington DC
PEF	Palestine Exploration Fund, London
RP	Rose Papers
SP	Stanmore Papers
TNA	The National Archives, London
TP	Tait Papers
TSP	The Sledmere Papers
UNA	United Nations Archives, New York
WP	Wordsworth Papers

Note on Transliteration

Most Arabic names and terms are transliterated in this book in accordance with the system adopted by the *International Journal of Middle East Studies*. But some words have been transliterated using the forms found in official documents produced in Western languages. Family names have been transliterated according to the pronunciation usually adopted by the family clans themselves. Words in Hebrew, as well as those in Ottoman Turkish, are almost always reproduced following a simplified phonetic system as close as possible to the Hebrew and Turkish of the present day.

Acknowledgements

This book is the result of a long, 'antifragile',[1] journey in and on the Middle East. It represents my research and thoughts on the root causes of a number of cultural, social, religious and political phenomena currently affecting the region.

During the years in which I worked on it I had the privilege of entering into contact with many remarkable persons who have contributed much to my knowledge and understanding of both the past and the present. I have many thanks to convey.

Thanks, first, to Moshe Ma'oz, Ilaria Porciani, Sara Roy and Salīm Anatī (my 'silent hero'). For different reasons, they have been and still are a source of inspiration: my gratitude towards them goes far beyond these few words.

I want to thank also a number of friends and colleagues who have read and commented on this work, and particularly Nicholas Doumanis, Beth Baron, Fanar Haddād, Daniela Huber and Isa Blumi. Their constructive feedback has been invaluable to me.

I am indebted to Roger Owen, Bill Granara and more generally to the Center for Middle Eastern Studies (CMES) at Harvard University, where I had the privilege to serve as a postdoctoral fellow for two years: this book started during my time there. I continued my work at the University of Freiburg's Institute for Advanced Studies (FRIAS), where I conducted research and lectured while serving as a Marie Curie Experienced Researcher. During the year I spent at FRIAS, my family was far away and I suffered. Yet I have had the chance to work in an outstanding environment and to rely on the support of Bernd Kortmann, Johanna Pink and a number of other friends and colleagues, who have been extremely generous towards me.

---

[1] N. N. Taleb, *Antifragile: Things that Gain from Disorder* (New York: Random House, 2012).

I owe a debt of gratitude also to the Fritz Thyssen Stiftung for a generous year's research grant, and to Nathalie Tocci, Dietrich Jung, Nazmī Jūbeh, Andrea Graziosi, Efrat Ben Ze'ev, Claudio Lo Jacono, Rabī'e Moḥammad Salāma, Brian A. Catlos, Paolo Capuzzo, Māha 'Izzat al-Khūlī, Karīm Makdisī, Arturo Marzano and Vittorio Vidotto. They have all supported my work in a number of ways. I am very grateful to them all.

A heartfelt thanks goes to the students who have taken my courses of History of Colonial and Post-Colonial Spaces at the University of Bologna, and particularly to Joanne Boustani, Mohamed Amer and Layla Hashemi: their sharp inputs have had a positive impact on the final result of this book, and were greatly appreciated.

Dimitris Kamouzis and Anestidis Stravos guided me in the research conducted at the Center for Asia Minor Studies in Athens, where I was assisted by a brilliant young student: Barbara Kontogiannis. Equally important has been the assistance received by Ayten Ardel and the staff of the Osmanli Başbakanlık Arşivi in Istanbul.

Mahmūd Ashqār, Director of the Center for Heritage and Islamic Research in Abū Dīs, gave me the opportunity to access a wide range of unpublished documents. The same applies to Mūsa Shteiwī and Rānia Mashāl at the University of Jordan's National Archives.

Ruth Benny guided me in the research conducted at the Lambeth Palace Library in London, where I have also benefited from the experience of Joe Maldonado (British Library Manuscript Collection) and Mark Dunton (The National Archives). Helena Vilensky, of the Israel State Archives, has been an invaluable source of help for my research for the past fifteen years. Maureen Grimshaw and David Pillegi assisted me in the periods that I spent at the Archives of the Israeli Trust of the Anglican Church of Jerusalem.

I am indebted to Rachel A. Lev (American Colony Archive Collections), Christos Kyriakides (Cyprus State Archive), Batia Leshem (Central Zionist Archive), as well as to the staff of Les Archives Nationales de Tunisie in Tunis, the Bodleian Library (Oxford), the Archivio Storico-Diplomatico del Ministero degli Affari Esteri of Rome, the National Archives and Records Administration in Washington and the Archivio Segreto Vaticano for their invaluable help and support.

This is also the place to thank my linguistic editors, Elizabeth Stone and Helen Johnston, for their meticulous work, and Nicola Ramsey, my editor at Edinburgh University Press: her enthusiasm and competence made the difference.

The final but most important thought is for my parents, who have always supported my dreams, and for *l'amore della mia vita*, Daniela, whom I met ten years ago in Jerusalem, in a place where I would have hardly imagined to meet the woman of my life. Without her and our children, Niccolò and Valerie, I would not have had the necessary inner stability for facing the many challenges encountered while writing this book.

To Niccolò

In what sense is it meaningful to distinguish, on the basis of ethnicity, between two people who speak the same language, eat the same food, laugh at the same jokes, share the same set of cultural references, and may even live in the same village, just because they happen to belong to different religious groups?

Elias Muhanna

The lumping together of different ethnic groups into one artificial unit is not the worst feature of colonialism. Its most obnoxious feature is the subsequent alienation of the colonized from their roots, from their culture, from their religion, from their language, from their laws and from their concept of justice. You cannot colonize a group without first dehumanizing them, enslaving them, and brainwashing them into believing that they are inferior. The colonial masters, through myths designed to show the inferiority of the oppressed and colonized people, through the imposition of language of the colonial masters, but mostly through the inclusive and frightening character of their authority managed to impose on the colonised a new religion, new ways of behaviour, new ways of seeing and, in particular, a pejorative judgment with respect to their original culture, religion, language, sense of right and wrong.

Chukwudifu Oputa

Introduction: The Past's Present

'The Turks weren't hurting us when we left, they were crying.'[1]

Basiliki Kalogeropoulou

The Thirty Years War started in 1618 as a conflict between various Protestant and Catholic states in the Holy Roman Empire. It brought devastation and major population loss to the heart of Europe. Many observers of today's Middle East have found similarities with that distant past.

The Polish-American diplomat Zbigniew Brzezinski, for instance, contended that several analogies exist 'between what's happening in the Middle East and what happened in Europe during the Thirty Years War several centuries ago, namely the rising of religious identification as the principal motive for political action'.[2] Similarly, the French geographer Fabrice Balanche argued that 'the global resonance of the Syrian war has a precedent from some four centuries ago: the conflict in Bohemia (1618–23), which initiated the Thirty Years War'.[3]

Many public figures have expressed similar opinions, including Leon Panetta ('we are looking at kind of a 30-year war'),[4] Andrew Sullivan ('the thirty years war brewing in the Middle East'),[5] and Brendan Simms, according to whom 'the root of the Thirty Years' War, just as with many Middle Eastern conflicts today, lay in religious intolerance'.[6]

Others have analysed how the Thirty Years War ended, deriving from it a 'model' that could be used to bring peace to the Middle East. Pulitzer Prize-winner Jack Miles wrote that 'the Peace of Westphalia [in 1648] re-drew parts of the map of Europe. Peace in the Middle East may yet do the same'.[7]

Each of these approaches is part of an ongoing process of the region's 'medievalisation', or the tendency to juxtapose an allegedly medieval Middle East with the modern, secular, normative West.[8]

The Thirty Years War had, indeed, little to do with 'religious identification'. Catholic France, for instance, supported the intervention of Protestant Sweden, led by Gustavus Adolphus (1594–1632), against the Holy Roman Empire and the Catholic League. Both the Thirty Years War (a non-proxy conflict) and the many proxy-wars in today's Middle East show that religious issues alone can explain little. Four centuries ago, France, the Habsburgs, the German princes (whose conversion had little to do with theology and much with asserting their power) and other regional players clashed mainly, although of course not only, for practical reasons.

The same applies to the present-day Middle East, where cleavages and sectarian strife have much to do with the socio-economic effects of globalisation, the short- and long-term effects of nationalism and ongoing geopolitical dynamics. In this respect, the decision to overthrow Saddām Hussein's regime in 2003 and, more recently, the United States' non-intervention in Syria and the 2015 nuclear deal with Iran, have been perceived by Saudi Arabia as indirect aid to Iran's strategies. Largely as a consequence of this, and particularly following the Arab uprisings of 2011, Riyadh has invested an enormous amount of resources in opposing the rise of any government or party that, in the Arab world, could have represented a credible alternative to the 'Saudi model'. This also explains Riyadh's decision to support the Egyptian army in its coup against former Islamist president Mohamed Morsi.

It is largely to these considerations, and thus to Iran's increased role in the region, that the continuation of the current Middle East's many proxy-wars should be linked.

On the other hand, to imply that the region should make up for the centuries that divide it from a normative West is not only orientalist but also tends to simplify a more complex picture. Early seventeenth-century Europe was facing the repercussions of the Protestant Reformation, which had started a century earlier. On top of this, the fanaticism that characterised relations between Catholics and their 'dissident brothers'[9] (that is, how Catholic clergy used often to refer to Protestants) has no parallel in the history of the Middle East.

Despite what the ongoing debates would seem to imply, Sunnis and Shi'as, but also Christians, Jews and other religious groups or confessions, have lived together for centuries in the region, reaching a level of coexistence[10] – a relatively new concept that does not erase the existence of boundaries but implicitly acknowledges that such boundaries are negotiable – higher than any registered in most of the rest of the world, Europe included.[11] It is significant, just to take an example, that as recently as 2003, about 40 per cent of Baghdād's population – that is, a quarter of the whole of Iraq – was composed of people born from Sunni–Shi'a mixed marriages; Baghdād's Iraqis call them 'Sushis'.[12]

The tangible reality of 'Sushis' has today been largely replaced by an alternative vision, which prefigures – and often advocates – a 'Balkanisation' of the region. This approach is rooted in the early 1990s and was expressed in an article ('Rethinking the Middle East') by Bernard Lewis in *Foreign Affairs* in 1992. Lewis contended that many states in the region are simply artificial Western creations (a common yet simplistic claim; see Chapter 6).[13] He also predicted as among the most likely future scenarios that the Middle East would collapse 'into a chaos of squabbling, feuding, fighting sects, tribes, regions and parties'.[14] Considering this potential chaos, it might be argued, it would have been much easier to force or convince the local populations to accept an order imposed from the outside.

To what extent have these predictions turned into self-fulfilling prophecies? The answer, from the perspective of three decades later, is open to debate. What it is certain, however, is that, particularly since the beginning of this century,[15] the remodelling of the 'greater Middle East' – that is, the division of large states into small homogeneous entities incapable of posing any coherent threat – has been advocated by a number of influential think tanks in Washington, including by Project for the New American Century (PNAC). Of the twenty-five political figures who signed PNAC's founding statement of principles, ten (including Dick Cheney, Donald Rumsfeld, John Bolton and Paul Wolfowitz) went on to serve in the administration of US President George W. Bush.[16] It is equally evident, from a less political and more academic and journalistic perspective, that a growing number of publications are describing the present-day Middle East in terms of a region 'splintered by sects and tribes'.[17] In these works, the whole area appears as a distant and somehow obscure and artificial region, in which local people are influenced by ancestral 'tribal' and religious cleavages, and live 'in a system based on opposition'. Peace, noted McGill Professor Philip Carl Salzman, 'is not possible in the Middle East because values ["kin, clan, and cult"] and goals other than peace are more important to Middle Easterners'.[18]

The sense of a largely artificial region, characterised by 'sealed-off' minorities (or a 'mosaic of minorities'[19]) and historical discontinuities, has become widespread, to the extent that the word 'stability' continues often to be paired with concepts such as 'division', 'partition' or 'natural borders' (that is, the adjustment of border features to mirror ethnic or religious differences).[20] Although several studies on the 'production of knowledge' about the Middle East – and related distortions – have been published since the turn of the millennium,[21] the challenging or deconstruction of the narratives linked to the process of 'Balkanisation' that is allegedly taking place in the Middle East is still limited.[22] One of the most compelling, indirect, exceptions can be found in Gerard Russell's *Heir to Forgotten Kingdoms*, in which the author, through an in-depth analysis of the almost inaccessible 'pagan religions' (Mandaeans, Zoroastrians, Druzes, Kalasha, Yazidis and many others) that have survived in the Middle East, challenges the perception of the region as inherently divided and violent.[23] Russell uncovers ancient rituals and sheds light on an extraordinary yet little known cultural and social patrimony that, until very recently, had remained largely intact for millennia. It is noteworthy that these groups survived under Islam, that is in a context (the medieval 'Muslim world') in which many aspects of Judaism as a religious civilisation 'were formulated, codified, and disseminated',[24] while no equivalent faith survived in Christian Europe. Despite having suffered disadvantages and various forms of oppression and, at times, persecution, these 'religious minorities' flourished in an environment that was 'perfectly capable of valuing diversity'.[25]

The original nucleus of this volume developed with the aim of providing a historical context for these considerations by shedding light on essentialised, ahistorical notions of religious and identity-related issues. More precisely, the book aims to assess what the region is currently experiencing by challenging the discourse of the 'medievalisation' of the Middle East. It provides a historical understanding of the transition from empire to sealed identities, that is, the process through which complex and multidimensional local contexts have been simplified (meaning the tendency to define, indeed rationalise, the other in terms more suitable and useful to the self), homogenised and denied in their historical continuities by a number of extra- and intra-regional actors. Against the backdrop of a milieu in which identities were largely flexible, multifaceted and 'hyphenated', the practice of politicising ethno-religious differences, through 'ascribing a nonmutable, culturally genetic profile to a group', often with the purpose of marginalising it, led to a reality of tendentiously sealed identities.[26]

The temporal focus of this attempt is mainly linked to the 'long nineteenth century' of the Middle East – framed by the late Donald Quataert between Bonaparte's invasion of Egypt (1798) and the beginning of the League of Nations' mandates (1922)[27] – that has also been dubbed by a number of scholars as the 'reform century': from the early reforms (1808–39) under Sultan Mahmūd II (1785–1839) until the 1908 Young Turk Revolution. These temporal and conceptual periodisations, as well as the choice of which historical facts or figures affected a given region the most, are of course always arbitrary, often 'self-centered',[28] and tend to unduly sharpen our sense of antagonism between different parties by ignoring centuries of earlier dynamics and continuities. This might result in a problematic process: it is in fact necessary, perhaps now more than ever, to instil (or re-instil) the concept of *continuity* in reference to the history of the region.

The relevance of 'continuities' has been evident throughout most of the millenary history of the region, and from a wide range of different angles. For instance, the 'Epic of Gilgamesh' (c. 2100 BCE), a literary product of Mesopotamia, includes a number of themes (including the flood myth adopted in the Noah's ark narrative) and motifs later on included in the Bible and other religious books. The history of Jerusalem represents another powerful example. As noted in a study published by the Bar-Ilan University's Ingeborg Rennert Center for Jerusalem Studies, 'Canaanite Jerusalem had two holy sites; both were above and outside the city walls. Shalem was probably worshiped in the area of the Temple Mount, which later became the holiest site for the Jews and the third most holy site for Moslems'.[29] These and a plethora of other possible examples are hardly surprising. Every 'invader', in fact, has, to some extent, left its mark upon the region and its inhabitants. In Jacques Weulersse's words, 'Hittites, Arameans, Assyrians, Sea Peoples [. . .] didn't vanish, they changed their capitals, sometimes altered languages and customs, they hardly touched the rural population, already bound to the soil [*déjà lié au sol*]'.[30]

Notwithstanding these and other related considerations,[31] a special attention to the historical span of time covered in this volume is at least partially justified by the fact that it favoured the rising of enduring dynamics that effectively prevented the persistence of flexible, multifaceted and hyphenated identities, a process whose echoes are still visible in the present of much of the Middle East. More generally, this specific historical phase influenced many of the attitudes that a meaningful percentage of people – from Japan to the United States, passing through Europe, the Middle East and other world regions – still maintain towards history (it was the century of the first museums, national libraries and archives but also of recorded sound and photography), science, culture and the forging of the relationships and balance of power between a number of world's areas.

The Book's Structure

Despite being focused on the relatively distant past, *The Middle East from Empire to Sealed Identities* speaks to and sheds light on the present, providing a deeper understanding of the dynamics that most of the region is currently experiencing. It is introduced by Chapter 1, which provides a conceptual frame, by contextualising a number of terms and concepts commonly adopted – and 'taken for granted' – when approaching the region. Particular attention is given to 'tribalism', 'sectarianism', 'minorities' and other key concepts that are often synonymous with uncompromising divisions and cleavages. Unsurprisingly, these aspects have come to prominence, without paying appropriate attention to the local historical context, in many (if not most) studies that focus on the modern and contemporary Middle East.

The three chapters that follow (2, 3 and 4) turn to three crucial junctures of the 'long nineteenth century', when exceptional circumstances worked to shape the region's ethno-religious, political, economic and cultural dimensions. The French historian Fernand Braudel (1902–85) noted that even a minor event 'could be the indication of a long reality, and sometimes, marvelously, of a structure'.[32] These three 'moments' likewise are significant beyond themselves and are essential components of a 'structure' that, in different forms and degrees, still echoes today throughout most of the region.

More specifically, Chapter 2 investigates the germs of competing ethno-religious visions in the Middle East, examining the 1830s, a decade that marked the passage from it being a tendentially insular region, inhabited by a 'cluster of communities' and characterised mainly by a large volume of intra-regional trade and commerce,[33] to one based upon a mosaic of competing nationalistic visions and major powers' antagonisms over supremacy.[34] The census of 1831 contains, for the first time in Ottoman history, a number of hints as to ethnic groups. The same year, Sultan Mahmūd II (1785–1839) founded *Takvim-i Vekayi* ('Calendar of facts'), the first fully Turkish language newspaper. Until then, and again from the 1840s until 1868's provincial yearbook, references were almost only provided according to large and encompassing religious affiliation. Yet, and despite the almost complete absence of any Ottoman counting of ethnic groups, European powers fostered a process of division and subdivision of the 'non-Muslim population, chiefly the Christians, in accordance with their national interests and subjective preferences'.[35] This period, which coincided with the first major conquest of an Arab-speaking country (Algeria) by a European power (France) (that is, a period in which Muslim-majority states and societies were compelled to live in a world dominated by 'others'), was also characterised by the establishment of municipal councils, a Western institution which carried unintended consequences for the political climate of 'Greater Syria' and the broader region.

Chapter 3 analyses the politicisation of ethno-religious differences ignited with the Tanẓīmāt, the Ottoman reformist period that witnessed the introduction in the region of a number of concepts – such as *waṭaniyyah* ('patriotism') – pointing towards the secular, Western, concept of nationality. The introduction of these concepts and a new 'stimulus to national improvement', to use an expression adopted by a number of intellectual and political figures of the time, had its roots in Lebanon and in Syria in the convergence of two main interests, those of Arabic-speaking Christian communities of those countries (in-out perceptions) and of Christian missionaries (the outside-in dimension). Believers of the different Christian denominations soon became the respective channels through which Western powers tried to impose their political, commercial and cultural influence over the region.[36]

The medium- and long-term effects of these processes coincided and often overlapped with the rising of *Osmenlilik* ('Ottomanism'), an expression of civic nationalism – that flourished in the 1870s and 1880s and ultimately faded with the Balkan Wars in 1912–13 – in which loyalty to the sultan, often erroneously perceived as 'the Grand Caliph of Islamism [Gran Califfo dell'Islamismo]' by the Roman Catholic authorities,[37] was replaced with loyalty to the Empire. Ottomanism, like 'Arabism', was, to a large extent, the result of the failure of the Ottoman Empire to keep pace with Europe.[38] The two approaches were not necessarily in contradiction with one another: most Arabists, while stressing Arab elements of identity, 'remained Ottomanists until 1918'.[39] In this sense, the main goal of Ottomanism was to provide political freedom and equality in exchange for loyalty to the Empire from all its citizens.[40] Nonetheless, Chapter 3 shows how this resulted in the sharpening of religious identities and ethnic-linguistic awareness, with long-lasting effects on the region and its inhabitants. Indeed, as noted by Hanioğlu, 'local resistance to the center's determined attempts to penetrate the periphery accentuated the fragmentation of identity throughout the empire. The unprecedented attempts to unify multiple religious, ethnic and regional groups only served to strengthen their splintered identities in defiance of central policies.'[41]

The 'sharpening process' and the related 'intercommunal dissonance'[42] were further exacerbated in the first two decades of the twentieth century, the phase under analysis in Chapter 4. The years that preceded the First World War witnessed, in fact, the deterioration of relations between Turks and Arabs – an occurence perceived in positive terms by several Western policymakers[43] – and the full 'appropriation' by some local leaders of a number of concepts considered of little or no value just a few years earlier: 'Our new kingdom', contended, for instance, Fayṣal (1885–1933), British-appointed King of Iraq from August 1921, 'is based on the sheer patriotism of her subjects'.[44]

In this same period, at the climax of 'war of Ottoman dissolution',[45] British authorities developed various policies aiming at enshrining religious differences and at promoting a Muslim communal identity, through the creation of a new 'millet system' – a self-serving variation of the previous 'system' of Ottoman administration of separate religious communities – and the establishment of a number of unprecedented communal institutions (such as the Supreme Muslim Council), both perceived as stabilising elements and useful instruments of control. In fact, Britain, whose empire was composed (in 1918) one fifth by Muslims,[46] understood the Middle East as tendentially fragmented in terms of religions and confessions.[47] Through the redefinition of the Muslim community as the largest and most influential millet (a concept, rarely used in the records, that until the early nineteenth century referred only to religious communities, while later on also being applied to non-religious 'nations'), British authorities succeeded at confining any form of dissent to religious issues.[48]

Religion indeed proved to be a useful tool for Western powers in their attempts to stymie and pre-empt the formation of multireligious nationalist movements. In the British Raj, on the one hand, London introduced the term 'Hinduism' and helped to construct a new version of the caste system, assigning social and political meanings to caste and enshrining these meanings in legal and political structures. The demographers of British India and their ethnographic advisers were 'obsessed with the ranking of castes'.[49] On the other hand, the promotion of Muslim communal identity was considered by London as a powerful tool to appease Muslim opinion throughout the Empire. These kinds of policy, that Niall Ferguson and a few other historians have tried to conceptualise in more positive terms in recent years, were aiming at preventing the emergence of a pan-Islamic rebellion – in Malaysia, India and later in Egypt and Palestine – against the British authority.[50] Muslim communal institutions were thus used, particularly in the Middle East, to relegate any expression of protest to religion or religious-related aspects.[51]

Chapter 5 turns the attention to another, if not the most, powerful expression of the politicisation of ethno-religious differences in the early twentieth century: the Balfour Declaration. This provided a vigorous boost to the growing tendency of ascribing ethnic or racial identities to local peoples, shaping a 'pattern' ('Balfour's pattern') that marked a point of no return in the process of homogenisation of the region's ethno-religious components.

The decision to perceive the whole area in racial and/or ethno-sectarian terms, and to ignore or underestimate the fears, ambitions and often the very existence of what was then about 90 per cent of the local population – often loosely referred to as 'non-Jewish communities'[52] or 'Palestine bédouine'[53] in the dispatches of the time – has had major repercussions, in some cases visible up to the present day. The approach shown by several prominent British figures towards Jews and Zionism was, particularly just before and during the First World War, determined by anti-Semitic feelings. Yet these feelings were expressed in the form of a deep-rooted philo-Semitism of evangelical and puritan memory. In both cases, Jews were reduced to their 'Jewishness'. In this sense, philo-Semitism and anti-Semitism often became two sides of the same coin.

On top of these considerations, it should also be noted that the Balfour Declaration, beyond its symbolic significance, did not in itself have any binding power. It became legally relevant when it was included in the British mandate for Palestine by the League of Nations. The latter denied, since its foundation, the inclusion of a clause for 'racial equality', proposed by Japan, within its founding charter. In theory, the underlying intention of the mandate system implemented by the League of Nations was to prepare the various populations for self-determination and self-government. In practice, it was an instrument used by the victorious powers to legitimise their own 'rights of conquest' in order to divide the spoils of ex-empires, as well as land holdings belonging to the defeated nations. This was an objective pursued through a paternalistic approach which, on the one hand, supported the idea that there was a hierarchy among the various 'races' – Jan Christiaan Smuts (1870–1950), a leading figure in Lloyd George's (1863–1945) War Cabinet, who is credited with authoring the international mandates idea, defined the African populations as 'barbarians' – and, on the other hand, was leveraged by an exaggerated emphasis on the need to establish well-defined borders based on ethnic principles.

Chapter 6 takes on board these aspects and, more specifically, the period of the post-First World War 'fissiparous conferences' and treaties. These represented a meaningful turning point that, on the one hand, provided the international legal legitimisation to ethno-sectarian processes of racialisation, sharpening the religious and ethnic identities examined in the previous chapters, and, on the other hand, enabled a 'cherry-picking process' – that is, the selection of a few 'natural representatives' of the local populations.[54]

London and Paris were granted their mandates by the League of Nations during the 'imperial sunset',[55] a historical phase that coincided with the collapse of the three main multinational empires – Habsburg, Ottoman and Russian – and the establishment of thirty new, largely homogeneous, nation-states.[56] Despite being an era of unprecedented criticism towards the empires (and their still enduring legacies), and the fact that the Wilsonian rhetoric of self-determination flourished in these years, tens of millions of Arabs and hundreds of millions of Muslims had no representative body that could give voice to their aspirations.[57] The sudden and, at times, impulsive empowerment of several 'trusted' representatives of local populations backfired on the British authorities on a number of occasions and contributed to fostering fragmentation, disunity and 'unrepresentativeness' within local societies. Fayşal, warned General Edmund Allenby (1861–1936) in March 1920, 'has begun to sign himself Grand King of the Arabs'.[58]

The 'cherry-picking process' went hand in hand with a growing emphasis on the need to establish well-defined borders based on ethnic and/or religious principles.[59] Western statesmen demonstrated themselves to be 'anxious to proceed immediately with the delimitation' of new confines.[60] Borders drawn at the time, ironically amounting to one of the most stable aspects of the Middle East in the last century, still today remain a contentious topic of debate. This is certainly largely due to the arbitrary way in which some of them were laid out: 'South of Sykes Picot line', noted British diplomat Robert Vansittart (1881–1957) in 1920, 'we can lay down the frontier as we wish'.[61] Chapter 7 problematises these aspects and the related 'bordering process', and sheds light on the efforts that peoples in the region – in the context of a new process of homogenisation of diversities – are exerting today in order to get *back* into history, regaining possession of their multifaceted pasts. Their efforts have the potential to deconstruct the many 'segmented identities' that are currently emerging. They have also the capability of bringing to light some of the hybrid identities and experiences that once flourished in Mediterranean spaces, prompting external observers to pay closer attention to their echoes in the realities of sufferance that affect the region today.[62]

Notes

1. Centre for Asia Minor Studies (CAMS), KP 328B, p. 12. Basiliki Kalogeropoulou, Potamia, 1921.
2. Interview with Z. Brzezinski in D. Rothkopf, 'A Time of Unprecedented Instability?', *Foreign Affairs*, 21 July 2014. Available at: http://foreignpolicy.com/2014/07/21/a-time-of-unprecedented-instability.
3. F. Balanche, 'The Levant: Fragmentation and Remapping', in A. J. Tabler (ed.), *100 Years of Sykes-Picot* (Washington DC: The Washington Institute for Near East Policy, 2016), pp. 3–25.

4. Interview with L. Pennetta, in *USA Today*, 6 October 2014. Available at: https://www.usatoday.com/story/news/politics/2014/10/06/leon-panetta-memoir-worthy-fights/16737615.

5. A. Sullivan, 'The Thirty Years' War Brewing in the Middle East', *Sunday Times*, 16 December 2006.

6. B. Simms, 'Ending the Thirty Years War', *New Stateman*, 26 January 2016. Available at: http://www.newstatesman.com/politics/uk/2016/01/ending-new-thirty-years-war.

7. J. Miles, 'How Will the Mideast War End? Christian History May Provide a Clue', *New Perspectives Quarterly* 32(2) (April 2015): 52–8.

8. Ussama Makdisi, conversation with the author, European University Institute, Florence, 5 June 2015. More recently, the topic has been addressed in U. Makdisi, 'The Problem of Sectarianism in the Middle East in an Age of Western Hegemony', in N. Hashemi and D. Postel (eds), *Sectarianization* (London: Hurst, 2017), p. 67.

9. Archivio Segreto Vaticano (ASV), Segr. Stato, rubricella 543, 'Pilgrimages', 1902, rubr. 17, fasc. unico. Bishop Giacomo Radini-Tedeschi (1857–1914) addressing Pope Pius X (1835–1914) on the occasion of Radini-Tedeschi's pilgrimage to the Holy Land from 16 September to 22 October 1902.

10. 'Coexistence' is a term that 'acquires special relevance and meaning when it is no longer possible. The search for an "Ottoman model" for coexistence, for instance, begins retrospectively, after the disintegration of the empire in the wake of Balkan and Arab nationalisms and the ethnic cleansing of Anatolia': R. Bryant (ed.), *Post-Ottoman Coexistence: Sharing Space in the Shadow of Conflict* (New York: Berghahn, 2016), p. 3.

11. 'Jews of Islam', in Mark R. Cohen's words, 'experienced much less persecution than did the Jews of Christendom': M. R. Cohen, *Under the Crescent and Cross: The Jews in the Middle Ages* (Princeton NJ: Princeton University Press, 1994), p. xix. Nothwistanding this, throughout history several 'Western rulers' have tolerated large numbers of Muslims and Jews who lived under their authority. Confirmation of this can, for instance, be found during the time of Alfonso VI of Castile-Leon (1077–1109), James I of Aragon (1213–76), and Roger II of Sicily (1130–54), better known as 'the baptized sultan'. Even then, however, it was possible to detect certain 'trends'. For instance, when Maimonides (1138–1204), one of the greatest Jewish scholars of all time, was expelled from Spain, he and his family decided to settle in Cairo, under the (at times cruel) rule of Saladin (1138–93), and not in any other area in Europe.

12. The precise rate of mixed marriages is hard to determine. Iraqi marriage certificates, in fact, do not state the 'sectarian ID' of the spouses but only the *madāhib* (religious schools) according to which the marriage was carried out. Fanar Haddād notes that the rate of mixed marriages in Baghdād 'was certainly widespread enough for it not to raise eyebrows' (F. Haddād, email exchange with the author, 10 October 2017). According to some sources, 'about 40 percent of Iraqis were from Sunni–Shia mixed marriages until 2003'. See, for instance, Monitor's Editorial Board, 'Iraq's opportunity in the battle for Mosul', in *The Christian Science Monitor*, 30 August 2017. Available at: https://www.csmonitor.com/Commentary/the-monitors-view/2016/0830/Iraq-s-opportunity-in-the-battle-for-Mosul.

13. Edward Said noted that 'nations are narrations. The power to narrate, or to block other narratives from forming and emerging, is very important to culture and imperialism': E. Said, *Culture and Imperialism* (London: Vintage, 1993), p. xiii.

14. B. Lewis, 'Rethinking the Middle East', *Foreign Affairs* 71(4) (Autumn 1992): 117.

15. A few precedents might be found in earlier decades. Already in 1982, for instance, a study published by Oded Yinon, a former senior official with the Israeli Foreign Ministry, 'explicitly endorsed Arab-state fragmentation or "dissolution" as Israel's modus operandi': V. Tilley, *The One-State Solution* (Ann Arbor: University of Michigan Press, 2005), p. 108. More specifically, a study that appeared in the quarterly periodical *Kivunim* ('Directions') contended that 'Lebanon's total dissolution into five provinces serves as a precedent for the entire Arab world, including Egypt, Syria, Iraq and the Arabian Peninsula, and is already following that track. The dissolution of Syria and Iraq later on into ethnically or religiously unique areas, such as in Lebanon, is Israel's primary target on the Eastern front in the long run, while the dissolution of the military power of those states serves as the primary short-term target': ibid. Similar claims, fostering the idea of establishing discrete areas defined in terms of ethno-national and religious identities, were made by other analysts, including Ze'ev Schiff (1932–2007) on *Ha'aretz* (5 February 1982).

16. The remodelling of the 'greater Middle East' has been advocated by a number of US officials, including former US President George W. Bush in his State of the Union speech on 20 January 2004. Similar considerations were expressed by President Bush at the American Enterprise Institute on 26 February 2004.

17. M. B. Russell, *The Middle East & South Asia* (Lanham MD: Rowman, 2014), p. 3.

18. Both quotations are taken from https://www.gatestoneinstitute.org/11117/middle-east-tribal-culture.

19. B. Lewis, *The Shaping of the Modern Middle East* (New York: Oxford University Press, 1994), p. 14.

20. The word 'invented' is one of those most commonly encountered in studies focused on the modern 'Middle East'. See, for instance, D. Fromkin, *A Peace to End All Peace: The Fall of the Ottoman Empire and the Creation of the Modern Middle East* (New York: Holt & Company, 1989), p. 224.

21. This is particularly relevant for the American context. See, for instance, D. Little, *American Orientalism* (London: I. B. Tauris, 2003); O. Khalīl, *America's Dream Palace: Middle East Expertise and the Rise of the National Security State* (Cambridge MA: Harvard University Press, 2016); Z. Lockman, *Field Notes: The Making of Middle East Studies in the United States* (Stanford CA: Stanford University Press, 2016); D. Yaqub, *Imperfect Strangers: Americans, Arabs, and U.S.–Middle East Relations in the 1970s* (New York: Cornell University Press, 2016). For a more general perspective, see D. Kandiyoti, 'Enduring Concerns, Resilient Tropes, and New Departures', in S. Altorki (ed.), *A Companion to the Antropology of the Middle East* (Hoboken NJ: Wiley Blackwell, 2015), pp. 3–14.

22. The parallel with the Balkans, however, seems vexed. Iraq is a good case in point. Unlike the case of Serbia and the Bosnian Serbs in the 1990s, Iraqi Shi'ites, for instance, show no interest in being represented by Iran, or in considering it as their regional representative.

23. For a recent example on the inherently divided and violent 'Muslim world', see G. Abdo, *The New Sectarianism* (Oxford: Oxford University Press, 2016). For a study on the 'struggle for the soul of Islam' and the 'tribal wars of ethnicities and identities', see V. Nasr, *The Shia Revival* (New York: Norton, 2006), p. 20.

24. See N. Stillman, 'The Jews in the Medieval Arabic-Speaking World', in A. T. Levenson (ed.), *Jews and Judaism* (Chichester: Wiley-Blackwell, 2012), ch. 12. Stillman notes that among the aspects mentioned there were 'the domains of [Jewish] liturgy, law, and theology'.

25. G. Russell, *Heirs to Forgotten Kingdoms* (London: Simon & Schuster, 2014), p. xxiv. Lebanese novelist Amin Maalouf went a step further, arguing that 'if my ancestors had been Muslims in a country conquered by Christian armies, instead of Christians in a country conquered by the forces of Islam, I don't think they would have been allowed to live in their towns and villages, retaining their own religion, for over a thousand years': A. Maalouf, *Les Identités meurtrières* (Paris: Grasset, 1998), pp. 67–8. According to Maalouf, '*Il y a dans l'histoire de*

l'islam, dès ses débuts, une remarquable capacité à coexister avec l'autre'. For a perspective more focused on the Palestinian context, see M. U. Campos, *Ottoman Brothers* (Stanford CA: Stanford University Press, 2011).

26. L. Peirce, 'An Imperial Caste', in M. R. Greer, W. D. Mignolo and M. Quilligan (eds), *Rereading the Black Legend* (Chicago: University of Chicago Press, 2007), p. 27.

27. D. Quataert, *The Ottoman Empire, 1700–1922* (Cambridge: Cambridge University Press, 2000), p. 54.

28. As noted by Jürgen Osterhammel, '"our" nineteenth century began only in the West', implying that much of the rest of the world followed other 'calendars' and gave pre-eminence to other historical processes. J. Osterhammel, *The Transformation of the World* (Princeton NJ: Princeton University Press, 2014), p. 49.

29. 'Y. Shalem, *Jerusalem: Life Throughout the Ages in a Holy City – History of Jerusalem from Its Beginning to David*, Bar-Ilan University's Ingeborg Rennert Center for Jerusalem Studies, 6 March 1997, available at: https://www.biu.ac.il/JS/rennert/history_2.html.

30. J. Weulersse, *Paysans de Syrie et du Proche-Orient* [Farmers in Syria and the Middle East] (Paris: Gallimard, 1946), p. 56. Maxime Rodinson (1915–2004), committed to exposing the approaches designed to deny or minimise any continuity in the region's history, broached the subject by focusing on the Palestinian context: 'A small contingent of Arabs from Arabia did indeed conquer the country in the seventh century [. . .] the Palestinian population soon became Arabized under Arab domination, just as earlier it had been Hebraicized, Aramaicized, to some degree even Hellenized. It became Arab in a way that it was never to become Latinized or Ottomanized. The invaded melted with the invaders. It is ridiculous to call the English of today invaders and occupiers, on the grounds that England was conquered from Celtic peoples by the Angles, Saxons and Jutes in the fifth and sixth centuries. The population was "Anglicized" and nobody suggests that the peoples which have more or less preserved the Celtic tongues – the Irish, the Welsh or the Bretons – should be regarded as the true natives of Kent or Suffolk, with greater titles to these territories than the English who live in those counties': M. Rodinson, *Israel and the Arabs* (London: Penguin, 1982), pp. 319–20. See also n.a., *Kitāb Tawārīkh Mokhtasar Yunbī Mamalek wa Bilad 'Edīdah wa mā Hadatha fiha men Qadīm al-Zamān 'ela 'Asrenā Hathā* [A Brief History Book Tells about Kingdoms and many Countries and what Happened in them from Ancient Times until Today] (Malta: n.p., 1833), p. 19.

31. When it comes to the Arab conquest of the seventh century, the region encountered the most pervasive – but also less 'forced' – of the invasions witnessed in the area. Through it, Arabs introduced the language, religion and type of government embraced by most of the local inhabitants. The majority of the latter remained predominantly Christian until the beginning of the eleventh century; as a general tendency, thus, Islam was not imposed. This does not mean that the conquest was greeted by the locals 'with open arms', and even less that the present-day populations are the direct descendants of the ancient ones – but, instead, that most of the local inhabitants were Arabised in a natural way, in a process of continuity, thus maintaining what in modern times would have been called a 'cultural basis'. This is so not only in consideration of the small number of new invaders, but also in virtue of the fact that the Arabic that was introduced markedly preserved the sound of the ancient tongues spoken in the region. See Al-Mubarrad, *Al-Kāmil* [The Perfect One] (Cairo: Dār Nahdat Misr, 1956), vol. 2, p. 439. As noted by Ra'ad, Arabic has the same 'sound system as Cana'nite, reflected in the twenty-eight-sign alphabets of both. Ugaritic also has the same sounds, except that the thirty-sign alphabet has three signs for the aleph: ā, ū, ē. As the only live language in the region for many centuries, Arabic can be said to be the storehouse containing the inventories of the earlier languages'. See B. L. Ra'ad, *Hidden Histories* (London: Pluto Press, 2010), p. 187.

32. Cited in R. Khālidī, *Brokers of Deceit* (Boston MA: Beacon Press, 2013), p. xi. Khālidī's book focuses on three key 'moments' related to the USA's role in the Middle East.

33. Karpat noted that until the 1830s there was not one Ottoman nation but 'a cluster of communities': K. H. Karpat, *Studies on Ottoman Social and Political History* (Leiden: Brill, 2002), p. 544.

34. Markaz al-Wathā'iq wal-Makhṭūṭāt (Centre for Documents and Manuscripts, from here: CDM), University of Jordan, 'Amman, file n. 2358 FO614312 T188. The folder contains also several reports by Western consuls based in the region. See, for instance, Angelo Durighello, American Consul in Aleppo (where he also represented Spain, France and other European powers), to the Secretary of State, 20 November 1837: 'Baghdad boasts an extensive trade with Damascus': ibid. Yet in 1848, the British Consul in Jerusalem, James Finn (1806–72), wrote to the British Secretary of State, Lord Palmerston (1784–1865), that 'English commerce can scarcely be said to exist here': British Library Manuscript Collection (BLMC), Rose Papers, vol. 26, add. 42797.

35. K. H. Karpat, *Ottoman Population, 1830–1914* (Madison: University of Wisconsin Press, 1985), p. 45. These policies had an increasing impact on the Ottoman authorities. It is enough to mention that thirteen different Christian categories were detected and included in the last Ottoman census of 1906–7. This mirrored the growing relevance that Christian groups held in the eyes of Western powers. Muslims, on the other hand, were not classified along confessional (Shi'ite or Sunni) or ethnic (for instance, Kurd or Arab) lines.

36. The Syrian Protestant University of Beirut, founded by American missionaries in 1866 and later known as the American University of Beirut, played a particularly meaningful role in articulating and spreading these new ideas. Lebanese-Egyptian author George Antonius (1891–1942) was among the first historians of Arab nationalism to study the influence of the Syrian Protestant University. See G. Antonius, *The Arab Awakening: The Story of the Arab National Movement* (London: Hamish Hamilton, 1938), ch. 3.

37. ASV, Segr. Stato, rubricella 576, 'Constantinople', 1909, Cardinal Secretary of State, Rafael Merry del Val y de Zulueta (1865–1930), to Pope Pius X, Istanbul, 27 April 1909.

38. Ottomanism, mainly triggered by the 'Tanẓīmāt process, became popular in a historical period in which the increasing 'flexibility' of Ottoman institutions made the Empire particularly vulnerable to foreign interference. In November 1878 – four months after the end of the Congress of Berlin, when Turkish possessions in Europe declined sharply and the issue of nationality acquired a new urgency within the Ottoman context – the US consulate in Istanbul made it clear that any Ottoman ruling or decision was 'so elastic as to permit of almost any' interpretation. CDM 2331 FO614285 T367. US consulate in Istanbul to US diplomat Charles Payson (1837–1913), third Assistant Secretary of State, 3 November 1878.

39. E. Dawn, *From Ottomanism to Arabism* (Urbana: University of Illinois Press, 1973), p. 173.

40. Armenians were among the first to be accused by the Ottoman authorities of unlawfully abandoning the 'Ottoman citizenship': Başbakanlık Osmanli Arşivi (BOA) ID.HUS 56/21, letter signed by Sultan Abdul-Hamid II's Chief Secretary, Süreyya Paşa, 29 January 1894.

41. M. Şükrü Hanioğlu, *A Brief History of the Late Ottoman Empire* (Princeton NJ: Princeton University Press, 2008), p. 108.

42. B. Masters, *Christians and Jews in the Ottoman Arab World: The Roots of Sectarianism* (Cambridge: Cambridge University Press, 2001), p. 130.

43. The Sykes–Picot Agreement, according to British stateman Lord Lamington (1860–1940) at the House of Lords, aimed 'to detach the Arabs from the Turks': The National Archives (TNA) FO 371/6379, House of Lord Proceedings, Lord Lamington (who served as Commissioner of the British Relief Unit in Syria in Spring 1919), 14 March 1921. The deterioration of relations between Turks and Arabs continued to worsen in the years that followed. On 9 July 1922, Bertha Vester (1879–1968), head of the American Colony in Jerusalem, argued that: 'People think of Palestine as Turkish. As a matter of fact, though the Government and heads of departments were Turks, there were hardly more than 100 of them, all told. The Arabs detested them': American Colony Archive Collections (ACAC), Jerusalem, Scrapbook of articles, 1922–6. Already in 1848, British consul in Jerusalem James Finn noted: 'I have seldom or never visited towns where Turkish soldiers are found': BLMC, Rose Papers, vol. 26, Add. 42797.

44. TNA FO 371/5034, Fayṣal speaking at the opening of the Syrian conference, Damascus, 6 March 1920.

45. D. A. Howard, *A History of the Ottoman Empire* (Cambridge: Cambridge University Press, 2017), p. 279. Howard described this phase as follows: 'A 600-year-old empire was coming apart, and the empire's diverse peoples, Turks, Kurds, Armenians, Greeks, Arabs, South Slavs and others, whose desires the revolution channeled, now fought intensely for control of its heritage': ibid., p. 295.

46. For long time the Catholic Church considered Britain as the 'role model in infiltrating among the people [maestra nel penetrare tra i popoli]' of the world. See ASV, Arch. Deleg. Apostolica in Iran, fasc. 24, b. 10, f. 249. Egidio Lari (1882–1965), apostolic delegate in Persia, to then Cardinal Eugenio Pacelli (1876–1958), 2 June 1932.

47. BLMC, Cecil Papers, Add. 51094, British orientalist Thomas Walker Arnold (1864–1930), 7 November 1918.

48. See also L. Kamel (ed.), *The Frailty of Authority: Borders, Non-State Actors and Power Vacuums in a Changing Middle East* (Rome: Nuova Cultura, 2017) and L. Robson, *Colonialism and Christianity in Mandate Palestine* (Austin: University of Texas Press, 2011).

49. Osterhammel, *The Transformation of the World*, p. 27.

50. Harvard history professor Niall Ferguson contended, for instance, that India 'owes more than it is fashionable to acknowledge to British rule': N. Ferguson, *Empire: The Rise and Demise of the British World Order and the Lessons for Global Power*

(New York: Basic Books, 2002), p. 358. These and other simplistic assumptions were published in the context of the US invasion of Iraq in 2003, when Ferguson and other scholars supported the invasion of the country.

51. It should be noted that the successful attempts of pre-empting the formation of indigenous multireligious nationalist movements did not necessarily imply a will to divide the region by ethnicity into sub-autonomous areas. For a long time, the British authorities in fact tried to avert any possible territorial partition: they did not have any interest in sharing frontiers with powers with large armies. The British approach aimed at creating friendly buffer states by means of influence, exercised through trade treaties, loans and cordial advice. The situation began to change with Germany's increasing influence, and the Franco-Russian alliance of 1894, the Fashoda Crisis (1898) and the British military frailty that was displayed during the Boer War (1899–1902). From then, and more precisely beginning with the agreement ('Entente Cordiale') that in 1904 granted freedom of action to Britain in Egypt in exchange for a free hand accorded to Paris in Morocco, the phenomenon of partitions among the major powers became increasingly common.

52. TNA CAB 23/4, Alfred Milner's (1854–1925) Memorandum, 6 October 1917.

53. French consul in Jerusalem, Jacques d'Aumale (1886–1979), to the French Minister of Foreign Affairs, Aristide Briand (1862–1932), 27 December 1931, Les Archives Nationales de Tunisie (LANT), Series: Mouvement National, Carton 24, Dossier 4 (1931–2), folio 25.

54. Editorial published on 'Palestine', the weekly organ of the British Palestine Committee (founded in 1916 with the aim of resetting 'the ancient glories of the Jewish nation in the freedom of a new British dominion in Palestine'), 29 January 1921: 'These international conferences are fissiparous in their progeny, for one had hardly begun before it delegates portions of the work that it was supposed to do to future conferences': ACAC, Scrapbook of articles, 1922–6.

55. Beloff noted that 'the war [First World War] had given a major impulse to anti-imperial feeling and weakened the self-confidence of the ruling elites. The desire to limit defence expenditure was a dominant factor in foreign policy'. See M. Beloff (ed.), *Britain's Liberal Empire 1897–1921* (London: Palgrave, 1987), vol. 1, p. 18.

56. Doyle defined 'empires' as 'relationships of political control imposed by some political societies over the effective sovereignty of other political societies': M. W. Doyle, *Empires* (Ithaca NY: Cornell University Press, 1986), p. 19.

57. In a book largely focused on the European context, Halperin and Palan note correctly that empires have 'infiltrated the modern state system in ways that may not be readily apparent': S. Halperin and R. Palan (eds), *Legacies of Empire* (Cambridge: Cambridge University Press, 2015), p. 15.

58. TNA FO 371/5034, Allenby, Cairo, 27 March 1920.

59. It should be noted that the largely disruptive influence exerted by nationalism reached the Eastern Mediterranean at a relatively late stage in comparison to the North African context. Countries such as Egypt and Tunisia, in fact, had been nearly independent political units since the nineteenth century. In this respect, the 'colonial' division of North Africa has been tendentially the result of a less 'alienating' and disruptive process than that which occurred in the Eastern Mediterranean.

60. TNA FO 371/6379, excerpt taken from a report produced by the British Foreign Office on 24 March 1921. The document clarified that 'His Majesty's Government are anxious to proceed immediately with the delimitation of that part of the boundary which lies between Ras el-Nakura on the Mediterranean and Imtar which is just south of Jebel Druze but the Mesopotamian section of the line cannot be delimited until after the hot weather.'

61. TNA FO 371/5245, Vansittart, private secretary to the Foreign Secretary, Lord Curzon (1859–1925), 28 July 1920.

62. On the 'liquid' experiences in the 'Mediterranean frontiers', see D. Bechev and K. Nicolaïdis, *Mediterranean Frontiers: Borders, Conflict and Memory in a Transnational World* (London: I. B. Tauris, 2010), pp. 1–12.

Beyond 'Tribes' and 'Sects': on Concepts and Terms

There are no tribes in the West; there are nations and ethnic groups. Only primitive, savage societies have tribes.[1]

Gerald Caplan

We have become so used to terms like 'collective identity', 'identity groups', 'identity politics', or, for that matter 'ethnicity', that it is hard to remember how recently they have surfaced as part of the current vocabulary, or jargon, of political discourse. For instance, if you look at the International *Encyclopedia of the Social Sciences*, which was published in 1968 – that is to say written in the middle 1960s – you will find no entry under *identity* except one about psychosocial identity, by Erik Erikson, who was concerned chiefly with such things as the so-called 'identity crisis' of adolescents who are trying to discover what they are, and a general piece on voters' identification. And as for ethnicity, in the *Oxford English Dictionary* of the early 1970s it still occurs only as a rare word indicating 'heathendom and heathen superstition' and documented by quotations from the eighteenth century.[2]

Eric Hobsbawm

This chapter contextualises some key concepts commonly adopted for approaching and understanding the Middle East. It shows how different ideas and assumptions have been perceived, imposed and/or adopted in different cultural and geographical contexts.

Concepts such as state, capital, border, citizenship, private property, sectarianism (or *Tā'ifīya*, a neologism introduced in Arabic in the nineteenth century) were of secondary importance and by no means certain of success in the pre-First World War Middle East and held heterogeneous meanings, until external actors, including Protestant missionaries, contributed to disseminating these and other ideas in the region.[3] Their limited adoption was, in a number of cases, confirmed by the absence of Arabic terms to express those same concepts.[4]

The common claim that Jerusalem has never served as the capital (from the Latin *caput*, head) of any Arab or Muslim entity, for instance, neglects the fact that the notion of *'āṣima* itself, which, in modern Arabic, refers to the capital of a state, was unknown in classical Arabic, at least in its contemporary political-administrative meaning; *Al-'āṣima* (singular form of *al-'āwāṣim*, defences, fortifications), literally 'the protector', indicated originally the line between southern Turkey, Iraq and northern Syria, which divided the Byzantine Empire from the caliphates.

All this is even more pertinent for citizenship, the concept that commonly indicates political belonging in the West and recalls the Greek *polites* (citizen) and Latin *cives*. Until the relatively recent past, Semitic idioms offered no word to indicate such concepts. If, in modern Arabic, in order to fill up this void, the term *jinsīya* has been adopted (from the root *j-n-s*, which in classical Arabic indicated gender, race and class, depending on the case), this may be linked to the necessity to translate concepts that were relevant in the European context and, at the same time, to the need to introduce an idea that would help outsiders to 'grasp' the locals' sense of self-perception. Such a process (see Chapter 2) began to take shape from the 1830s: an identity transition phase in which the region witnessed unprecedented penetration by external actors and the embracing of a number of 'sciences',[5] as well as terms expressing collective belonging (such as '*hubb al watan*', meaning, with a political connotation, 'love of the homeland', as well as 'Syrian' and others).[6]

All this does not imply that notions for expressing one's own identity were non-existent in the region, or that the particular importance of a certain city ('*a'zama medīna*', the 'greatest city') was not recognised (not only Baghdād or Damascus but also Jerusalem, in the first period of Islam, played a role comparable with that of a 'capital').[7,8] Concepts such as *'aṣabīya* (reciprocal solidarity), developed by Ibn Khaldūn in the fourteenth century, *qawmīya*, which may be interpreted as a 'neutral' loyalty[9] to a community held together through cultural and linguistic bonds, and *wataniya*, or loyalty to a community residing in a certain region, demonstrate a linguistic and cultural articulation that is worth noting.[10] These and a number of other related concepts, however, held meanings strikingly different from the secular ones acquired in more recent times, and were hardly perceived as linked to identity politics.[11] The idea that individuals could assemble and be organised in accordance with non-religious criteria was in fact largely considered to be inherently opposed to the Islamic concept of community. Influential Iranian-born philosopher Jamāl al-Dīn al-Afghānī (1838–97) contended, for instance, that Islam itself provided a far superior means of socio-political organisation. Such ideas were echoed by a number of other followers of Al-Afghānī, including Egyptian jurist Muḥammad ʿAbduh (1849–1905), one of the key founding figures of Islamic modernism and a direct witness of the British occupation of Egypt – which lasted, in different forms, for seventy years – in 1882.[12] It might be an irony of history that these and other similar claims were made in a historical phase in which these religious scholars and political activists were questioning the compatibility of Islam and modernity: their attempts, in fact, undermined an established belief system[13] and fostered the ideological conditions needed for the penetration of secular, nationalist ideas in the region (see Chapter 3).

'Tribalism', Sectarianism, Ethnicity: Deconstructing Simplified Versions of the Past

'It was an uprising ("Awakening" or Sahwa) of Iraqi tribes that had pushed back the growing threat of IS' [Islamic State] predecessor in 2006'.[14] Impressions such as this are commonly conveyed in analyses on the contemporary Middle East and North Africa. They are often mirrored in works more focused on countries in sub-Saharan Africa, where 'tribes' have historically been depicted with somewhat similar clichés: 'Few African tribes', argues, for instance, Aylward Shorter, 'are so well known as the Masai of East Africa. With their striking physique and noble bearing, they are the obvious choice for the cover photo of a travel brochure or as a symbol of all that is romantic and singular about Africa'.[15]

These repeated references to tribal societies, which are undermined and criticised by a number of African scholars, are still based on a perception defined by outsiders during colonial times.[16] The modern and contemporary use of the concept of the tribe – tied to classical and biblical/quranic images, and with minor points of connection with Ibn Khaldūn's original understanding of *'aṣabīya* (the term was already familiar in the pre-Islamic era)[17] – has often been erroneously used to refer to autonomous, uncompromising social units, loyalty to which relies solely on family and blood-ties.[18] It conveys a negative connotation – like, for that matter, the abovementioned concept of 'awakening', which implies that someone was sleeping – associated with primitiveness and conservative backwardness. Historically, this has been functional from the perspective of European powers. Indeed, for colonialism to take root it was deemed important that African peoples and others would think of themselves in terms of small clans and tribes without any collective, or more 'elaborated', identity.[19] These kinds of approach – from which a number of newly crafted 'tribes' and/or 'races' stemmed, like, for instance, the Hutu and the Tutsi in Rwanda and Burundi – did not successfully represent 'the actual activity of the society they depicted, nor were they intended to; they represented only that slice of it that interested the official observer'.[20] As argued by Stephen Chan, in a book based on years of field research in a number of African countries:

> It is now possible to say that there were seldom such entities as African 'tribes', except that they were the creations of colonial administration [. . .] which needed to define, categorize and then administer people, often balancing the interests and benefits gained from one group against another.[21]

Admittedly, concepts such as 'tribes' (*qaba'il*) – that, contrary to what it is common at present, was rendered as 'nations' in a French dictionary dated 1844[22] – or 'tribalism' (*qabalīya*) do not, in the Eastern Mediterranean, bear the same negative connotation as in the African context. On top of this, they might sometimes be useful in providing a more 'immediate' and 'easy' identification of subethnic societal divisions, that also includes the *fukhdh* (clan), *khams* (five generations of male heirs) and *beīt* (house). And yet the common explicit or implicit reference to a 'Middle East's Tribal DNA'[23] (more recently used to 'explain' the 31 December sexual assaults in Germany[24]) remains as problematic as it is simplistic, and tends to overlook the fact that the rising of Islam itself (and the *fiqh*, or Islamic jurisprudence) represented a sort of revolutionary rupture between the pre-Islamic ('tribal') Arab 'world' and the ensuing 'Arab-Islamic *ummah*'.[25]

As Confucius (551–479 BCE) contended, 'if names be not correct, language is not in accordance with the truth of things. If language is not in accordance with the truth of things, affairs cannot be carried on to success.'[26] The choice of using concepts such as 'tribe' – at times conflated with the concept of 'nomad' but adopted also to refer to non-nomadic people – certainly has semantic relevance.[27] Yet the *problématique* goes beyond this (highly relevant) aspect in as much as its largely acritical usage downplays or ignores also how 'tribes' developed over time and how they tend to provide the image of societies that are eternally conflictual and rigid. More than this, it occludes accurate views of African and Middle Eastern realities and fails to take into account that the so-called tribal groups 'are not social organisations whose integrity receded into a remote past; rather the tribalism displayed is a reaction to more recent events and conditions'.[28] This applies particularly to the most recent past of the region, when widespread social and physical insecurity forced individuals to rely on extended family networks. Even in time of great uncertainties, 'tribes' appear in any case much less relevant than what is often implied. For instance, according to a poll conducted in Iraq in April 2004, that is, right after the overthrow of Saddām Hussein's regime, 'only 1 per cent of those questioned gave their tribe as the most important expression of identity'.[29]

It is fair to assume that, in the near future, concepts such as 'tribe' will be considered by scholars no more acceptable than the one of 'race', a concept, rooted in medieval Europe[30] and widely perceived as derogatory and misleading today, that was acceptable and common until a relatively recent past. This appears yet more likely if we consider that many, although of course not all,[31] intellectuals and public figures who are originally from 'tribal countries' refuse to be encapsulated within these loaded and divisive analytical frames. For example, Prince Hassan bin Talal, brother of King Hussein of Jordan, notes that 'portraying Jordan simply or mainly as a tribal context does not give justice to a more articulated country, history and society'.[32] In other words, a growing number of public figures in the region appear increasingly aware that the use of this concept 'reflects widespread but outdated

19th-[and twentieth-]century social theory',[33] while others have noted that, from the perspective of Arab writers, the concept of *qaba'il* was often used, throughout much of the nineteenth century, to refer to modern nation-states:

> *Qabīla* could refer to a political faction in ancient Athens, the Basques in Spain, the inhabitants of a Swiss canton, the seventeenth-century colony of Pennsylvania, or the post-revolutionary French nation. In the 1858 Paris international fair, for example, one could see – according to a Lebanese eyewitness – 'various *qaba'il* of people,' including Americans, Englishmen, Italians, Turks, Arabs, and others. [. . .] Around the middle of the century this term was highly popular. One newspaper spoke of a 'Europe unified, despite disagreement among some of its *qaba'il*', and referred to the *London Times* as 'the English people's mouthpiece – *lisan ḥāl al-qabīla*.[34]

Avoiding terms and concepts such as 'tribes' is thus, on the one hand, a way of saying that the way we recount history and the words we use matter a great deal, and, on the other hand, a mode of exposing the many times when 'tribalism' has replaced what in Western countries would have been referred to using concepts such as ethnic awareness, extended families, regionalism, kinship groups, ethnic separatism and movements.[35] It is significant that concepts such as 'tribes' and 'tribalism' have always been explicitly avoided by European scholars when referring to European contexts, despite the fact that Roman gentes, Basques, migrant populations coming from Central Asia in the fourth century CE, Celtic clans, to name only a few, would easily 'comply' with the category of 'tribes'. Anyone familiar with the societal milieu of places such as Sicily or Lucania is aware of the existence of extended families and of their pervasive influence throughout such societies. In many cases, these family networks also include a large number of external members (*'parenti acquisiti'*), often co-opted for economic, cultural or political interests. This in no way denies the peculiarities of different contexts, for instance the existence of extensive families that, at times (for instance in the case of the Saudi Arabian National Guard Forces – and contrary to the regular Saudi army) also contribute to the formation of local armies or militias (in the case of the Saudi Guard Forces, families loyal to the 'House of Saud'). Yet extended families in non-Middle Eastern or African contexts are hardly ever described or imagined as 'tribes', nor are they perceived as inherently violent and 'sealed-off' entities, or approached through what the late Tel Aviv University Professor Joseph ('Yossi') Kostiner defined as unchangeable 'tribal values'.[36]

Writing in 1971, African anthropologist Archie Mafeje (1936–2007) noted that 'if tribalism is thought of as peculiarly African [or Middle Eastern], then the ideology itself is particularly European in origin'.[37] His words appear particularly pertinent if considering that for many centuries 'tribal' identities 'did not operate in such a rigid and exclusive way'.[38] In other words, they never represented rigid and impermeable units. What completely changed in the region (and in most of the rest of Africa) from the mid-nineteenth century onwards is that a previously slowly developing, fluid ethnic self-awareness shifted into a new, harder 'tribal' structure, to the extent that 'tribalism' was stronger and more politically relevant in 1981 than it was in 1881.[39]

The latter is the analytical aspect that better links 'tribalism' to 'sectarianism', or *Ṭā'ifiya* – a neologism, considered as an 'essentially contested concept' today,[40] introduced in Arabic in the nineteenth century to render the common European concepts ending in '-ism'.[41] The Middle East has always been a region in which religious boundaries – as in the case of 'tribes' – were shifting, blurred and ambiguous. The minority/majority dichotomy, so fraught with significance today, is, for instance, very much the result of newly created mental and physical divisions.

Yet, in his *Minorities in the Arab World* (1947), the celebrated historian Albert Hourani (1915–93) defined 'minority' simply as a community that was either non-Sunni Muslim or non-Arabic-speaking, or both, living within a Sunni Arab majority and with a well-established presence in the region. The alleged existence of separate, clearly identifiable and long-standing minorities persisted for many decades and is still today mirrored in a number of books, some of them rooted in the idea that 'the concept of religious minorities historically preceded nationalism and national minorities both in the Orient and in the Occident'.[42] These kinds of argument have been increasingly deconstructed and rejected however (it is fair to assume that a similar process will occur in reference to 'tribes' and 'tribalism'). As noted by Benjamin White, 'the nation-state form creates the objective conditions in which people begin to consider themselves as minorities and majorities: however, these remain subjective categories'.[43]

The 'millet system', often misrepresented as a static and rigid top-down structure implemented for organising the life of 'Ottoman minorities', was, in reality, hardly something that could be considered a 'system' at all, and had indeed very little in common with the 'process of minorisation' started in the late nineteenth century.[44] In Aaron Rodrigue's words, 'nothing in the political system of the Ottoman Empire called for different groups to merge into one [. . .] That particular arrangement, therefore, renders invalid all our terms for debate about minority/majority, which are all extraordinarily Europe-centered'.[45] Indeed, before the first decades of the twentieth century, neither the local populations nor the Western powers used the term 'minority', or 'majority', to describe the ethno-religious composition of the region.[46] It should also be added that belonging to a certain 'sect' has for centuries been just one, often secondary, way of expressing one's identity. Today, many ethnicities in Middle Eastern countries still have Sunni and Shi'a branches that exist parallel to confessional identity.

The fluid human and cultural intersections that for centuries have characterised the daily life of different religious groups and confessions in the region have been 'covered' by layers of history, mainly related to the homogenising effects of divisive ideologies inspired by nationalism. In this sense, it is important to remember that unlike medieval societies, characterised as a sum of particularisms, the era of the nation-states tended towards the homogenisation of diversities; and this has had a major impact on the Middle East as well, where religious and identity-related 'borders' have historically been much more nuanced than in Europe. As witnessed by French governor of Algeria Jules Cambon, in 1897, '*les frontières sont, malgré tout, idéales*'.[47]

In many documents of the 1700s and 1800s, it is possible to find a distinction between *ibn 'Arab* (Arab son) and *ibn Turk* (Turkish son). This means that local people often considered the non-Arabic-speaking Turks as foreigners: a further confirmation that 'all identities' are, to a large extent, 'reactive'.[48] At the same time, the origin from a certain village, belonging to a *ḥamūla* (family clan) and the local customs were all factors that marked a certain distinction between the protonations present in the region. And yet, until the relatively recent past, local 'tribes' and 'sects' were not in need of clear-cut borders that could divide their *Heimat* – which in German does not refer to one's country or nation, two abstract ideas that are too broad and distant, but rather to a place in which our most profound memories are rooted. But this should not suggest that the various fluid local identities were deprived of peculiar, if not 'protonational', characteristics.

All this brings us to the third analytical layer of this chapter, connected to ethnicity and more generally to the several ethnic and other local nationalisms present in the Middle East. These ethnic groups hold nationalist ambitions that are sometimes expressed very strongly, as with the Kurds, whose communal mobilisation revolves around a (multi)ethnic pole rather than a confessional one. Yet the case of the Kurds, certainly not an isolated one, reveals much on ethnicities and, more broadly, identity-related aspects of the region. With the possible exception of the seventeenth-century philosopher Ahmad-i Khani (1650–1707), there is no evidence that any Kurd thought in terms of a whole Kurdish people until the end of the nineteenth century.[49] There is an almost complete consensus among scholars that the Kurdish people – indicated in several British documents produced in the first half of the twentieth century as individuals lead by a 'tribesman',[50] or as 'a tribe who keep very much to themselves'[51] – have represented an identifiable group for perhaps two millennia, but it is equally clear that it was little more than a century ago that they, like Arabs and Turks, acquired an ethnic sense of identity. This happened in place of the idea of Ottoman citizenship and membership of a religious community,[52] and did not result in any clear-cut sense of 'political loyalty'.[53]

Why, then, unlike many other ethnic groups in the region, did the Kurds not identify themselves as the Kurdish people until relatively recently? Anthony Smith provides an indirect answer to this by focusing on the 'rudiments of a nation',[54] that is, a set of identifiers so fundamental and so long in existence – so taken for granted – that virtually no one felt any need to investigate them further. Meron Benvenisti goes a step beyond this, and posits that 'the whole game of identity definition reflects the immigrant's lack of connection. Natives don't question their identity'.[55]

Among local people, different senses of identities (connected to religious, local, transnational, land and family-related aspects) coexisted, without any contradiction between them. For instance, a Kurdish woman, Asemath Barzani (1590–1670), was the first known female rabbi; her 'Jewishness' did not prevent her from experiencing and living other identitary dimensions. It is not uncommon to read claims that would seem to foster opposite understandings of the local reality: 'The Kurds', contented for instance Oriental Secretary Vyvyan Holt (1896–1960), 'are anti-Persian, friendly to the British and pro themselves'.[56] Yet and contrary to these kinds of impression, Barzani's various identities – like those of millions of other Kurds in modern and contemporary times – were both distinct and overlapping.[57] As Barnett and Telhami point out, one of the ways in which the entire region differs from others 'is that the national identity has had a transnational character'.[58]

This transnational character and overlapping identities were not in contradiction with a strong attachment to the land. At the same time, emphasis on the transnational character should not be overstretched and (mis)used to imply that most nations and/or states in the Middle East are 'artificial', or recent Western creations. Indeed, a number of local states and nations (in the sense of cultural communities, or, to borrow a term from the Indian context, *Rashtra*) are more ancient and 'rooted' than some in the West. Countries such as Oman (where a state was established in 751 CE with its first Ibadi imam), Yemen (a state founded in 900 CE by a descendant of 'Ali ibn Abi Talib) or Egypt (a state rooted in the ancient Naqada II culture of Upper Egypt), to name a few, remind us of a millenary and often-neglected 'statual' background,[59] while Morocco, Tunisia and others have been nearly independent political units since the nineteenth century. Simultaneously, Iraq and Syria,[60] but also Palestine (see Chapter 7) and others, show a deep-rooted 'self-awareness' that is lacking among certain European countries. All this is not meant to suggest that local peoples were actually in need of well-defined borders.[61] When crossing new borders, merchants became, often in the space of a few days, smugglers; laborers were transformed into refugees; and goods became contraband. On top of this, local people strongly opposed any possible division of the land; 'no political or economical frontiers' pointed out for instance the Pan-Syrian Congress to Fayṣal in May 1919, 'will ever exist between Syria and Mesopotamia'.[62]

Yet in spite of these and other related considerations it is important to emphasise that, to stick to the 'Mesopotamian context', the modern and contemporary Iraqi identity has been 'imagined' and 'constructed' like any other identity in history and that it is that complex and shared identity – often stronger than sectarian divisions – towards which a considerable majority of the local population still looks (70 per cent, according to a survey conducted in 2008 by the Iraq Centre for Research and Strategic Studies).[63] This further confirms that the main roots of the crises that are plaguing large areas of the Middle East should be found in the lack of inclusive social contracts, and not in the alleged 'artificiality' of the region's states, or in largely 'artificial' problems connected to 'state identities' and state-centred narratives, on which Chapter 7 will focus.

A Note on Geographical and Semantic Scope

In relation to what has been argued so far, a brief overview of the geographical and semantic scope of this book appears necessary. Bernard Lewis noted that 'the term "Middle East" was invented in 1902 by the American naval historian Alfred Thayer Mahan [. . .] This new geographical expression [. . .] soon passed into general use'.[64] The same stance was adopted by a plethora of other scholars, including Fred Halliday, who contended that 'the very term [Middle East] was invented in the early twentieth century (1902)'.[65] Unlike geographical names used to refer to other regions or continents – such as the Americas, Africa or Europe – the 'Middle East' refers to an area of the world largely defined from the perspective of those living on the two sides of the Atlantic: the expression bears no real cultural or geographical connotations on the ground. However, the same allegation (the 'accusation' of 'centrism') is rarely applied to other geographical terms that are no less widespread. *Maghreb* (Arabic: 'the West'; its trilateral root, *gha-ra-ba*, hints also at the concept of being 'a stranger') might, for instance, be linked to an 'Orientalcentric' perspective and projection that has Egypt – and, more generally, the Eastern Mediterranean 'Arab heart' – as its centre of gravity.

No natural or ideal regions exist, all are the result of deductions and interpretations based on subjective judgment.[66] In other words, the process of naming and 'imagining' regions is never neutral. Human beings have always tended to name areas through their own geographical and cultural perspective. Almost always, this common attitude has been accepted without resorting to any allegation or artificiality-related argument. For instance, *Anatolia* (from Greek Ἀνατολή, or 'Sunrise'), which makes up most of modern-day

Turkey, was named as such from a Greek perspective, while *Nippon*, or 'Sun Origin', is rooted in a Chinese perception: seen from the latter, the sun rises from Nippon/Japan. Asia, on the other hand, is speculated to come from the Akkadian *'asu'* ('to go out, to rise'), in reference to the sun: 'Asia is a term indicating the east of the region that is considered one of the cradles of human civilization'.[67]

To return to the more specific area covered in this book, *Eber-Nari* ('Beyond the River', in the Akkadian language spoken in ancient Mesopotamia) was the term used by Assyrians and Persians to refer – from an 'Assyrian-centric' and 'Persian-centric' perspective – to the land beyond the Euphrates, that is, modern Syria. For centuries – and still at present – that same area has been known by Muslims as *Bilād al-Shām*, the 'land to the left', meaning, turning the eyes towards where the sun rises, the land on the left-hand side of Mecca. The 'land to the right' (*Bilād al-Yemen*) of Mecca is still known today, both in and outside of the region, as Yemen.

A clear indication of the perspective of the 'interested observer' might be found in dozens of other terms used to refer to most or part of these and other areas, including 'Outre-Mer' ('Beyond the [Mediterranean] sea', or 'Overseas', from the perspective of the Crusader states), 'Holy Land' (the area between the Mediterranean Sea and the Jordan River, which boasts a rich millenary history, antecedent to the three monotheistic religions), 'Levant' ('Mediterranean lands east of Italy', a recognition of the strategic role played by the Republic of Venice and other maritime city-states), 'Mashreq' (in Arabic and Persian: 'The East'; as in the case of *Bilād al-Shām*, and contrary to the other terms mentioned above, Mashreq was born within the region).[68]

Despite the fact that most of these expressions have promoted a simplified and often misleading perception of the region (or part of it), none of them has suffered a 'stigma process' comparable to what might be seen in relation to the Middle East.

It may rightly be suggested that over the last century the term Middle East has been hijacked, resulting in a more defined idea of what it means and acquiring some colonial connotations that, despite being perceived in positive terms by a few scholars,[69] have prompted many observers to use less loaded alternatives (including Eastern Mediterranean, or WANA: West Asia and North Africa).[70] Yet despite what has been often argued, this expression has far older and deeper roots than almost all the geographical terms mentioned up to this point, a fact attested by both Islamic and European sources.

In his *Historiae Adversum Paganos* (416 CE), the Roman historian Paulus Orosius (375–420), a native of today's Portugal, made a reference to a Spanish delegation stationed in Babylon (present-day Iraq) using the expression 'medio Oriente [middle East]' ('Hispanorum Gallorumque legatio in medio Oriente apud Babylonam'),[71] translated fourteen centuries later by French historian Joseph Toussaint Reinaud as '*le cœur de l'Orient*' ('the heart of the East').

Similar expressions – often, as it is also the case in our times, not in relation to a clearly defined area – have been used by a number of other scholars and intellectuals over the centuries, including Goethe – who used the term 'Mittler Orient' in his *West-östlicher Diwan* (1819) and, thanks to his internationally recognised influence, contributed to making it popular – in reference to Hafez's land (1315–90), that is, to Persia and its neighbouring areas. Contrary to what it is often argued, these and other similar expressions were not 'coined in the course of the 19th century' but are instead the fluid outcome of a deep-rooted historical background.[72]

Deconstructing the common assumptions surrounding the expression 'Middle East' – used, in this book, mainly to refer to areas encompassing present-day Egypt, Jordan, Syria, Lebanon, Israel, Palestine, Turkey, Iran, Iraq and Saudi Arabia – has the positive effect of elucidating the many ways in which this part of the world has been known and perceived throughout much of its history, enabling a better grasp of the relevance of the point of observation of the 'beholder'. At the same time, it provides further evidence to tackle the widespread, yet simplistic, 'artificiality thesis' (see Chapter 7).

Notes

1. G. Caplan, *The Betrayal of Africa* (Toronto: Groundwood Books, 2008), p. 14.
2. E. Hobsbawm, 'Identity Politics and the Left', *New Left Review* 217(1) (May–June 1996): 38–47. Before the end of the nineteenth century, human beings never felt the necessity to prove their identity. Identity cards were introduced in some Western countries in the early twentieth century (Italy in 1926), but the expressions 'collective identity' or 'identity politics' were simply non-existent until relatively recently.

3. Gaiser noted that early Muslims 'tended not to use binary, tertiary, or relational terminology ("church-sect-cult" or "sect-denomination"), but rather to abstract the main groups using a singular concept [. . .] casting all of them together as firqas': N. Hashemi and D. Postel (eds), *Sectarianization* (London: Hurst, 2017), p. 67.

4. The absence of a number of terms used at a later stage to express collective belonging was the mirror of a fluid reality in which self-versus-other constructions were less expressed or needed. In this sense, the relatively recent introduction in the region of concepts such as 'refugee', 'smuggler' or 'contraband', so fraught with meaning today, are also very much the result of newly created mental (ethno-sectarian 'races') and physical (borders) divisions.

5. As noted by Pollard, 'in the 1830s, translations of texts on geography – which was defined as being a science through which nations could be ranked and ordered – reinforced the notion that the globe was divided into civilized and uncivilized, clean and unclean nations. During the 1830s, a number of French texts on descriptive geography; cosmography; physical geography; religious, political and historical geographies, as well as moral geographies were all translated into Arabic, including al-Tahtawi's translation of Malte-Brun's Géographie universelle in 1838': L. Pollard, *Nurturing the Nation* (Berkeley: University of California Press, 2005), p. 28.

6. A. J. Rustum (ed.), *Al-Usūl al-'Arabīyya li-Tā'rikh Sūriyah fī 'Ahd Muhammad 'Alī Pāshā* [Materials for a Corpus of Arabic Documents Concerning the History of Syria under Muhammad 'Alī Pāshā] (Beirut: Al-Maktaba al-Būlusiyya, 1987), pp. 99–100.

7. The expression 'the greatest city' is a common way of referring to the prominence of a given city. It might be found in modern and pre-modern books produced by authors within the region, as well as in Western publications targeting local people. In relation to Damascus, see for instance n.a., *Kitāb Tawārīkh Mokhtasar Yunbī Mamalek*, p. 18.

8. See K. 'Athāmina, *Le premier siècle de l'Islam: Jérusalem, capitale de la Palestine* [The First Century of Islam: Jerusalem, Capital of Palestine], in F. Mardam-Bey and E. Sanbar (eds), *Jérusalem: le sacré et le politique* [Jerusalem: The Holy and the Political] (Arles: Sindbad, 2002), pp. 115–48.

9. Ibn Khaldūn 'did not have a dichotomous notion of self and other, or an aggressive manifesto for political action. And yet, he became a major reference point in the discourse of Arab nationalists, in particular [. . .] when Arab nationalism was sponsored by British and French imperial strategists': A. Adib-Moghaddam, *Psycho-nationalism* (Cambridge: Cambridge University Press, 2018), p. 29.

10. The concept of *'aṣabīya* was introduced by Ibn Khaldūn in the *Muqaddima*. It may be linked to what Said Nursi (1877–1960) defined as 'positive nationalism', a predisposition that 'arises from an inner need of social life and is the cause of mutual assistance and solidarity; it ensures a beneficial strength'. S. Nursi, *Letters, 1928–1932* (Istanbul: Sözler, 1993), p. 381. *'Aṣabīya* is not, then, a concept comparable to nationalism. Baron De Slane (1801–78) translated it as 'esprit de corps', while Hellmut Ritter (1892–1971) interpreted it with a more convincing 'solidarity feeling'.

11. As noted by Wael Abu-'Uksa, with the rising of the language of nationalism in Arabic (first half of the nineteenth century), a number of concepts expressing collective belonging (including *milla, jins, sha'b, watan, jumhūr, umma*) experienced 'frequent fluctuations in the morphology [. . .] extending the semantic field of some and dismissing the use of others': W. Abu-'Uksa, *Freedom in the Arab World* (Cambridge: Cambridge University Press, 2016), p. 127.

12. 'Abduh's conservative understanding of these and other related issues did not prevent him from denouncing the 'extremism' of some Islamic doctrines, including fringes of Wahhābism. See M. 'Abduh, M. 'Imarāh (ed.), *al-A'māl al-kāmila lil-Imam Muḥammad 'Abduh* [The Full Works of the Imam Muḥammad 'Abduh] (Beirut: al-Mu'assasat al-Arabīyya, 1972), vol. 3, pp. 536–40. See also M. 'Abduh, M. 'Imarāh (ed.), *Al-Islam wa al-Mar'ah fi Ra'i al-Imam Muḥammad 'Abduh* [Islam and the Woman in the Opinion of the Imam Muḥammad 'Abduh] (Cairo: Al-Qāirah li al-Thaqāfa al-'Arabīyya, 1975).

13. Al-Afghānī advocated for the reopening of *Ijtihād* (independent religious-legal judgment). Hourani noted that 'in Afghani's mind, Islam means activity. The true attitude of the Muslim [. . .] is not one of passive resignation to whatever might come, as coming directly from God; it is one of responsible activity in doing the will of God': A. Hourani, *Arabic Thought in the Liberal Age 1798–1939* (Cambridge: Cambridge University Press, 1983), pp. 128–9.

14. J. Vennekens, 'The Influence of Tribalism in the Middle East', *International Perspective* (22 September 2015). Available at: http://www.internationalperspective.be/insight/2015/09/the-influence-of-tribalism.

15. A. Shorter, *East African Societies* (London: Routledge, 1974), p. 30.

16. Zambian historian Mose Kaputungu Sangambo, for instance, noted that 'We [Luvale, Lunda, Luchazi, Mbunda and Chokwe] were once brothers at Inkalanyi; we have separated to found different tribes but now we are coming back together again in our new Zambian nations': M. K. Sangambo, *The History of the Luvale People and their Chieftainship* (Zambezi: Mize Palace, 1984), p. 91.

17. See R. al-Sayyid, *Min al- shu'ūb wa al-qaba'il ila al-umma. Dirāsa fi takawwn mafhm al-umma fi al-Islam* [From Peoples and Tribes to the Nation. A Study about the Concept of the Nation in Islam] (Beirut: n.p., 1984), pp. 17–88.

18. A. Yossef and J. R. Cerami, *The Arab Spring and the Geopolitics of the Middle East* (London: Palgrave Macmillan, 2015), p. 4.

19. Hollywood movies are especially revealing in this respect, particularly a number on the America of the 'Indians' (Native Americans), where the 'white man' invented the 'redskins', attempted to assimilate the indigenous population to human types more familiar to him, forged the myth of Pocahontas (a falsely constructed sexy and 'good Indian'), and, more generally, projected his hopes and fears on the 'West'. See L. Kamel, *Imperial Perceptions of Palestine: British Influence and Power in Late Ottoman Times* (London and New York: I. B. Tauris, 2015), pp. 176–82.

20. J. C. Scott, *Seeing like a State* (New Haven CT: Yale University Press, 1998), p. 7.

21. S. Chan, *Grasping Africa: A Tale of Tragedy and Achievement* (London: I. B. Tauris, 2007), pp. 39 and 44.

22. '*Qaba'il*' was literally translated as 'nations' while '*Ibn al-Tā'ifa*' was rendered as 'national, par rapport aux personnes'. J. Berggren, *Guide français-arabe vulgaire des voyageurs et des francs en Syrie et en Égypte: avec carte physique et géographique de la Syrie et plan géométrique de Jérusalem ancien et moderne, comme supplément aux voyages en orient* (Uppsala: Leffer et Sebell, 1844), p. 580.

23. See P. C. Salzman, 'The Middle East's Tribal DNA', *Middle East Quarterly* 15(1) (Winter 2008): 23–33. Available at: http://www.meforum.org/1813/the-middle-easts-tribal-dna.

24. M. Molinari, *Da dove viene il branco di Colonia*, in 'La Stampa', 10 January 2016. Available at: http://www.lastampa.it/2016/01/10/cultura/opinioni/editoriali/difendere-leuropa-dal-ritorno-delle-trib-fl3u3Wh0fpyzgEdDi81ycN/pagina.html.

25. Many peoples, noted David Maybury-Lewis, are 'stigmatized as being "tribal" because they insist on being marginal': D. Maybury-Lewis, *Indigenous Peoples, Ethnic Groups, and the State* (Boston MA: Allyn and Bacon, 1997), p. 55.

26. Cited in W. Zhang, *Confucianism and Modernization* (New York: Palgrave, 2000), p. 61.

27. 'One prominent feature of interwar discussions of "nomads" and "tribes" was the conflation of the two terms'. R. S. Fletcher, *British Imperialism and 'the Tribal Question'* (Oxford: Oxford University Press, 2017), p. 52.

28. M. H. Fried, 'The Notion of "Tribe" and "Tribal Society"', in J. Helm et al. (eds), *Proceedings of the 1967 Annual Meeting of the American Ethnological Society* (Seattle: University of Washington, 1968), pp. 3–20.

29. T. Dodge, 'State Collapse and the Rise of Identity Politics in Iraq', in G. Montserrat and J. Rex (eds), *The Ethnicity Reader* (Cambridge: Polity Press, 2010), p. 115. The poll, commissioned by *USA Today* and *CNN*, questioned 3,444 people across Iraq.

30. See G. Heng, *The Invention of Race in the European Middle Ages* (Cambridge: Cambridge University Press, 2018).

31. See for instance K. H. al-Naqeeb, *Society and State in the Gulf and the Arabian Peninsula* (London: Routledge, 1990). Korany contends that 'Tribalism is still there in its old/new form'. B. Korany, 'Analyzing Change in the Middle East: A Framework Revisited', in C. Jones (ed.), *The Politics of Change in the Middle East*, Durham Middle East Papers, no. 78, March 2017, p. 35. See also F. Jabar, 'Sheikhs and Ideologues: Deconstruction and Reconstruction of Tribes under Patrimonial Totalitarianism in Iraq, 1968–1998', in F. Jabar and H. Dawod (eds), *Tribes and Power: Nationalism and Ethnicity in the Middle East* (London: Saqi, 2003), pp. 72–3. It should be noted that King Abdullah II also pointed out that the tribe is 'a basic pillar of this society'. 'Amman, 8 June 2010, available at: https://kingabdullah.jo/en/speeches/celebration-accession-throne-anniversary-great-arab-revolt-and-army-day. As noted by Davidov and Andersen, 'despite the problematic status of "tribes" as precolonial political forms, in the postcolonial milieu, tribes have emerged as indigenous units formed for the purposes of cultural preservation, lobbying, activism, and advocacy'. V. Davidov and B. Andersen, 'Mimetic Kinship: Theorizing Online "Tribalism"', in T. L. Adams and S. A. Smith (eds), *Electronic Tribes* (Austin: University of Texas Press, 2009), pp. 21–2. We may call this attitude 'pollera syndrome', in reference to the Bolivian context. As in other South American countries, Andean women consider it very fashionable to dress in the *pollera* – a skirt from Spanish farming culture that was imposed on the local indigenous women by the Spanish colonial authorities. Over time, the *pollera* became a sort of status symbol in the eyes of Bolivian Andeans. Along with the bowler hat imported from Great Britain, it is today the emblem of Andean native pride.

32. Conversation with the author held at the prince's private residence, 18 July 2016. The meeting took place at the end of an international conference ('Re-Ordering the Middle East? Peoples, Borders and States in Flux') organised by the author at the University of 'Amman's Center for Strategic Studies.

33. C. Lowe, 'The Trouble with Tribe', *Teaching Tolerance* 19, Spring 2001, available at: https://www.tolerance.org/magazine/spring-2001/the-trouble-with-tribe. Lowe clarifies that 'in English, writers often refer to the Zulu tribe, whereas in Zulu the word for the Zulu as a group is *isizwe*. Zulu linguists translate isizwe as "nation" or "people". Isizwe refers both to the multi-ethnic South African nation and to ethno-national peoples that form a part of the multi-ethnic nation. When Africans use the word "tribe" in general conversation, they do not draw on the negative connotations of primitivism the word has in Western countries.'

34. A. Ayalon, *Language and Change in the Arab Middle East: The Evolution of Modern Arabic Political Discourse* (Oxford: Oxford University Press, 1987), pp. 25–6.

35. Gula-Ndebele noted the following: 'I am not denying the existence of smaller clans whose identities and culture invariably poured into the greater collective. What I take issue with is the deliberate avoidance of identifying the conglomeration of said clans as an ethnic group'. E. Gula-Ndebele, '"Tribalism": A Scar Today, a Wound Tomorrow', *Conversation Zimbawe*, 30 November 2014. Available at: https://conversationzimbabwe.com/2014/11/30/tribalism-a-scar-today-a-wound-tomorrow.

36. J. Kostiner, *The Making of Saudi Arabia, 1916–1936: From Chieftaincy to Monarchical State* (Oxford: Oxford University Press, 1993), p. 141. Distinguished scholars such as Avraham Sela still contend that 'Palestinians are highly divided into tribes and [. . .] this poses a major obstacle to their self-determination': A. Sela, conversation with the author, Mandel School for Advanced Studies, Jerusalem, 19 July 2017. Uzi Rabi, whose edited collection nonetheless has the merit of showing differences between highly heterogeneous contexts, argued that 'tribal leaders are siding with different parties, further deepening the cleavages in Syrian society [. . .] It's high time to bring the tribe back into the analysis of states in the Middle East'. U. Rabi (ed.), *Tribes and States in a Changing Middle East* (London: Hurst, 2016), pp. 8 and 10. Mordechai Kedar went so far as to propose a 'tribal solution' to the Israeli-Palestinian conflict, that is the creation of eight 'Palestinian tribal emirates' (Gaza Strip, Jenīn, Nāblus, Rāmallāh, Jericho, Tūlkarem, Qalqīlya and the Palestinian part of Hebron/al-Khalīl). Concerning the Iraqi context, Kedar noted that 'tribes continue to fight each other' and that 'all this dream of creating an Iraqi nation [. . .] fails in replacing the traditional loyalties and this is the source of all evil in Iraq'. Excerpts from Kedar's lecture at Rochester (New York), available at: https://www.youtube.com/watch?v=cxY37JD2Pr8. The problems connected to the 'tribal approach' and the importance of overcoming the 'fragmentation' of the local milieu were

highlighted to me by, among others, Palestinian political activist Sam Bahūr. Interview with the author, al-Manāra, Rāmallāh, 12 October 2011.

37. Cited in F. U. Ohaegbulam, *Nationalism in Colonial and Post-Colonial Africa* (Washington DC: University Press of America, 1977), p. 60.

38. T. Ranger, *The Invention of Tribalism in Zimbawe* (Gweru: Mambo Press, 1985), p. 17.

39. R. Papstein, 'From Ethnic Identity to Tribalism: The Upper Zambezi Region of Zambia, 1830–1981', in L. Vail (ed.), *The Creation of Tribalism in Southern Africa* (Berkeley: University of California Press, 1991), p. 373. On the codification of group differences within state structures in Africa and India, and the way through which it transforms and hardens group identities, see M. Mamdani, *Citizen and Subject: Contemporary Africa and the Legacy of Late Colonialism* (Princeton: Princeton University Press 1996) and N. Dirks, *Castes of Mind: Colonialism and the Making of Modern India* (Princeton: Princeton University Press, 2011).

40. See F. Haddād, '"Sectarianism" and its Discontents in the Study of the Middle East', *Middle East Journal*, 71(3) (Summer 2017): 362–83. Haddād notes that 'not only can political behavior be sect-centric (and thereby perceived as "sectarian") without "the deployment of religious heritage as a primary marker of modern political identity", it can also be sect-centric while standing militantly against any such deployment', p. 369. Makdisi contends that 'sectarianism refers to the deployment of religious heritage as a primary marker of modern political identity': U. Makdisi, *The Culture of Sectarianism: Community, History, and Violence in Nineteenth-Century Ottoman Lebanon* (Berkeley: University of California Press, 2000), p. 7.

41. See Mneimneh, 'From Communitarianism to Sectarianism', pp. 62–82.

42. M. Apostolov, *Religious Minorities, Nation States, and Security* (Aldershot: Ashgate, 2001), p. 15. See also J. Eiber (ed.), *The Future of Religious Minorities in the Middle East* (Lanham MD: Lexington Books, 2018), pp. ix–xx.

43. B. White, *The Emergence of Minorities in the Middle East* (Edinburgh: Edinburgh University Press, 2011), p. 209. As noted by White: 'The communities that emerged as "minorities" during the mandate cannot simply be mapped back onto the millets or Christian and Jewish communities of the Ottoman period. A minority is a modern phenomenon, a millet pre-modern', p. 45. It should be added that the so-called 'millet system' was neither unitary, nor static. In Latif Tas's words: 'It was also not a "system", which implies something structured to come top-down from the centre as part of a representation of authority,

but rather something that emerged bottom-up in different ways from the various communities'. L. Tas, 'The Myth of the Ottoman Millet System', *International Journal on Minority and Group Rights* 21 (2014): 497–526.

44. The millet practice ('system' implies a top-down structure coming from the centre as part of a representation of authority) emerged as a bottom-up process from the various communities, representing their different ways of life. This practice, often highly localised and unevenly applied, registered a process of institutionalisation and centralisation in the second half of the nineteenth century. Laura Robson notes that 'the idea of minorities (and, for that matter, majorities) arose outside the Middle East, in a post-Enlightenment Europe': L. Robson (ed.), *Minorities and the Modern Arab World. New Perspectives* (Syracuse NY: Syracuse University Press, 2016), p. 3.

45. A. Rodrigue, 'Difference and Tolerance in the Ottoman Empire: Interview by Nancy Reynolds', *Stanford Humanities Review* 5(1) (Spring 1996): 81–92. Rodrigue clarifies that 'it is fundamentally wrong to conceptualize the Ottoman Empire, and the Middle East more generally, before the modern period in terms of majorities and minorities': ibid.

46. Stephen Hemsley Longrigg (1893–1979) points out that 'the oft-drawn picture of Syria as a "mosaic of minorities" can be misleading, and this is not only by ignoring the immense preponderance of the Sunni Muslim population, but also by unduly emphasizing the elements which separated this majority from the rest, and minimizing the wide common ground which all shared': S. H. Longrigg, *Syria and Lebanon under French Mandate* (London and New York: Oxford University Press, 1958), p. 11. Wehrey noted that 'sectarian differences have [often] coexisted with, or been subsumed by other affinities': F. Wehrey (ed.), *Beyond Sunni and Shia* (London: Hurst, 2017), p. 2.

47. LANT, Series: E, Carton 550, Dossier 5 (1890–1912), folio 35, French governor of Algeria Jules Cambon, Tunis, 11 January 1897.

48. J. Massad, *Colonial Effects* (New York: Columbia University Press, 2001), p. 275.

49. D. McDowall, *A Modern History of the Kurds* (London: I. B. Tauris, 2007), pp. 1–2.

50. TNA FO 624/28/152, R. W. Bullard, British Legation, Tehran, 28 October 1942.

51. TNA FO 624/28/240, Letter from the Nawab of Bahawalpur to the Viceroy and Governor General of India, Lord Linlithgow, 15 December 1941.

52. D. McDowall, *A Modern History of the Kurds* (London: I. B. Tauris, 2007), pp. 1–2.

53. When European imperialists tried 'to create a Kurdish state at Sèvres [1920], many Kurds fought alongside Ataturk to upend the treaty. It's a reminder that political loyalties can and do transcend national identities in ways we would do well to realize today': N. Danforth, 'Forget Sykes-Picot. It's the Treaty of Sèvres that Explains the Modern Middle East', *Foreign Policy*, 10 August 2015. Available at: http://foreignpolicy.com/2015/08/10/sykes-picot-treaty-ofsevres-modern-turkey-middle-east-borders-turkey.

54. A. Smith, *Ethno-symbolism and Nationalism* (London: Routledge, 2009), pp. 25 and 72.

55. M. Benvenisti, *Son of the Cypresses* (Berkeley: University of California Press, 2007), p. 233.

56. TNA FO 624/28/152, Kirkūk, 1 August 1942. Holt was the 'Oriental Secretary' at the British Embassy in Baghdād.

57. 'Some Yazidis', noted for instance Yazidi scholar Murad Ismail, 'consider themselves Kurds while others consider themselves ethnically Yazidi or as an ethnoreligious group distinct from the Kurds': M. Ismael, 'Kurdish Independence and the Unheard Yazidi Voice', *Al-Arabiya*, 22 September 2017. Available at: https://english.alarabiya.net/en/views/news/middle-east/2017/09/22/Kurdish-Independence-and-the-unheard-Yazidi-voice.html.

58. S. Telhami and M. Barnett (eds), *Identity and Foreign Policy in the Middle East* (New York: Cornell University Press, 2002), p. 19.

59. See Y. al-Qaradāwī, *Al-Hulūl al-Mustawrada wa Kayfa Janat 'ala Ummatinā* [The Imported Solutions and How they are Rooted in our Community] (Cairo: Maktabat Wahba, 1977), vol. 1. Despite providing some interesting inputs, Al-Qaradāwī is known for his uncompromising views and for considering anyone who does not fully comply with his views as 'not concerned with the problems of Islam': ibid., pp. 6–7.

60. Modern-day Syria and Iraq both have several significant antecedents in the pre-Islamic world. Focusing, for instance, on the thesis of a 'divided and artificial Iraq', what nowadays would be referred to as a non-sectarian patriotism has indeed more complex roots in the Iraqi context than is often claimed. For a long time, such feelings proved tendentially stronger and more rooted than sectarianism. A study conducted by a group of Iraqi intellectuals for a Norwegian think tank clarified this aspect, pointing out, for example, that the claim that

Iraq is an artificial creation concocted by the British after the First World War overlooks the fact that 'the separation between the three Ottoman provinces that was in place in 1914 dated back only 30 years, to 1884' (see 'More than "Shiites" and "Sunnis" – How a Post-Sectarian Strategy Can Change the Logic and Facilitate Sustainable Political Reform in Iraq', in *Norwegian Institute of International Affairs Report*, February 2009). For much of the eighteenth and nineteenth centuries, those same three Ottoman provinces – Basra, Baghdād, Mosul – were governed as a single entity, with Baghdād as their centre of gravity. Even at the time, numerous local intellectuals indicated the area as 'Iraq', while the expression 'the region of Iraq' (*iklim-i Irak*) can be found in early eighteenth century Ottoman chronicles such as *Gulshan-i khulafa* (1730). See L. Kamel, 'Artificial Nations? The Sykes-Picot and the Islamic State's Narratives in a Historical Perspective', *Diacronie Studi di Storia Contemporanea* 25(1) (2016): 1–20.

61. For instance, the annual Nabi Musa festival, which gathered thousands of people, primarily from areas in present-day Israel and the Palestinian territories, was the expression of a clearly emerging 'proto-national cohesion' aiming at commemorating the traumatic events related to the Crusades. See K. al-Asali, *Mawṣim al-Nabi Musa Filastīn: tā'rīkh al-Mawṣim wa 'l-Maqam* [The Nabi Musa Festival in Palestine: the History of the Festival and of the Shrine] ('Amman: Dār al-Karmil, 1990), and U. S. Barghūti, *Al-Marahil* [Turning Points] (Beirut: al-Mu'assasat al-Arabīyya, 2001), pp. 76–7.

62. TNA FO 371/5034, Pan-Syrian Congress to Fayṣal, 19 May 1919.

63. It is interesting to note that the support for Haider al-Abadi – the current prime minister and a Shi'a – is today highest among the Sunni Arab population. See M. al-Dagher, 'A Striking Positive Shift in Sunni Opinion in Iraq Is Underway. Here's What it Means', *Washington Post*, 14 September 2017. Available at: https://www.washingtonpost.com/news/monkey-cage/wp/2017/09/14/iraqi-sunnis-are-impressed-by-the-defeat-of-isis-heres-what-that-could-mean/?utm_term=.7fadc3aabe5c.

64. B. Lewis, *The Shaping of the Modern Middle East* (Oxford: Oxford University Press, 1994), p. 3. One year after (1903) the term was allegedly invented, the 'annuario' (yearbook) of Bocconi University clarified that 'Middle East is not just a geographical expression [*non è soltanto una espressione geografica*], but also a geographical, political end economic entity formed by a certain number of States': Università Commerciale Luigi Bocconi, *Annuario* (Milan: Società Tipografica Editrice Popolare, 1903), p. 137.

65. F. Halliday, *The Middle East in International Relations* (Cambridge: Cambridge University Press, 2005), p. 77.

66. See R. Hartshorne, *The Nature of Geography: A Critical Survey of Current Thought in the Light of the Past* (Lancaster PA: Association of American Geographers, 1939).

67. Y. Lee, 'Asia as a Methodology', in O. Grau (ed.), *Museum and Archive on the Move* (Berlin: De Gruyter, 2017), p. 124.

68. After a visit to the region, Henry van Dyke (1852–1933), professor at the University of Princeton, argued that 'the Jordan is not a little river to be loved; it is a barrier to be passed over': H. van Dyke, *Out-Of-Doors in the Holy Land* (New York: Scribner, 1908), p. 132. On the following page, van Dyke defined Jordan an 'everlasting symbol of division, of separation', p. 133. This is what happened to Felice Bovet during his pilgrimage in 1858: 'I wanted to swim across the river [Jordan] to gather *Idumea palms*. But the current was so strong that it quickly carried me away. I fought with all my strength, until, finally too tired to go on, I began to call for help'. F. Bovet, *Viaggio in Terra Santa* [A Voyage to the Holy Land] (Florence: Tipografia Claudiana, 1867), p. 175. The US explorers William Libbey (1855–1927) and Franklin Hoskins (1858–1920) went beyond, arguing that, until bridges were built on the river, the residents on both sides of it would remain 'strangers or enemies, to each other'. W. Libbey and F. E. Hoskins, *The Jordan Valley and Petra* (New York: Putnam, 1905), vol. 1, p. 89. Such considerations were in line with the impressions reported by the British consul in Jerusalem, John Dickson, in July 1892: 'The "Mutasereflick", a minor province, of Palestine, is bounded in the North by a line which runs from the river Awja (a little to the north of Jaffa) past the village of Sinjel (between Jerusalem and Nāblus) and down to the fords of the Jordan, near Jericho, and is separated from Eastern Syria by the river Jordan and the Dead Sea'. Israel State Archives (ISA) RG 160/2881-P, British consul in Jerusalem, John Dickson (1847–1906), to the Marquis of Salisbury (1830–1903), 19 July 1892.

69. Bruce Gilley, for instance, went so far to claim that 'Western colonialism was, as a general rule, both objectively beneficial and subjectively legitimate in most of the places where it was found': see B. Gilley, 'The Case for Colonialism', *Third World Quarterly*, e-version (September 2017): 1–17.

70. This point was made to me also by Majeda Omar, director of the Royal Institute for Interfaith Studies in Jordan. Conversation with the author, 'Amman, 18 July 2016.

71. 'A delegation of Spanish and Gauls in Babylon, in the middle of the Orient'. P. Orosius, *Historiarum adversum paganos libri* (Leipzig: Teubner, 1889), vol. 6, pp. 19–20.

72. D. Foliard, *Dislocating the Orient: British Maps and the Making of the Middle East, 1854–1921* (Chicago: University of Chicago Press, 2017), p. 209. Despite providing several interesting insights, Foliard's book does not include any reference to pre-nineteenth-century use of the expression 'Middle East'.

2

The First Moment – 1830s: The Germs of Competing Ethno-religious Visions

In the previous 500 years, the 'multi-ethnic' nature of Ottoman society had rarely been considered problematic: Scholars have demonstrated that conflict along lines of communal differences constituted extraordinary moments in an otherwise well-oiled administration that capitalized on the heterogeneous composition of society. After the 1830s, however, it becomes increasingly clear that the world order was changing and what was once the empire's strength became its potential weakness. Its diversity would be used as a wedge.[1]

Isa Blumi

In his classic book *A History of the Arab Peoples*, Albert Hourani chose the first major conquest of an Arab-speaking country, Algeria, by France (1830–47) as the key turning point of his analysis on the 'age of European empires'.[2] From then on, Hourani contended, Muslim states and societies could no longer live in a self-sufficient system of inherited culture: 'Their need was now to generate the strength to survive in a world dominated by others'.[3] The historical context that paved the way for this epochal outcome was nonetheless rooted in earlier imperial dynamics, of which Napoleon's invasion of Egypt (1798) – the first modern incursion by the West into the Middle East – was the most celebrated example.[4]

Napoleon, like most of the major statesmen of his time, aimed to take advantage of the growing instability of the Ottoman Empire, whose initial regression can be traced back to a number of causes, including the abolition of the Timar,[5] and the outcomes of cold and drought during the Little

Ice Age, when the rising population pressure and resource shortages created the conditions for the outbreak of the Celali Rebellion (1595–1610) – a turning point in Ottoman fortunes, particularly in terms of agriculture and economy.[6]

Since then, the Ottoman Empire gradually transformed itself into a form of land of conquest for the increasingly aggressive European powers: 'This is an odd Country', British diplomat John Bidwell stated from Istanbul in 1809, 'where every foreign minister enjoys, from the Porte, absolute power over the Subjects of this Sovereign [. . .] His house is a sanctuary, the violation of which by the Turks would instantly produce a war between the two Countries.'[7]

Napoleon's intervention had a long-lasting impact on the region. Yet it was not that incursion but rivalry with Russia, exacerbated in the last decade of the eighteenth century, that prompted the final arbiter of the region's fate prior to the Second World War – Britain – to intervene more directly in the Eastern Mediterranean. The presence of a powerful Ottoman state was considered by Tsarist Russia as an obstacle for accessing Black Sea and Mediterranean ports. Britain, on the other hand, perceived Tsarist policies in the Balkans and Asia as a threat to its trade routes to the Far East and made it a priority to preserve the territorial integrity of the 'sick man of Europe'. France also supported the dismantling of the Ottoman Empire and aimed to establish an independent Arab state in the area, under its direct influence, that could hinder British trade routes to India. Indeed, India was the cornerstone of Britain's imperial strategies towards the region and, due to geopolitics, history and its unique status within the Empire, had a decisive influence on a chain of overseas agencies that stretched from southern Persia to eastern Africa.

Building on this historical background characterised by competing imperial perceptions and dynamics, this chapter sheds light on a number of political and identity-related developments that, from the 1830s, started to permeate large parts of the Middle East, mapping out the early transition from porous identities to competing ethno-religious visions. The sections that follow analyse the cultural, ideological, political and commercial implications of the 'opening process' of the region, a historical phase ignited by the 1831 invasion of Greater Syria by the army of Muḥammad 'Alī (1769–1849). The chapter ends by assessing the significance of the process of rearrangement of multidimensional and multifaceted local communities into what might be seen as the archetype of the nineteenth-century nation-state.

From Porous Identities to Competing Ethno-religious Visions

A number of historical phases – including those related to Fakhr-al-Dīn (1572–1635), Genghis Khan (whose soldiers swept through the region in the thirteenth century), the Safavid Empire, as well as a few other dynasties – left significant traces on the demographic and confessional equilibrium of the region. It was, however, the third decade of the nineteenth century that came to represent a sort of watershed, with enormous consequences for much of the area. In the years following the invasion (1831) of Syria and Palestine by Ibrahīm Pasha (1789–1848), the region, hitherto largely impermeable to these and other related processes, experienced growing religious and 'sectarian' cleavages, as well as an increasing militarisation and the rising of new dynamics of competition between the great powers;[8] until the 1830s, as Roger Owen remarks, the Syrian coast had 'no direct trade with Britain'.[9] In other words, as European states strived to expand their influence, they worked to sharpen local identities and peculiarities in order to bring down competing powers. It was then, in the same decade in which Ottoman Turkey started to have permanent diplomatic postings in European capitals, that Greater Syria witnessed the rising of protonationalisms rooted in conflicting confessional visions:

> Ibrahim Pasha's establishment of municipal councils, a Western institution, carried unintended consequences for the political climate of Greater Syria [. . .] Their establishment enabled the development of a political body whose membership was allocated along sectarian lines [. . .] These councils altered the political landscape, forcing marginalized muqata'jis to decide between losing their privileged lifestyle by opposing Egyptian rule or siding with their fellow elites against 'commoners.' This sectarian institution demonstrated an open challenge to the traditional political discourse within Greater Syria, as they operated outside of the traditional vertical non-sectarian subject–ruler paradigm embodied in the muqata'ji system.[10]

It is significant that it was during those same years, coinciding with a period of unprecedented Western penetration and of 'early' confessionalisation of a few local cities,[11] that the concept of *dawla* – linked in the Quran and in later sources with the meaning of circulation of power and fortune – appeared for the first time in its modern connotation of the 'state'.[12] Meanwhile, the term *jinsīya* – translated in an English dictionary of the early nineteenth century as 'the correspondence of a kind, species, or genus' – started to be employed,[13] by a (still limited) number of people in the region, in connection with the idea of 'nation'.[14] In Wael Abu-'Uksa's words:

> In correspondence between Ibrahim Pasha and Syrian notables regarding the confirmation of Jasper Chasseaud's appointment as the American consul in Syria in 1833, Ibrahim expresses his wishes for Chasseaud's success in conducting the matters of his compatriots, *'abnā' jinsihi'* (literally, those who belong to his kind) [. . .] During the 1830s nationalism became a prominent factor in conceptualizing history in Arabic.[15]

The developments that, from the 1830s onwards, started to occur across large parts of the Middle East were ignited by a mixture of factors, a number of them linked to the influence exerted by Western powers and their conflictual geopolitical and commercial interests. Even more consequential, however, were the first effects, partially visible already from the early 1820s, of the rising of nationalism from 'West-to-East' in the Ottoman Empire.[16] This followed a geographic and temporal course that involved Greeks, then Serbs, Romanians, Bulgarians, Armenians, Albanians (an exception in the West-to-East course), Kurds and, last but not least, Arabs, whose centres of nationalism were Damascus, Baghdād and Cairo – capitals of colonised countries – and not, for instance, Riyadh or Mecca, cities of independent states.[17]

Muḥammad 'Alī's '*khurūj*'

From a more intra-regional perspective, the major developments witnessed in the 1830s were largely connected to the self-declared *khedivé* of Egypt and Sudan, Muḥammad 'Alī,[18] whose policies ushered in a new era perceived by many as 'a sign of the weakening of the Ottoman Empire'.[19] He came to power in 1805, exploiting the power vacuum that followed the expulsion of the Napoleonic troops from Egypt (1801).[20] Like Napoleon, Muḥammad ʿAlī was committed to separating Egypt from the rest of the Ottoman Empire. A modern organisation of the state, an efficient centralised administration, an efficient army and industry: these were the main tools through which the 'enlightened despot' strived to implement his policies.[21] In order to speed up his plans, he took advantage of several scientists and experts, primarily French and Italian, as well as of a number of young officials who were sent on training missions to Europe (among them Niqula El Massabki, a Maronite, originally from Damascus, who studied the art of printing in Milan and succeeded, in 1820, in establishing the first official press in Egypt: *Al-Amīriya*).[22]

In 1831, after securing his grip on power and succeeding in thwarting the threat posed by the Mamluks,[23] the Egyptian *khedivé* decided to exploit the growing weakness of the Ottoman authorities by starting what documents of the time defined as a 'rebellion' (*khurūj*) against the sultan.[24] The rebellion was ignited by the invasion of Syria and Palestine: two strategic buffer zones, coveted by Muḥammad ʿAlī for a long time, useful, among other things, to guarantee the access to the raw materials needed for Egypt's economic growth.[25] It should be noted that the permission to establish a governorate in that strategic area, as well as to have a free hand in Egypt itself, had already been formally granted by Sultan Mahmūd II to Muḥammad ʿAlī in 1822. In exchange, the latter agreed, the same year, to send his troops to quell several attempted revolts by Greeks who wished to gain independence from Ottoman control.

Muḥammad ʿAlī's army – led by his eldest son Ibrahīm Pasha, with the support of French-born Egyptian commander Sulaymān Pasha (1788–1860)[26] and the assistance of a number of local Greek Catholics[27] – invaded Syria and Palestine on behalf of Mahmūd II, although, paradoxically, this was contrary to the wishes and interests of the sultan himself.[28] Ottoman forces proved, nonetheless, to be too archaic to be able to organise a serious opposition. The region was conquered almost at a stroke. An organised opposition was encountered only in ʿAkkā (Acre), but its seemingly impregnable fortress, which Napoleon failed to capture three decades earlier, was overcome within six months of the siege commencing, on 27 May 1832.[29]

The troops lead by Ibrahīm Pasha took possession of Damascus in the weeks that followed, reaching Adana (southern Turkey) in August. Egyptian forces crossed the Taurus Mountains and, on 22 December, defeated at Koniah (Central Anatolia) an army of 60,000 soldiers sent by the Ottoman sultan to repel the attack.[30]

The progression of Ibrahīm Pasha's troops ended 150km from Istanbul. Muḥammad 'Alī, in fact, did not intend to bring about the full collapse of the Ottoman central authority and accepted to withdraw in exchange for the full control of Adana and the Syrian regions. This decision was largely taken also due to the pressure exerted by Great Britain, France and Russia: these powers were interested in maintaining the political status quo, fearing that the Ottoman government might have fallen under the direct control of a less influenceable local player.[31] Although these fears were destined to persist, Muḥammad 'Alī managed (partially) to obviate them by adopting, over the years, a dual course. On the one hand, as a warning, he made a deliberate use of violence against local populations (Muslims, Christians and others).[32] On the other hand, he implemented openly liberal and flexible policies towards foreigners residing in the region, personally engaging in the appointment of foreign consuls in a number of urban centres in Syria and Palestine.[33] 'Mohammed Ali', noted Lord Anthony Ashley-Cooper (1801–85) in 1839, 'and his ferocious son-in-law Ibrahim Pasha, though terrible to their own, are mild as sucking doves towards independent Europeans; their savage violence has opened Egypt and Syria to the traveller from distant lands, and rendered his journey easy and secure'.[34]

'Opening' the Region

From the partial withdrawal of Muḥammad 'Alī's army, until 1840, for a total of eight years, Greater Syria remained under full Egyptian control, with a central administration located in Damascus.[35] Never more than in this brief historical phase, the region was opened to Western powers' influence and missionaries' activities,[36] as well as to major explorations (also laying the groundwork for the field of inquiry commonly known as 'Biblical archaeology').[37] These epochal occurrences foreshadowed and, to a certain extent, prepared the ground for a new, largely Western-inspired, reformist era (see Chapter 3) that, between various failures and a few successes, involved progressively the whole area, present-day Syria included. 'I now call your attention', wrote *New Yorker* columnist Sarah R. Haight (1808–81) while touring the region in that very period, 'to the important and beneficial changes which might result from the subjugation of these regions to the rule of Western nations'.[38]

Within a few years, a number of reforms were implemented, ranging from the centralisation of the taxation system to the development of the roads network and the reorganisation of the agricultural sector. On top of this, thanks mainly to the efforts of a wide number of Protestant missionaries, Jerusalem, Beirut, Cairo, Istanbul and several other urban centres in the region (including Iranian cities such as Tabriz and Urmia) registered the opening of new hospitals and schools –long considered as propaganda tools by the Ottoman authorities[39] – as well as the development of tourism, banks, commerce and initiatives linked to exploration and cartography.[40] These and other related phenomena were hastened also by the evolution of an articulated system of communication: telegraph wires, mail services, undersea cables, expanding rail infrastructures and, from 1835, fast passenger steamers that connected Britain (and then France and the Austrian Empire)[41] with what an 1837 House of Commons report defined as 'the uncivilized nations of the earth'.[42] The latter, on a number of occasions, expressed their strong opposition to the ways in which these new systems of communication tended to depict local people and dynamics. An editorial published on 'Souriya' (Syria) in 1875 – when 'signs of disaffection' were 'being reported at the Porte [in] every corner' of cities such as Aleppo,[43] Damascus and Beirut[44] – contended, for instance, that it was well known:

> that the various Christian confessions [. . .] have continued to this day to enjoy perfect security and peace under the protection of the Sultan without regard to their distinctive creeds and ceremonies, except the Protestants, who have a peculiar desire to spread inflammatory news here as it is their habit everywhere [. . .] it is the character of the Protestants from whatever nation [. . .] they lie to deceive simple and ignorant people by diffusing such false reports in order to bring them under their own community. This is also the case with the London newspapers [they] fill their pages with lies and inventions [in order to] inform their readers that Protestantism is spreading and prospering in all parts of the world.[45]

Notwithstanding the cultural but also ideological relevance of these kinds of local perception, it is important to stress that the new developments, in some cases, simply helped to accelerate processes that were already going on and, for the same reason, did not trigger major upheavals in the life rhythms of local people. It should also be added that, in a number of cases, the 'encounter' with the West actually served to strengthen traditional customs and practices and did not affect all areas equally: rural districts, in particular, initially remained almost completely immune to the epochal processes mentioned above.[46] Finally, it is necessary to consider that, at least in the first phase, the local productive fabric succeeded in maintaining its competitiveness and continued to generate considerable internal trade, that is, commercial exchanges with other parts of the Empire, more than with foreign trading partners.

Despite all these considerations, the broader scenarios that resulted, influenced by factors that went well beyond economic aspects – the Eastern Mediterranean was experiencing a sort of invasion of goods (mainly textiles) from Europe from the 1820s – contributed to an accumulation of pressure on a variety of equilibria that had been consolidated over time.[47] In the medium and long term, those who would be caught up in the net of a global economic system dominated by Europe were, in fact, not only the local elites and merchants – immediately ready to adjust their lifestyles to external influences – but also many other segments of the local population. In several districts of Syria and Palestine, for instance, the gap that divided the low-income classes from the most prosperous ones widened in the course of one generation. Moreover, these occurences did not succeed to alter the tendentially conservative nature of the local social and cultural milieu, despite, however, having significant repercussions for its subsequent development.

Among these repercussions was also the contribution of economic conditions to demographic growth: Istanbul, for instance, increased its population from about 375,000 inhabitants in the 1830s to over than a million at the outbreak of the First World War; while Beirutis, whose number was around 6,000 in the early 1830s (300,000 in 1910), started in that same decade to establish a number of neighbourhoods outside the Old City, including Ashrafiye, Ra's Beirut and Zokak el-Blat (which was home also to a Jewish community until the mid-twentieth century). Nonetheless, major differences occurred between the economic growth of Muslims and non-Muslim groups within the empire. This had much to do with a number of interconnected factors that favoured *Ra'āyās* (non-Muslims) at the expense of Muslims.[48] As noted by Karpat:

> The non-Muslim population actually grew at a fairly fast rate after the 1830s – probably 2 per cent annually; the Muslim population declined or remained the same in number. There are indications, however, that fertility rates among the Muslims began to increase after 1850. The causes of the disproportionate fertility rates among the two groups are to be found in the special economic and social conditions which favored non-Muslims and penalized the Muslims, especially Turks. Male Turks spent their peak reproductive years in military service and were unable to marry and settle down to take advantage of economic opportunities. Then, when in the nineteenth century the Ottoman state was exposed to the influence of the European capitalist economy and to intensified internal and international trade, several non-Muslim groups became the early recipients of the economic benefits. Although numerically a minority, the non-Muslims, who had no military obligations, throve under the changed economic, cultural, and social conditions, and this had a positive effect on the size of their populations.[49]

The Process of Re-Ottomanisation

'The intended realization by [Muḥammad] Alī', noted the British Consul-General for Egypt Patrick Campbell (1779–1857) in 1838, 'of his long-meditated plan to declare his independence, has at length been unequivocally communicated by him, both to M. Cochelet, the Consul-General of France, and myself'.[50] Muḥammad 'Alī's long-term ambitions were thus made clear: he intended to obtain the full control of Egypt (including succession rights) and Syria (without succession rights).

The governments of Great Britain, Russia, Austria and Russia looked with great apprehension at the extraordinary results – including the capitulation of the Turkish fleet – achieved by the Egyptian army in Nezīb on 24 June 1839. To tackle the situation, the four European powers, with the presence of a few Ottoman emissaries, met in London on 15 July 1840, for what later became known as the London Straits Convention. It was then agreed that Muḥammad 'Alī would be offered permanent control (not, however, sovereignty, which would still be subject to the sultan) over Egypt and the *sanjak* of 'Akkā, while asking for his withdrawal from the coastal regions of Mount Lebanon and the inland areas of Syria. Yet Muḥammad 'Alī's prevarications – he was convinced of being able to count on France's backing – prompted the European powers to shift from diplomacy to military action, in order to guarantee the stability of an Ottoman Empire that was weak but instrumental to their strategic interests.

In September 1840, the British Navy, led by Admiral Robert Stopford (1768–1847), and flanked by the Austrian fleet, docked near Beirut and started to shell Sidon and 'Akkā. Ibrahīm Pasha's forces did not put up much resistance. The entire area was brought back under the authority of the Ottoman sultan; Muḥammad 'Alī was forced to reduce his claims, accepting the title of *suzerain* of Egypt and Sudan.

Once its authority was restored over Syria and Palestine, the Ottoman Empire, weakened but still intact, faced two main external challenges: a further proliferation of the activities of Christian missionaries in the region; and the increasing intrusion of Western governments, on which the Tanẓīmāt (see Chapter 3) tried to put a limit. The price imposed by the great powers for the re-establishment of the sultan's sovereignty in the Syrian context appeared, in fact, clear: Istanbul was bound to recognise European influence on the Eastern Mediterranean. It is within this frame that we should consider the many consular offices that were opened in the 1840s in a number of cities in Syria and Palestine – where the first hoisting of a national flag (French) occurred in 1843, in Jerusalem. The faculty granted to Western consuls to try and, in some cases, to arrest subjects residing in the Ottoman Empire but holding citizenship of their respective countries was further proof of the encroaching influence of external actors.

1830s: Echoing Ideas, Shaping Commerce

Writing in 1837, Anglo-Irish author Robert Montgomery Martin (1801–68) noted being 'aware that the period in which we live is one of the most momentous epochs which mark the progress of our species in the ascending scale of knowledge, virtue and happiness', adding that Britain would be the nucleus around which all world nations would 'form themselves in concentric circles'.[51] Just a year later, the British Parliament established the Public Record Office ('to keep safely the public records' and shed light on the legacy of Britain's past), while the year after that (1839), Britain succeeded in establishing a permanent settlement in Aden – a major Yemenite hub of transportation for the entire region – and in opening the first con-sulate of a Western country in Jerusalem; from then on, for over a century, London was the pre-eminent strategic actor in the region.[52]

The history of European, and particularly British, imperialism(s) did not, of course, start in the nineteenth century but grew organically out of a long narrative of imperial expansion – that also includes the Crusades – characterised by interconnected histories, rather than sudden ruptures. Yet the 1830s marked what might be viewed as the starting point of the global phase of imperialism, that is, the moment in which the latter, in John Darwin's words, 'ceased to be an affair of colonial patronage and mercantile lobbies and turned instead into a global programme, the "imperialism of free trade"'.[53] In this decade, and for the first time, average numbers of migrants from Britain, mainly from the south of England (Kent, Hampshire, Somerset and Surrey), regularly exceeded 100,000 people, including a large number of merchants and missionaries. The average emigration of those years reached, in some contexts, nearly four times that of the previous decade.[54] Additionally, in 1830, the East India Company opened the Red Sea route. Before then, passengers, goods or letters heading for Asia had no alternative but to circumnavigate Africa (from 1835, mail for India was sent through the Middle East rather than around the Cape of Good Hope). All these aspects further contributed to hasten the spread of a number of ideas and concepts in the Middle East (and elsewhere).

The 'global programme' to which Darwin referred was directly linked to the increasing strengthening of 'informal imperialism', that is, the indirect control of large parts of the region, usually though trade treaties and loans, by external powers: a system, far less expensive than formal imperialism, that triggered the conditions for the creation of a number of colonial or semi-colonial states and the access to bigger markets and more resources – including fuel, cotton and rubber.

In this sense, the 1838 Treaty of Balta Liman, a formal trade agreement between the British and Ottoman authorities, played a particularly important role. While Britain continued to apply strict protectionist policies to its agricultural markets, the Porte granted equal taxation to local and external merchants, expanding the old British capitulatory privileges and placing London in a pre-eminent position in the Empire's foreign trade (a number of similar free trade treaties were signed between the other major Western powers and the Ottoman authorities between 1838 and 1841).

The expansion of the Ottoman market for British manufactured goods became an increasing necessity in the years following the dissolution of the Levant Company (1825) – the English chartered company that had been established in 1592 – when the strategic importance of the region and the increasing presence of British merchants pushed the British authorities to take routes and local resources under more direct and stricter control. This was a decision with far-reaching impacts that further contributed to raise British trade revenues (imports and exports combined) from around £4 million in 1830 to nearly £15 million by 1860.[55] Yet the mindset through which British consuls approached the region from the 1830s onwards went beyond merely commercial calculations:

> The change in the character of British consuls in Syria during the 1830s is noticeable. The old Levant Company agents had been almost wholly concerned with trade but the new breed of consuls sought to justify their position by political activity. All European consuls endeavoured to interfere in the government of the region in the hope of advancing the interests of their own governments, or in some cases of furthering their personal ambitions or enthusiasms.[56]

'Archetypal' Entities

The Treaty of Balta Liman was negotiated and signed at a time when the Ottoman authorities were facing huge challenges, including suffering a series of territorial losses in Europe. In 1830, following the intervention of France, Britain and Russia, the Ottoman authorities granted Greece full independence, bringing to an end four centuries of imperial rule and almost nine years of war against the Ottoman forces. This represented a major result for hundreds of thousands of ordinary Greeks and particularly for Orthodox Christian Ottoman subjects, to which the new Hellenic Kingdom, thanks mainly to the support it enjoyed from the Great Powers, began to extend the scope of its nationality (the practice of extra-territoriality): 'Among the competing foreign nationalities', noted Ayşe Özil, 'the particularity of Greece was that its ties of nationality were mainly based on Orthodox Christianity'.[57] Besides epitomising a new and, in many respects, promising era, these outcomes also represented the first of a long series of successful attempts through which Western powers worked to rearrange the multidimensional and multifaceted Greek-Ottoman community as a European kingdom, establishing a sort of archetype of the nineteenth-century nation-state. This was a powerful linking element in the context of the passage from empire to the era of 'sealed identities'. It should be noted that variations of this same 'archetypal model' were fostered in the years to follow in several other Ottoman contexts, most notably in the Lebanon, where European powers, downplaying the geographic overlapping of the different local communities, urged the partition of Mount Lebanon into micro 'religious entities'. The proposal, known as 'double *qaimaqamate*' and adopted by the sultan on December 1842, brought about the establishment of a Christian district in the north and an area under Druze control in the south, further contributing to the homogenisation and violent polarisation witnessed in the area thereafter.[58] These kinds of policy were implemented in a context in which a number of Western observers – like the French consul in Beirut, Henri Guys, author of a novel in the 1830s dealing with Beirut's inclusive religious diversity – tried to distinguish between Muslim and Christian habits, often ending up failing to spot meaningful differences, lumping them together as simply 'Syrian' or 'Eastern'.[59]

Notes

1. I. Blumi, *Foundations of Modernity: Human Agency and the Imperial State* (New York: Routledge, 2012), p. 48.
2. The colonisation of Algeria, its subsequent annexation as a French département, and the imposition of a French administrative model, led to the destruction of all the indigenous administrative apparatus and traditional elites, without their being replaced by new ones. Chalcraft contends that 'almost half the Algerian population was killed directly or indirectly by the French': J. Chalcraft, *Popular Politics in the Making of the Modern Middle East* (Cambridge: Cambridge University Press, 2016), p. 113.
3. A. Hourani, *A History of the Arab Peoples* (London: Faber, 1991), p. 263.
4. The invasion coincided with among other things the '(re)discovery' of the Rosetta Stone and the importing of the first Arabic moveable-type printing press (seized by Napoleon from the Vatican): an occurrence destined to further stimulate the expansion of Arabic reading and writing. Its first printed document, a circular in Arabic distributed in Cairo, was a proclamation by Napoleon himself in which he claimed to be a defender of Islam.

5. The Timar system, almost abandoned in the seventeenth century and formally abolished in 1831, foresaw that the conquered territories would be distributed among the participants of the military campaigns in the form of temporary rights over the land. See B. Lewis, 'Some Reflections on the Decline of the Ottoman Empire', *Studia Islamica* 9 (1958): 111–27.

6. B. Fagan, *The Little Ice Age: How Climate Made History, 1300–1845* (New York: Basic Books, 2000).

7. BLMC, EP, vol. 4, Add. 41315, John Bidwell to 'Miss Sally', Istanbul, 28 September 1809.

8. During the rebellions that occurred in Palestine in 1834 to oppose the compulsory conscription imposed by Ibrahīm Pasha, a certain number of Muslims attacked a group of Jews of Safed. Some sources attest the killing of over 500 Jews. See N. Shur, *Toldot Sfat* [History of Safed] (Jerusalem: Ariel, 1983), p. 189 and M. Abir, 'HaMered neghed haShilton haMitzri beÈretz Yisraèl biShenat 1834' [The revolt agaist the Egyptian domination in Èretz Yisraèl in 1834] (MA thesis, the Hebrew University, 1961). The same year, Muslims and Jews in Hebron suffered violent attacks committed by Ibrahīm Pasha's troops. According to John Nicolayson (1803–56) Palestine experienced in that phase a 'sad state of confusion [. . .] the Moslems [of Jerusalem] are in great consternation'. [Archives of the] Israeli Trust of the Anglican Church (ITAC) – *Palestine Mission Journal* – 1833–8, vol. 2, 19 May 1834. As for the 'increasing militarization', it is noteworthy that 24,000 men were serving in the Ottoman army in 1837. Their number reached 120,000 five decades later. See Quataert, *The Ottoman Empire*, p. 63.

9. R. Owen, *The Middle East in the World Economy, 1800–1914* (London: I. B. Tauris, 2002), p. 86.

10. G. A. Francioch, *Nationalism in Ottoman Greater Syria 1840–1914: The Divisive Legacy of Sectarianism* (California: Naval Postgraduate School, 2008), p. 36. Cit. in A. Beshara (ed.), *The Origins of Syrian Nationhood: Histories, Pioneers and Identity* (London: Routledge, 2011), p. 2.

11. Yazbak noted, for instance, that the 'communal division of Haifa may be said to date back to the 1830s'. M. Yazbak, *Haifa in the Late Ottoman Period, 1864–1914: A Muslim Town in Transition* (Leiden: Brill, 1998), p. 193.

12. As noted by Al-Barghūti, in its verbal form, *dawla* meant 'to turn, rotate or alternate'. It then assumed the meaning of 'dynasty' and, finally, of 'state'. T. Al-Barghuti, *The Umma and the Dawla* (London: Pluto Press, 2008), p. 21.

13. J. Richardson, *A Dictionary, Persian, Arabic, and English* (London: Bulmer, 1806), vol. 1, p. 348.

14. Rustum, *Al-Uṣūl al-'Arabiyya*, pp. 96–8. See also A. J. Rustum, *Hurūb Ibrāhīm Pāshā fī Sūriyah wa'l-Anāḍūl* [The Wars of Ibrāhīm Pāshā in Syria and Anatolia], 2 vols (Beirut: Al-Maktaba al-Bulusiyya, 1986).

15. Abu-'Uksa, *Freedom in the Arab World*, pp. 126 and 133. Abu-'Uksa noted also that 'the politicization of *jins* and its use as equivalent to the modern concept of 'nation' became evident around the mid-1800s; thus, for instance, the Italian quest for national unity was rendered in the newspaper *al-Jawā'ib* in 1861 as *wiḥda jinsiyya*', ibid., p. 134.

16. Hourani contended that 'feudal Lebanon disappeared in the convulsions of the generation which stretched from 1831 to 1860. In order to impose disarmament and conscription in obedience to the command of Ibrahim Pasha, Bashir [Emir of Lebanon from 1789 to 1840] began to play off Christians against Druzes': A. Hourani, *The Emergence of the Modern Middle East* (Berkeley: University of California Press, 1981), p. 157.

17. W. W. Haddād, *Nationalism in a Non-National State: The Dissolution of the Ottoman Empire* (Columbus: Ohio State University Press, 1977), p. 20.

18. The term *khedivé* is often rendered as viceroy. Muḥammad 'Ali was at that time (1831) a *de facto khedivé*, in as much as the title was granted with a *firman* by Sultan Abdülaziz I (1830–76) only in 1867.

19. 'Ādil Mannā, in a roundtable transcribed in P. Scham, W. Salem and B. Pogrund (eds), *Shared Histories* (Walnut Creek CA: Left Coast Press, 2005), p. 58. 'Ali, an Albanian born in Macedonia (present-day Greece), arrived in Egypt in 1801 at the head of a division, composed of irregular Albanian soldiers, established by Selīm III (1761–1808) with the purpose of expelling the 'French invaders'.

20. After Napoleon's withdrawal, Ali managed to secure the support of a number of influential figures, including *'ulamā'*, *tujjār* (merchants) and local notables. The sultan was then prompted to appoint Muḥammad 'Ali as Egypt's *wāli* (governor). The request was received in July 1805, after three consecutive governors sent by the Porte had been previously expelled.

21. A. K. Rafeq, 'A Different Balance of Power: Europe and the Middle East in the Eighteenth and Nineteenth Centuries', in Y. M. Choueiri (ed.), *A Companion to the History of the Middle East* (Oxford: Blackwell, 2005), p. 242.

22. A. Radwān, *Tarīkh Matba'ah Būlāq* [History of the Būlāq Press] (Cairo: Al-Amīriya/Būlāq, 1953), p. 56.

23. In 1881, with the aim of stabilising his power, Muḥammad 'Ali ordered the killing of hundreds of Mamluks. The latter, actually about 3,000 in number, were invited for a banquet at Qaṣr al-Gawhara (the Jewel Palace), in Cairo's Citadel, where many of them were massacred.

24. Rustum, *Al-Usūl al-'Arabīyya*, p. 71.

25. See A. D. Belliard and G. Douin (eds), *Une mission militaire Française auprès de Mohamed Aly* [A French Military Mission to Mohamed Aly] (Cairo: Institut français d'archéologie orientale pour la Société royale de géographie d'Égypte, 1923), p. 79.

26. S. Urban, 'The Gentleman's Magazine', vol. 31, Januray–June 1840, London, Nichols (1849): 81.

27. For an assessment of the role of Hānna Bahrī (from Homs) and a number of other Greek Catholics chosen by Ibrahīm Pasha as special advisers for administrative tasks during his stay in Syria (in Egypt, Copts were usually preferred for these kinds of task by his father, Muḥammad 'Alī), see A. J. Rustum, *al-Mahfūzāt al-Malikīya al-Misrīya* [A Record of State Papers from the Egyptian Royal Archives] (Beirut: Al-Maktaba al-Bulusiyya, 1986–7), vol. 2.

28. A. Al-Raf'i, *'Asr Muḥammad 'Alī* [The Age of Muḥammad 'Alī] (Cairo: Dār al-Ma'ārif, 1989), pp. 215–16. See also J. De Haas, *History of Palestine – The Last Two Thousand Years* (New York: Macmillan, 1934), p. 391.

29. S. Abū-'Izzedīn, *Ibrahīm Pasha fī Sūrīya* [Ibrahīm Pasha in Syria] (Beirut: al-Matba'ah al-'Ilmīya, 1929), pp. 79–80.

30. Muḥammad Sabrī contended that in 1831 Ibrahīm Pasha was welcomed in Syria and Palestine as a savior: M. Sabrī, *L'empire égyptien sous Mohamed-Ali et la question d'Orient* [The Egyptian Empire under Mohameud-Ali and the Eastern Question] (Paris: Geuthner, 1930), p. 24. A number of documents, many of them hosted in the Egyptian archives, show, on the contrary, that he was received by the local populations with marked hostility.

31. G. Biger, *Erets rabat gvulot* [The Land of Many Borders] (Sde Boker: ha-Merkaz le-moreshet Ben-Gurion, 2001), pp. 20–5.

32. The 1834 uprising, for instance, was quelled with violence and by imposing heavy new taxes. The main instigators were brutally killed; many others were sent into exile to Egypt to work in local mines. See Rustum, *Al-Usūl al-'Arabīyya*, pp. 162–3.

33. Ibid., p. 66.

34. *The Quarterly Review*, January–March (London: John Murray, 1839), vol. 63, p. 171.

35. At the beginning of the nineteenth century, Jerusalem was encompassed within the *eyālet* (district) of Damascus, while Galilee and the North-Western Palestinian coastal area were part of Sidon's *eyālet*. In 1840, when the Ottoman authorities succeeded to resume their control over Palestine, the latter was divided into

administrative units (*eyālet, sanjaks, kaza, nahiye*), aiming at providing better control of the area. In 1841, the *sanjaks* of Jerusalem, Gaza and Nāblus were united within a separate district (*mutasarriflik*), encompassed in the jurisdiction of the *eyālet* of Sidon. During the Crimean War, Jerusalem was briefly transformed into an independent *mutasarriflik*, whose governor was subject to the direct authority of the sultan. With the administrative reorganisation implemented by the Ottoman authorities in 1864, the Holy City returned to being an independent *mutasarriflik*, subject directly to Istanbul.

36. A plethora of documents produced by the Ottoman authorities describe the unprecedented opportunities granted to missionaries working in the region from the 1830s on – and the related growing concern expressed by the Porte. See, for instance, BOA HR.TO. 231.38.2.3, unsigned, 10 October 1858.

37. In 1839, American biblical scholar Edward Robinson (1794–1863) laid the foundations for modern 'Biblical archaeology'. He identified, taking advantage of (at times fallacious) linguistic deductions and without conducting excavations on the spot, more than 200 biblical sites. He dedicated his first book to Karl Ritter (1779–1859), who, despite never having visited Palestine, distinguished himself for his contributions aimed at shedding light on a number of shortcomings in works produced on the area: Y. Ben-Arieh, *The Rediscovery of the Holy Land in the Nineteenth Century* (Jerusalem: Magnes Press, 1979), p. 146.

38. S. R. Haight, *Letters from the Old World* (New York: Harper and Brothers, 1840), vol. 1, p. 269. Haight also noted that 'Mohammedanism, in its rapid decline, is pulling down with it every country in which it predominates, and the time is almost present when the lowest point must be reached', p. 270.

39. ASV, Segr. Stato, rubricella 257, fasc. 1. Apostolic delegate to Istanbul, Angelo Maria Dolci (1867–1939), to the Cardinal Secretary of State Pietro Gasparri (1852–1934), 12 December 1914.

40. A few pioneering expeditions had already taken place in the previous decades. Among them, that of German explorer Ulrich Jasper Seetzen (1767–1811), the first person who succeeded to scientifically explore the area beyond the River Jordan. After him came the Swiss traveller Johann Ludwig Burckhardt (1784–1817). Charles-Leonard Irby (1789–1845) and James Mangles (1786–1867) provided further important contributions regarding 'Irāq al-Amīr (near 'Ammān) 1817–18.

41. In 1835, Britain was the first power to set up steam navigation in the region, connecting cities such as Beirut and Alexandria with Liverpool and other British

ports. France (and then Austria) started to provide similar services in the years to follow, fostering the rapid expansion of Beirut and its trade with Marseille. See D. Chevallier, *La société du mont Liban à l'époque de la révolution industrielle en Europe* (Paris: Geuthner, 1971), p. 183.

42. The Select Committee, 'The Aborigines of British Settlements', *The Asiatic Journal and Monthly Miscellany* 24 (1837): 89.

43. Writing about the unprecedented clashes and mobs that occurred in Aleppo from the 1850s, Sharkey remarks that 'among the poorer Muslims of Aleppo, the sense of deteriorating privileges appears to have sharpened [. . .] [also] because many Christians in the city were becoming visibly wealthier as a result of alliances with foreign firms. These wealthy Chritistians were mostly Melkites who had accepted Catholicism under the earlier influence of French and other missionaries': H. J. Sharkey, *A History of Muslims, Christians, and Jews in the Middle East* (Cambridge: Cambridge University Press, 2017), p. 147.

44. CDM 2331 FO614285 T367, Payson, 3 November 1878.

45. TNA FO 165/1067, unsigned editorial published on 'Souriya', 12 February 1875.

46. An exception to this might be found in the Ottoman education system, which, prior to the 1830s, consisted mainly of religious training, while from 1839 on, with the opening of the *rusdīye* (advanced primary level) public schools, also included a more practical curriculum. See Y. Atasoy, *Turkey, Islamists and Democracy* (London: I. B. Tauris, 2005), p. 28.

47. In reference to the district of Nāblus, Beshara Doumani pointed out that 'at least until the early 1850s, Nabulsi merchants had sufficient tools at their disposal to hold on to the lion's share of their hinterland's agricultural surplus [. . .]. Beginning in the 1850s, the power of local councils to affect the outcome of commercial disputes was steadily eroded, as commercial tribunals became dominated by Europeans': B. Doumani, *Rediscovering Palestine: Merchants and Peasants in Jabal Nablus, 1700–1900* (Berkeley: University of California Press, 1995), p. 118. Writing about mid-eighteenth-century Egypt, Peter Gran noted that internal forces were pushing the country towards a capitalist transformation long before the advent of the Western entrepeneur. See P. Gran, *Islamic Roots of Capitalism* (Syracuse NY: Syracuse University Press, 1979).

48. From the end of the eighteenth century on, the term '*Ra'āyās*' was used by the Ottoman authorities only in reference to non-Muslims. Jews were often listed separately. Yet, Palmerston clarified to the British consul in Jerusalem, James Finn, that the Ottoman authorities were not opposed 'to the conversion of Rayahs of the Jewish persuasion to Christianity': TNA FO 78/2068, 19 May 1847.

49. Karpat, *Studies on Ottoman Social and Political History*, p. 11.

50. TNA FO 226/87, Campbell to Palmerston, 25 May 1833.

51. R. M. Martin, *Colonial Policy of the British Empire* (London: Allen & Co., 1837), pp. 80–1.

52. House of Commons, *Reports from Commissioners*, band 26 (London: House of Commons, 1838), p. 126. It is only in the nineteenth century that documents of historical value started to be systematically archived and examined.

53. See J. Darwin, 'Widening the Gap: British Imperialism and The Great Divergence, 1830–1880', paper available at: http://www.lse.ac.uk/economicHistory/Research/GEHN/GEHNPDF/WideningTheGap.pdf.

54. In 1830, for instance, the total emigration 'from the United Kingdom to North America was 55,000, in 1831 it rose to 71,000, and in 1832 was over 99,000'. See I. Ferenczi, *International Migrations* (New York and London: Gordon and Breach, 1969), vol. 2, p. 250.

55. M. Lynn, 'British Policy, Trade, and Informal Empire in the Mid-Nineteenth Century', in A. Porter, *The Oxford History of the British Empire* (Oxford: Oxford University Press, 1999), vol. 3, p. 111.

56. M. Yapp, *The Making of the Modern Near East 1792–1923* (London: Routledge, 1988), p. 133.

57. A. Özil, *Orthodox Christians in the Late Ottoman Empire: A Study of Communal Relations in Anatolia* (New York: Routledge, 2013), p. 98.

58. Writing a century later, assistant secretary of the Palestine Government Max Nurock (1893–1978) noted the following: 'I remember the constitution of an independent Druze Community in Syria had caused criticism amongst Moslems. In the circustances, no hasty decision should be taken in this respect'. ISA 5040/16-M. Dispatch written by Max Nurock on 17 June 1936.

59. See H. Guys, *Beyrouth et le Liban: Relation d'un séjour de plusieurs années dans ce pays* (Paris: Dār Lahad Khater, 1850), 2 vols, and L. Fawaz, *Merchants and Migrants in the Nineteenth-Century Beirut* (Cambridge MA: Harvard University Press, 1983), ch. 8.

3

The Second Moment – The Tanẓīmāt's Long Waves: Politicising Ethno-religious Differences

Hatt-ı Hümayun provided that the equality of taxes entails equality of burdens, as equality of duties entails that of rights.[1]

Edward Stanley

The Historical Background

The Crimean War (1853–6) played an influential role in shaping the geopolitical order of large parts of the Middle East up to the First World War. It forced the Ottomans to become indebted to the European powers, pushed the region into the world economy,[2] and served as a watershed in the history of several Mediterranean countries. It can be associated with the first protodemocratic reforms to be introduced in some countries with Muslim majorities (in 1861, the *bey* of Tunis introduced – for the first time in the Islamic world – a written constitution; five years later, the first elections were held in Egypt; in 1876, the first Ottoman constitution was enacted).[3]

Furthermore, it was the first war in which Ottoman and European soldiers fought side by side against a common enemy; it was the first time, in fact, that a Protestant power (Britain) sided with a Muslim empire (Ottoman) in fighting a Christian empire (Russia). Moreover, it represented the first major armed clash in which news from the fronts was communicated by telegraph and printed in newspapers almost in real time: a novelty that, thanks also to the first photographs taken on battlefields, gave an unprecedented weight in the public consciousness to the victories of the Western powers against the 'despotic' Russian Empire. In the more limited context of Palestine, the

Crimean War constituted a no less important turning point. It was from that moment on that the idea of a 'Jewish client state' in Palestine increasingly became established;[4] a client state that was 'vital to British colonial interests, particularly to India'.[5]

The year that marked the beginning of the Crimean War was also particularly significant for the Persian Gulf: the local Arab sheikhdoms signed the Perpetual Maritime Truce, recognising Britain as the dominant power in the Gulf (oil in the Persian Gulf was discovered in 1908 and acquired a central role for Western powers in the 1930s, when major finds were made). The year that the conflict ended, however, coincided with the second reformist phase, inaugurated by the *Hatt-ı Hümayun* ('Imperial decree') in 1856, when the Ottoman authorities, under direct influence of the two powers that had fought alongside the Porte during the Crimean War (Britain and France), coined and introduced the concept of *vatandaş* ('patriotism', or 'compatriotism'), that is, a common bond between all Ottoman subjects: a decisive step towards the secular, Western, concept of nationality.[6]

Just a few months after the conclusion of the Crimean War, a second major shift unfolded. The outbreak of the Indian Rebellion against the rule of the British East India Company pushed London to reorganise its naval communications to India. The opening of the Suez Canal by France on 17 November 1869 significantly increased the international importance of the land bordering the naval corridor between India and Europe. Prime Minister Benjamin Disraeli – who secured a large percentage of the shares in the Suez Canal in 1876 – signed a crucial agreement with Istanbul in which, in exchange for control over Cyprus, London pledged to guarantee protection to the 'territories in Asia of His Imperial Majesty the Sultan'.[7]

The agreement, signed on 4 June 1878, and followed four years later by London's occupation of Egypt and Sudan – the two areas that, together with Palestine, represented the strategic banks of the Suez Canal – marked the historical phase in which London realised that the region, and particularly its 'most important [Mediterranean-Indian] corridor',[8] would be worth fighting a war for if necessary. More specifically, the entry of Cyprus into London's sphere of influence marked the moment at which Disraeli felt that, sooner or later, 'the step would bring Palestine and Syria within the orbit of British control'.[9]

The purchasing of the Suez Canal – 80 per cent of the traffic in the Canal was made up of British boats – ushered in 'a quarter-century of imperial expansion unequal since the conquest of Alexander the Great'.[10] During this period (known as 'New Imperialism'), throughout the late nineteeth and early twentieth centuries, Afghanistan, Burma, the Transvaal, Egypt and a number of other strategic regions fell under British influence, and Germany, which rightly claimed 'that it has never annexed a single square mile of Muhammadan territory', replaced Russia as London's main imperial rival.[11]

The German Reich, shaped during the long years of Otto von Bismarck's ascendancy, existed from the unification of Germany (1871) until the abdication of Kaiser Wilhelm II (1918). It appeared to Sultan Abdul-Hamid II (1842–1918)[12] as a potentially less dangerous ally than Britain, whose ambitions, even more so after the Cyprus Convention and the occupation of Egypt, alarmed the Ottoman authorities. Berlin, on the other hand, had no historical presence in the region and the prestige of the Second Reich was clearly on the rise, as the Berlin Congress of 1878 confirmed. These and other factors led the Porte to back what would turn out to be the wrong horse: the Ottoman and German Empires collapsed, one after the other, against the backdrop of the disastrous effects of the First World War.

Building on this historical background, the present chapter analyses the politicisation of ethno-religious differences during the Ottoman 'reformist process' in the post-Crimean War phase. The next section sheds light on the long-lasting economic, political and identity-related repercussions of this era. The sections that follow focus on the introduction of a number of identity-related concepts in the region, as well as on the role played in this process by both internal and external factors and actors. The chapter concludes by investigating the reasons why these ideas and concepts were accepted and 'absorbed' at that specific historical juncture, and why they resulted in the sharpening of religious identities and ethnic-linguistic awareness.

Whose Reforms?

The 'Tanẓīmāt era' refers to a period of reorganisation within the Ottoman Empire. Its inception followed the Russo-Turkish War of 1768–74, when even the more conservative Ottoman administrators felt an increasing stimulus to foster Western-style reform in the army. It ultimately came about through a series of reforms implemented from 1839 until 1876, when Abdul-Hamid II, sultan from 1876 to 1909, blocked the reformist process, taking advantage of the rivalry between the European powers, and introduced authoritarian controls that delayed Turkey's development by several decades.

A number of forerunners to this 'reformist era', however, might already be detected in the late 1820s, when Sultan Mahmūd II succeeded in dismantling the Janissaries (1826), the conservative elite infantry units which, until then, had always represented a major obstacle to any reformist initiative. In 1829, with the aim of erasing any visible physical marker of differentiation among Ottoman subjects and fostering religious and social homogeneity/uniformity among them, the sultan proclaimed the 'clothing reform'. From then on, clarified the sultan, *Je ne veux reconnaître désormais les musulmans qu'à la mosquée, les chrétiens qu'à l'église et les juifs qu'à la synagogue* [I do not wish to recognise Muslims outside the mosque, Christians outside the church and Jews outside the synagogue]'.[13] Particularly impactful in a society in which clothing – including the use of different colours of headgear and types of hats – had been for centuries an important means of expressing identity was the requirement imposed on all members of the bureaucracy to wear the fez, and banning, at the same time, the use of turbans. These practices, which coincided with the Ottoman Empire increasingly losing its grip on a number of non-Muslim communities, have been framed by some historians as the beginning of 'Ottoman modernity'.[14] They did not succeed at fully eroding distinctions based upon religion or social criteria but prepared the ground for the reformist Zeitgeist that followed:

> The 'clothing reform' undermined the sartorial order based on difference that had existed for centuries. In the past [. . .] clothing laws in the Ottoman Empire, western Europe, and China all had sought to maintain class, status, ethnic, religious, or occupational distinctions among both men and women. In a sweeping enactment, the 1829 law sought to eliminate the visual differences among males by requiring the adoption of identical headgear.[15]

With these kinds of policy, Ottoman strategists sought solutions for the growing internal conflicts, while expressing, at the same time, their concern at the progressive penetration by European powers: 'The European effect upon Jerusalem as a centre during the past year', noted British Consul James Finn (1806–72) in 1856, 'has been very great'.[16] The first period of the Tanzīmāt, which opened with the *Hatt-ı Şerif* of Gülhane of 1839, was focused on security issues, on the tributary system, as well as on stopping the growing processes of administrative peripheralisation through a system of centralisation and systematisation of all bureaucratic and organisational affairs. Jerusalem, in particular, enjoyed relative economic prosperity in this phase, accompanied by significant demographic growth.[17] The process of transformation that took hold in those years was nonetheless weak and had little impact on the Muslim population at this stage. The reforms, in fact, targeted and affected the institutional structure, providing little or no beneficial effects to the common people. This explains why they were only temporary and doomed to disappear once Muḥammad ʿAlī was forced to withdraw from Palestine in 1840. A striking example of the failures in this historical phase concerns the attempt to eliminate the *iltizām* – a taxed farming system by which the feudal lord collected the *ʿUşr* (a tenth), a tithe paid in kind, and certain other taxes – considered to plague the Empire. Though the Porte had promised its abolition in 1839 and again in 1856, it continued to be practised, due to the absence of a specialised tributary system.

If the *Hatt-ı Şerif* of 1839 was partly related to Islamic tradition (this was also mirrored in the wording and vocabulary adopted), and partly inspired by the European powers, the second reformist phase, inaugurated by the *Hatt-ı Hümayun* in 1856, was by many accounts carried out according to an Anglo-French imposition – that is, a policy prompted by those two powers that had fought alongside the Porte during the Crimean War. Notwithstanding its positive effects connected to the development of communications, the improvement of security and increasing the rights of minorities (the reforms aimed also at integrating non-Muslims and non-Turks into Ottoman society, guaranteeing them civil liberties and equal rights), the historical phase that started in 1856 modified and, in some cases, shattered several well-established equilibria.[18] Though the Empire's initial regression can be traced back to earlier times, it is reasonable to claim that the new policies undermined a functioning system without providing sustainable alternatives. As the Turkish economist Omer Clal Sarç wrote in regard to the industrial sector:

> The Tanzimat had shaken our oil industry by changing some of the needs of the population and thus had been instrumental in its decline [. . .] The Tanzimat, although instrumental in the decline of old industry, could not create a modern industry to take its place.[19]

The second reformist period, as with the previous 'reformist eras', proved, to a large extent, to be a failure.[20] Besides giving limited results, it created the conditions for the reinforcement of local powers and contributed to undermining the status quo between the various religious denominations. In addition, it coincided with a growing intrusion of European powers into Ottoman affairs, as well as with the dissolution of the feudal order, largely based on social status, that for centuries had characterised the power dynamics between several prominent Maronite, Druze, Sunni and Shi'i families (who were often in charge of, among other tasks, collecting taxes from peasants in Mount Lebanon and elsewhere).[21]

The reforms' failure to deliver was, to a large extent, connected to a generational issue. Only at the turn of the twentieth century, through the post-reformist generation formed in public schools created in the Tanzīmāt period – a generation that had no direct ties with the previous ruling class – was it possible to enter into a concrete reformist phase and to witness the rise of political movements such as the Committee for Union and Progress (CUP; the so-called Young Turks).

Notwithstanding its failures, the Tanzīmāt era did spark epochal changes that were destined to shake the foundations of the Ottoman Empire. The preamble of 1856's *Hatt-ı Hümayun* – that, as already mentioned, introduced the concept of patriotism or compatriotism – is a case in point. It was, however, precisely the failure of the reform process, in its exacerbation of the sense of alienation of minorities in the Empire, that drove such people to put an increasingly strong emphasis on the different dialects spoken by the various communities.

The negative effects referred to above became more evident over time, even to European governments. 'During eighteen years of residence here, as Consul', commented the British consul of Aleppo in 1875, 'I do not hesitate to say that I have never seen the Turkish Rule fall so low as it is at the present'.[22] In Greater Syria and other areas of the Empire, the reforms reinforced the power of local notables, accentuating the existing gap between the urban elite and the *fellaḥīn* (farmers). This facilitated a growing concentration of land in the hands of urban families and, thus, a decrease in the influence of dignitaries and *ālim* (religious scholars) in the villages. The new situation paved the way for a progressive dependence of the countryside on the cities and for internal fracture/competition among urban and rural notables.

Though the key socio-cultural characteristics of local society remained, for the most part, intact, the unnatural injection of other norms and traditions shaped the conditions for the subsequent weakening of local societies. It was a far-reaching process, which Divine describes, taking Palestine as a case study, in the following terms:

> In the last quarter of the [nineteenth] century, military, administrative, and fiscal reforms locked Palestinian Arabs into an imperial political system with stipulated cultural norms. [. . .] The first three decades of Ottoman reforms changed Palestine's imperial status and position and required major adjustments on the part of the population. [. . .] Social relations became less stable [. . .] Inequities in market relationships were more visible than ever before.[23]

Patriotism: cui prodest?

'There is not to be found among them that great stimulus to national improvement, which exists more or less in every country in the world – patriotism'.[24] When, in 1849, Colonel George Gawler (1795–1869) wrote these words to Lord Palmerston in reference to the Arabs of Palestine, the influence of 'patriotism', often defined as a 'non-aggressive form of nationalism',[25] was still unknown in most of the Middle East.[26] British Consul in Jerusalem James Finn went so far as to claim that *fellaḥīn* in the region 'are influenced by no patriotism for Turkey. The very name is unknown to them.'[27]

In the eyes of these and other external observers, the lack of 'stimulus to national improvement' was not only linked to a weak socio-cultural attachment to a particular place, but also to what they perceived as the absence of any religious or ethnic homogeneity. Still, in July 1912, British Consul-General of Egypt, Lord Cromer, who fostered an uncompromising understanding of divided religious affiliations in the colonial context of the country, contended that 'the Egyptians are not a nation [. . .] they are a fortuitous agglomeration of a number of miscellaneous and hybrid elements'.[28] Various primary sources reflect similar impressions regarding a number of other areas in the region: for instance, in Palestine, argued British Consul to Jerusalem John Dickson, 'none are able to report the existence of anything like a homogeneous feeling of nationality among the people'.[29]

The alleged lack of interest in any form of 'patriotism' or 'stimulus to national improvement' on the part of local populations – often described as unable to 'understand our metaphysical problems, our introspective questions'[30] – was perceived as even more disgraceful considering that, conversely, patriotism towards various of the region's areas was stronger than ever in far-off England:

> This Holy Land, although no longer an object of bloody ambition, has lost none of the deep interest with which it once inspired the most vehement crusader. The first impressions of childhood are connected with that scenery; and infant lips in England's prosperous homes pronounce with reverence the names of forlorn Jerusalem and Galilee. *We still experience a sort of patriotism for Palestine*, and feel that the scenes enacted here were performed for the whole family of Man. Narrow as are its boundaries, we have all a share in the possession: what a church is to a city, Palestine is to the world. [emphasis added][31]

The Archbishop of York himself, William Thompson (1819–90), had been clear on his feelings during the inaugural meeting of the Palestine Exploration Fund in 1865: Palestine, he claimed, 'is the land to which we may look with as true a patriotism as we do to this dear old England'.[32] It follows that local Arabs were generally depicted as foreigners in their own land and their 'unpatriotic' attitudes were often described using offensive tones:[33]

> The Arabs who are superficially clever and quick witted, worship one thing, and one thing only – power and success. [. . .] The British Authorities [. . .] knowing as they do the treacherous nature of the Arab, they have to watch carefully and constantly that nothing should happen which might give the Arabs the slightest grievance or ground of complaint. [. . .] the fellah is at least four centuries behind the times, and the effendi (who, by the way, is the real gainer from the present system) is dishonest, uneducated, greedy, and as unpatriotic as he is inefficient.[34]

'Imported Solutions'

'Stimulus to national improvement' – as Gawler and a number of others defined patriotism – was an 'imported solution' (*hal mustawrad*),[35] one largely influenced by interaction with the West. This is not to say that the concept of 'nation' was alien to the region.[36] Yet before the adoption or imposition of Western nationalist ideologies and the emergence of exclusivist approaches, the aspect considered most relevant by those living in the region was not political identity but, besides religion, provenance from a certain village (which often represented a sort of 'protonation within the protonation'), or the belonging to a specific *ḥamūla*, the use of a particular dialect, a way of dressing, a local product, a religious festival, a dance. In this sense, it was mainly external observers, or people originally from the region but with long exposure to outer contexts or ideologies, who felt the necessity of expressing their belonging to broader identity-related definitions.

From an outside-in regional perspective, European and American missionaries played a leading role in spreading ideas related to 'national improvement' and 'patriotism'; for instance, the impact of institutions such as the Protestant University of Beirut, founded by American missionaries in 1866 and later known as the American University, can hardly be overestimated. On the other hand, from an inside-out regional point of view, much influence was exerted by certain Turkish and Arab scholars, such as Rifāʿa al-Ṭahṭāwī (1801–73) and Buṭrus al-Bustānī (1819–93), who had lived in Europe for a few years before bringing back revised, European-inspired, versions of ideas and concepts – including a political and territorial-based understanding of 'nationality' – to their lands.[37] Before focusing on these two dimensions, it is important to stress that both patriotism and the possession of a national consciousness are in no way preconditions for feeling a strong attachment to a certain place, area or historical heritage.

Outside-in: The Influence of the Missionaries

In 1957, American historian Joel Carmichael pointed out that 'the crowning anomaly of the contemporary Arab "national" resurgence surely lies in the fact that its seed was sown by Christian missionaries, chiefly from Britain, France, and America'.[38] Indeed, Christian, and especially Protestant, missionaries played a seminal role in introducing seeds of competing national visions and the 'stimulus to national improvement' in large parts of the Eastern Mediterranean. The believers belonging to the local Christian denominations represented the respective channels through which European powers sought to impose their political, commercial and cultural influence over the region. Before 1798, the capitulations system – 'emblem of the Ottoman weakness' – allowed France to take care of the security of Catholic institutions and worshippers (including Maronites and Jacobites) in the region.[39] From 1774 on, Russia too, through the Treaty of Küçük Kaynarca, concluded at the end of the war between the Ottoman Empire and Russia, obtained similar prerogatives as far as the protection of the heterogeneous Orthodox community was concerned. The other two great powers of the time, Britain and Prussia, which more than any others influenced the development of the region in much of the historical period under examination in this book, would have found in the local Protestant community their natural outlet to counter the influence of 'degenerate form[s] of Christianity' and to strengthen their ascendancy over the Porte.[40]

Though at the beginning of the nineteenth century a third of Jerusalem's population was Christian, there was then no permanent presence of Protestants in loco. This was in spite of the central role that the Holy City held for millions of Anglicans and Lutherans. British Vice-Consul Young wrote in a dispatch sent to Secretary of State Lord Palmerston: 'There are my Lord two Parties to be noticed who will doubtless consider themselves entitled to some voice in the future disposition of affairs here. The one is the Jew – to whom God originally gave this land [. . .] and the other, the Protestant Christians, his legitimate offspring'.[41]

It was only in 1833, thanks to John Nicolayson (1803–56), a missionary of Danish origins educated at the Danish Lutheran Church, that the first permanent residency of a group of Protestants was established in Jerusalem. Seventeen years later, in 1850,[42] when the sultan granted them independent status with the recognition of their own millet, it is estimated that about fifty Protestants were residing in Jerusalem.[43] At the end of the century, their number had risen to about 1,000, becoming the third-largest Christian confession in the city, after Greek Orthodox (5,000 members) and Catholics (2,850).

Nicolayson had been sent by the London Society for Promoting Christianity among the Jews, better known as London Jews' Society (LJS), a missionary organisation as uninterested in the local Muslim populations as obsessed with the firm intention of converting 'God's ancient people'.[44] Jews, according to Nicolayson himself, nourished 'personal prejudices against the truth':[45]

> A wrong direction has been given to qualifications calculated to form an exalted character, and it is this that has rendered the Jews so depraved and despicable. [. . .] The circumstance of their being so degraded should not discourage, but increase our attempts for their conversion [. . .] The example of Christ should excite us to labour for the spiritual benefit of Israel.[46]

Established in London in 1809 as an independent voluntary company aiming at 'instructing the ignorant, especially such as are of the Jewish nation',[47] the LJS had worked since 1815 'in strict conformity to the liturgy and formularies of the Church of England and Ireland'.[48]

Although the LJS was not the first organisation to send missionaries to the Eastern Mediterranean, it was the first that succeeded in establishing a permanent residency in that place. Furthermore, it was the organisation that, thanks to the peculiar historical moment in which it flourished, had the most major impact on the subsequent development of the region. Two more decades passed before the second (among a final total of ten) British missionary organisations started to operate in the area. Then another three decades passed before the Church Missionary Society (CMS),[49] another organisation destined to leave its mark on Greater Syria, succeeded in making permanent entry into the region. The names of these organisations, the dates in which they started their activities, as well as the number of students enrolled in the schools opened by them, are included in a report outlined during the 'Conference of Missionary Societies in Great Britain and Ireland' hosted in Edinburgh in 1917:[50]

> The British Churches and Missionary Societies carrying on work in Syria and Palestine include the following: London Society for Promoting Christianity amongst the Jews (1823). The Presbyterian Church in Ireland (1843). Church Missionary Society (1851). British Syrian Mission (1860). Edinburgh Medical Missionary Society (1861). The Church of Scotland (1864). Friends' Foreign Mission Association (1869). The United Free Church of Scotland (1884). Jerusalem and the East Mission (1889). The Presbyterian Church of England (1895). [. . .] In connection with the Churches and Societies named there were at work in these countries before the war [i.e. in 1913] 180 missionaries of British nationality.[51]

Concrete results from activities carried out by missionaries started to be observed thanks to the changed political conditions witnessed in the 1830s. As we have seen, this was an important decade, in which Egyptian authorities created a more favourable climate for missionaries, including by removing the Ottoman ban (at times circumvented) on the construction of new churches and guaranteeing free access to holy places.[52] As noted by Nicolayson himself, 'only when the Egyptian forces headed by Ibrahim Pasha first entered Palestine [1831] could I really settle down in Jerusalem [. . .] and therefore the permanent Protestant mission in Jerusalem proper could first be founded

Statistics of the Work of British Churches and Societies in Syria and Palestine.

	European Staff	Native Staff	Pupils in Schools	Hospital In-Patients	Hospital Out-Patients
London Society for Promoting Christianity amongst the Jews	29	34	780	3000	64,500
The Presbyterian Church in Ireland	5	20	538	—	—
Church Missionary Society	45	233	2,848	3138	88,879
British Syrian Mission	20	100	3,108	—	6,464
Edinburgh Medical Missionary Society	8	11	—	857	19,987
The Church of Scotland	6	—	370	—	—
Friends' Foreign Mission Association	18	49	1,360	155	2,661
The United Free Church of Scotland	18	25	550	465	23,700
Jerusalem and the East Mission	27	25	1,300	484	21,598
The Presbyterian Church of England	—	—	—	—	—
	176	497	10,754	7,109	227,779

Figure 3.1 Document signed by the presidents/secretaries of the mentioned churches and missions. (Source: LPL, DP 400, ff. 86–94)

only in 1833'.[53] That same year, Nicolayson managed to rent a small apartment on behalf of his organisation, just a few metres away from Jerusalem's 'Jewish quarter' (which, until the late nineteenth century, was never homogeneously Jewish). 'Began to arrange the house,' Nicolayson wrote on 24 October 1833, 'which will be a long affair'.[54]

Since then, and in the decades to follow, the activities carried out by missionaries grew exponentially and became progressively more rooted in the area. Among the most significant consequences of these processes was a greater emphasis on the role of Arabic – due also to the translation of the Bible into Arabic, and then as the medium of a periodical press – and a growing familiarity of elites and other segments of local societies with concepts such as nation, homeland, state, capital, private property.[55]

A crucial role in the whole process was given to education. In the Palestinian context alone, for instance, the Protestant Bishop of Jerusalem from 1846 to 1879, Samuel Gobat (1799–1879), found both the means and the favourable Zeitgeist that allowed him to inaugurate an unprecedented number of new schools, from that in Jerusalem, opened in 1847, to those in Nāblus, Zabābdeh, Bethlehem, Lydda (al-Lud), Bayt Jālā, Ramla, Rafīdya, Shafā ‘Amr, Jaffa and a number of other cities and villages.[56] Thanks to the tireless work of the missionaries – mainly British, American and German men – and the use of education and medical care as tools to promote proselytism, Protestant missions in the region saw an exponential growth. This became a concomitant cause in leading London to assume a larger role in the region – even more so, considering that those schools were (and continued to be) run as much as possible 'in the same manner as are the National Schools in England'.[57]

These activities had major repercussions also on the policies adopted by the Ottoman authorities. Suffice to mention that until the middle of the 1800s, the urban elites received a traditional Muslim education. In 1869, that is, in the final historical phase of the Tanẓīmāt, the Porte launched a new mass education programme – based on the guidelines contained in a report drafted by the French government a few years earlier – which obliged all males in the Empire to undergo three years of study in Ottoman schools.[58] This was intended to counterbalance the influence exercised by upper-level mission schools – such as the Robert College (est. 1863) in Istanbul and the Syrian Protestant College (est. 1866) of Beirut – and other missionary institutions such as the Université Saint-Joseph (established in Beirut by French Jesuit missionaries in 1875), while reinforcing a feeling of loyalty to the Empire. Between 1876 and 1909 alone, the Ottoman authorities established almost 10,000 schools and academies.[59] Despite the original intentions, these schools also contributed to exacerbating the us-versus-others perception within the Empire and played a significant role in laying the ground for the increasing ethnocentric drives (see Chapter 4) witnessed in the late nineteenth and early twentieth centuries.

Introducing *wataniyyah*: Inside-out Perceptions

Competing national visions and the 'stimulus to national improvement' were largely the result of outside-in interactions. Yet they started to become more pointed through the influence exerted by a number of local intellectuals.

Some of them were struggling to find alternatives and solutions to the 'crisis of modernity' and the penetration of Western ideas. Others were linked to, and inspired by, missionary societies, or personally acquainted with Western contexts and perspectives. Among the latter category was the case of Rifāʿa al-Ṭahṭāwī, the first historical figure to introduce the concepts of *watan* (fatherland) and *wataniyyah* (patriotism) into Arabic (but also the likes of 'steamship' and many others).[60] This Egyptian intellectual, who studied at an educational mission in Paris between 1826 and 1831, published the first comprehensive analysis of the European (mainly French) societies, prompting a growing number of people to become acquainted with European 'sciences and research'.[61] He was the first of a limited number of Arab (mainly Egyptian) and Turkish scholars who, from the 1830s on, started to place increasing emphasis on the importance of providing a political significance to the attachment to one's birthplace (in German, *Heimat*).[62] In his influential *al-Murshid al-Amīn li al-Banāt wa al-Banīn* ('The Trustworthy Guide for the Education of Boys and Girls'), he went so far as to link women's education to the stability of the nation.[63] The experience gained by al-Ṭahṭāwī in France played a key role in influencing the assimilation of new concepts and in spreading a notion that was previously overlooked by most of the people residing in the area: the relation between territoriality and nationality.

For much of history, millions of Muslims have considered Islam as a perfect and complete (two words that in Arabic are close to each other but not interchangeable in meaning) system in itself: the revelations received by the Prophet Muhammad contained everything a Muslim was required to observe in order to conduct a righteous and prosperous life. For centuries, the interactions between the 'West' and the 'Orient' did not manage to undermine these certainties, nor to stimulate any will to emulate concepts and ideas popular in France or elsewhere in Europe. And this was in spite of the great interest that the European 'other' had had for centuries in the eyes of countless observers residing in – or travellers coming from – the Arab and Islamic world.[64]

Experiences such as the one of al-Ṭahṭāwī in France, therefore, were not necessarily bound to result in a process of osmosis, or in generating any sort of wider influence. It is certainly true that the will to come to terms with ideas and visions rooted in the history and traditions of Western countries was prompted by the growing presence of Western subjects in Ottoman lands, as well as of Ottoman citizens in Europe. The ideological bases, however, were rooted in the need to find sustainable solutions to tackle the progressive weakening of the cultural, economic and social fabric of the Ottoman Empire. In the context of this decline, increasingly visible already since the mid-eighteenth century, when Habsburg Austria and Romanov Russia achieved military parity with Istanbul, concepts such as homeland, nation, state and such like would have most likely been considered with the same contempt reserved to other traditions, ideas and customs that flourished in the European milieu in previous centuries.

Al-Ṭahṭāwī was among the first to grasp the importance of applying those concepts and, in particular, of the notion that a nation was intimately rooted and bound to a specific territory: this perfectly applied to the Egyptian 'nation', described in a number of works as his 'fatherland'.[65] Moreover, he was also one of the first people to link the progress and the well-being of France to patriotism, as well as to the attachment shown by French people to their country:

> Without the astronomy [that is, science] of the people of Paris, their wisdom, their accomplishments, their good administration, and their concern with the interests of their land, their city would be nothing at all.[66]

Buṭrus al-Bustānī (1819–83), known for being the first intellectual in the region to deal with issues related to Syrian nationalism, also played an important role in adapting European concepts to the context of his land. Born into a Christian Maronite family from present-day Lebanon, al-Bustānī was employed for long time by American Protestant missionaries as a teacher of Arabic, a commitment that – as in the case of Syrian Armenian scholar Gregory Wartabet and many others – prompted his conversion to Protestantism. Author of the first Arabic encyclopaedia (*Muḥīṭ al Muḥīṭ*, 'The Ocean of Oceans'), al-Bustānī published a treatise in 1849 in which he fostered the importance of promoting women's education. It should be noted, however, that his attentions, opinions and efforts were directed almost exclusively to the benefit of Arab Christians and Western subjects residing in the region.[67]

Overall, the work of al-Ṭahṭāwī, al-Bustānī and others remind us that the 'stimulus to national improvement' in Lebanon and in Syria was rooted in the convergence of two main interests: that of the Christian missionaries and of the Arabic-speaking Christian communities of those countries. Among the latter, Beiruti poet and journalist Khalīl al-Khūrī (1836–1907), a close acquaintance of al-Bustānī, played a particularly significant role. He was, in fact, the most prominent figure among a group of Arab Christian intellectuals committed to promoting both the revival of Arabic culture and the idea of a (sectarian, yet increasingly circumscribed) Syrian identity and *watan*. His ideas became relatively popular thanks to *Hadīqat al-Akhbār*, the first Syrian weekly, that he established in 1857, a year after the beginning of the second Ottoman reformist phase inaugurated by the *Hatt-ı Hümayun*. The journal, styled as a 'civil' (*madanī*) and scientific publication, was the first to obtain, outside of the Istanbul area, a formal licence by the Ottoman authorities.

Al-Khūrī and his fellow intellectuals were not only providing answers to new inputs and challenges faced in their times, but also coming to terms with a certain growing resentment towards Ottoman Turks, now considered one of the main historical reasons for the decline of the 'Arab nation'.[68] This growing attitude was not yet meant to foster Arab nationalism, nor separatism, but had, nonetheless, a certain influence on the later developments of both.[69] In Joel Carmichael's words:

> the initial impulse to what has since become Arab nationalism was furnished by the attempt of Arabic-speaking Christians to burst their constricting social bonds. It was the Arabic-speaking Christians who were the first to offer themselves as political leaders to the 'Arab world'.[70]

A number of prominent local Muslim scholars resented the idea of a 'Christian-led' Arabic revival process and offered an alternative vision of how to respond to the 'crisis of modernity' in the sphere of ideas. While expressing appreciation for Europe's technological and social improvements, Jamāl al-Dīn al-Afghānī, Muḥammad 'Abduh, Rashīd Ridā and other 'Islamic modernists' tried to reconcile them with their own ways of perceiving local societies. They espoused strong support for the revival of Arabic language (the language of the Quran), as well as of the Ottoman sultan (as caliph), and a marked emphasis on the need for returning to the original Islam – still perceived as superior to other religions but corrupted by wrong actions and interpretations.

During this period, known as the *Nahḍa* ('Rebirth') or Islamic modernism, slogans such as *Al-Badeel al-Islāmī* (Islamic alternative), *Al-Ihya al-Islami* (the Islamic revival), or *al-Usuliyya al-Islamiyya* (the Islamic fundamentalism), all advocating the return to the original meanings and sources of Islam, became increasingly common, contributing to igniting a process that, with some variations, would be witnessed a number of other times in the region in the following century, and especially in the last decades of the twentieth century (particularly after Egypt's defeat in the 1967 Six-Day War).

In light of these considerations, it might appear as a paradox that figures like al-Afghānī and ʿAbduh – whose home in Beirut became a meeting place for intellectuals of all religions, including Jews – were among the intellectuals that contributed the most to lay the ideological foundations for the penetration of secular, nationalist ideas in the region. While questioning the compatibility of Islam and modernity, and stressing the relevance of human reasoning, these scholars allowed the penetration of established religious conceptions and the legitimisation of innovation and change in the sphere of ideas. More specifically, scholars like al-Afghānī – who fostered a pan-Islamic identity as an expression of national solidarity – and ʿAbduh – who stressed the Arab character of early Islam – created the ideological milieu in which secular Western ideas could integrate and live side by side with an ideal form of Islam: a major contribution to the later rising of a number ideologies – including Arab nationalism – destined to shape the region and the daily life of most of its inhabitants.

Ottomanism's Side-effects

The revival of Arabic and the introduction of the concept of *wataniyyah* coincided with the rising of Ottomanism among Ottoman Turks – a phenomenon ignited by the Tanẓīmāt process that became widespread, particularly in the 1870s and 1780s. This form of civic nationalism was, to a large extent, a reaction against the failure of the Ottoman authorities to keep pace with Europe but also a tool to provide practical answers to the nationality laws – that increased the religious homogeneity of the Ottoman Empire – passed by newly established Christian states in the Balkans (Greece included).

The aim of keeping pace with Europe was fulfilled by fostering economic development and providing more political freedom and equality, in exchange for loyalty to the Empire from all its citizens.[71] This overarching Ottoman citizenship was meant to supersede religious, ethnic and linguistic cleavages among the Empire's diverse subjects. It should be noted that Ottomanism was interpreted in different (often conflictual) ways by non-Muslims and the 'Turkish Empire'.[72] Notwithstanding the different interpretations, Ottoman sources confirm that, with the passing of time, those who did not comply with its 'official' objectives were increasingly and repeatedly prompted, or threatened, to acquire an 'Ottoman mindset'.[73] 'Those who refuse to become Ottoman citizens', noted a document produced by the Ottoman authorities in 1898, 'must sell their land and return to the place where they came from'.[74]

Yet the idea of an inclusive Ottoman citizenship was rooted in the distant past and had its most powerful expression in the relations between Jews and Muslims, closely linked to each other in the daily life of the Ottoman Empire. Already, in 1420, Rabbi Shlomo Ben Yitzhak, ha-Tsarfati ('Solomon son of Isaac, the French') had send a missive from the Ottoman city of Edirne (close to present-day Turkey's border with Greece) to a group of persecuted German Jews, proposing them to join him in Ottoman lands:

> Your cries and laments have reached us. We have been told of all the sorrows and persecutions which you suffer in German lands. Listen, my brothers [. . .] if you [. . .] knew even the tenth of what God has blessed us with in this land, you would give heed to no further difficulties. You would embark at once to us [. . .] Here the Jew is not compelled to wear a yellow hat as a badge of shame [. . .] You will be free of your enemies. Here you will find peace.[75]

Italian Jewish merchant David dei Rossi went a step further, writing from Ottoman Safed in 1535 that 'the Exile [Galut] here is not like in our homeland. The Turks hold respectable Jews in esteem. Here and in Alexandria, Egypt, Jews are the chief officers and administrators of the customs, and the king's revenues. No injuries are perpetuated against them in all the empire'.[76] A plethora of similar testimonies can be found in archives spread throughout former Ottoman lands, where, despite tensions and problems, local subjects belonging to different communities tended often to perceive each other as *adelfia* (siblings).[77] This, of course, does not imply that all local communities had equal rights.[78] As noted by Ussama Makdisi in relation to the second half of the nineteenth century, 'at the same time as the United States struggled with slavery and black emancipation, and Europe with the emancipation of Jews, the Ottoman empire was confronted with the question of the place of non-Muslims in what had long been a Muslim empire'.[79] In the latter, non-Muslim citizens had been historically treated as *dhimmis*: they were protected as long as they paid the *jizya* (a tax required only from free, sane, adult males) and observed certain rules.[80] The *dhimma* was, in other words, a system of protection characterised by discriminations, in some cases resulting in 'great abuses', which, however, had nothing to do with the persecutions registered in the same historical periods in Europe. In theory, non-Muslim communities were prevented from building new places of worship and restoring those that had been damaged.[81] They were forbidden from accessing public office, carrying weapons or professing their religion in public. They also had to differentiate themselves regarding their language and clothes. However, as noted by Brenner apropos the centuries preceding the rise of the Ottoman Empire:

> Although horse riding was forbidden to Jews, the exilarch rode on a horse through Baghdad in a showy public ceremony during his inauguration. The documents that have come down to us from the tenth, eleventh, and twelfth centuries lead one to surmise that Jews dressed exactly the same way as their Muslim neighbors. New synagogues were built almost everywhere Jews lived, and there were even some churches whose rebuilding would surely have been forbidden if the letter of the law had prevailed.[82]

It should also be noted that local equilibria, particularly in late Ottoman times,[83] were not perceived by all observers, particularly external ones, in the same way. In 1839, William T. Young, first British Vice-Consul in Jerusalem, noted that a Jew in Jerusalem was not considered 'much above a dog'.[84] Young himself, however, had to acknowledge that, in case of need, a Jew would have found shelter 'sooner in a Mussulman's house than in that of a Christian'.[85] Just a few years after Young, in 1857, British Consul to Jerusalem James Finn pointed out that 'there are few countries in the world where in spite of appearances to the contrary, there is so much of practical religious tolerance as in Palestine'.[86]

Finn's words were mirrored in the following decades in a wide number of publications produced by pre-eminent Ottoman Jews, including İzmir poet Reuven Qattan, who wrote to the Judeo-Spanish paper *Liberty*, reminding its readers that 'before everything we should live Ottoman lives, cultivate the language of the Ottomans, form an integral part of the Ottoman nation, and sincerely love the Ottoman patria'. According to Qattan, 'We are Ottomans and nothing else'.[87]

Nowhere more than in judicial records it is possible to assess to what extent local communities perceived themselves, in different periods of Ottoman history, as being constructive elements of the Ottoman milieu.[88] American historian Amnon Cohen, who spent years studying documents stored in the archives of the sharia religious court (*sijil*) of Ottoman Jerusalem, found 1,000 Jewish cases filed from the years 1530 to 1601. Jews preferred to use Islamic sharia courts, rather than their own rabbinical courts:

> The Jews went to the Muslim court for a variety of reasons, but the overwhelming fact was their ongoing and almost permanent presence there. This indicates that they went there not only in search of justice, but did so hoping, or rather knowing, that more often than not they would attain redress when wronged. [. . .] The Jews went to court to resolve much more than their conflicts with Muslim or Christian neighbours. They turned to Shari'a authorities to seek redress with respect to internal differences, and even in matters within their immediate family (intimate relations between husband and wife, nafaqa maintenance payments to divorcees, support of infants etc.) [. . .] the Sultan's Jewish subjects had no reason to mourn their status or begrudge their conditions of life. The Jews of Ottoman Jerusalem enjoyed religious and administrative autonomy within an Islamic state, and as a constructive, dynamic element of the local economy and society they could – and actually did – contribute to its functioning.[89]

As argued by French historian Fernand Braudel regarding everyday phenomena, the practices of intercommunal interaction were taken for granted and only indirectly – as in the case of the religious courts – reported in the sources.[90] Indeed, interaction was not only a feature of societal exchanges, but was also often reflected in religious practices, particularly in borderlands and on frontiers. Most of the shared shrines of the Mediterranean that are still visited today, in fact, 'are situated on its eastern shores; their presence reflects a common past, a long coexistence of culturally mixed populations'.[91]

Emphasising shared practices and spaces, 'constructive elements' and hybrid identities and experiences that once flourished at the Mediterranean frontiers – like for instance the 'mixed pilgrimages' to the tomb of biblical prophet Ezekiel in Kifl (south-eastern Iraq) – is not meant to deny or downplay differences, however. The Ottoman milieu can, in fact, be characterised as having been a sum of particularisms. Indeed, it is to the homogenisation of those particularisms that ethnocentric drives, and the related strengthening of religious and ethnic-related cleavages, should largely be ascribed. This is not relevant only in the Ottoman context. Writing in reference to the homogenisation of Western societies, Patrick Girard noted, for instance, that 'modern anti-Semitism was born not from the great difference between groups but rather from the threat of absence of differences'.[92] Alain de Benoist took this argument further in pointing out that 'modernity could no longer accept a particularism that was, on the contrary, perceived as acceptable in a society characterised by a sum of particularisms. Modernity, in other words, abolished an array of distances that, conceived as impassable, had also played a protective role.'[93]

All this brings us back to Ottomanism and the political will, further fostered by the first Ottoman constitution issued in December 1876, of developing an inclusive Ottoman citizenship. Despite being ideologically rooted in centuries of interactions, Ottomanism soon became associated with the danger of erasing differences, and for this was highly feared by a wide range of non-Muslim and non-Turk Ottomans. Unsurprisingly, it also resulted in the sharpening of religious identities and ethnic-linguistic awareness:

> Christians, in particular, interpreted Ottomanism as a project meant to impose Islam on their communities, and they increasingly turned to European powers for support (for example, the Maronite community in Syria looked to the French). Thus, Ottomanism unwittingly politicized ethno-religious difference, raised minorities' awareness of that difference, and created the conditions for proto-nationalist revolts that ultimately contributed to the erosion of the Empire.[94]

Notes

1. TNA FO 881/3089, British Secretary of State Edward Stanley (1826–93), 20 November 1876.
2. In many cases, the 'encounter with the West' did not change but instead strengthened local customs and traditions. Moreover, a number of innovations introduced in this historical period went on to accelerate processes that were already taking place and did not succeed in altering the rhythms of life of most of the local populations (particularly in rural areas). Yet, in the medium and long term, the penetration of Western ideas and practices would contribute to shattering a number of well-established equilibria.

3. L. Kamel, *Imperial Perceptions of Palestine: British Influence and Power in Late Ottoman Times* (London and New York: I. B. Tauris, 2015).

4. Clayton defined it as a 'key link (and a buffer against the French) in the Middle Eastern chain': A. Clayton, *The British Empire as a Superpower, 1919–39* (Athens: University of Georgia Press, 1986), p. 138.

5. G. M. Levine, *The Merchant of Modernism* (New York: Routledge, 2003), p. 48.

6. The failure of the reform process exacerbated the sense of alienation of 'minorities' in the Empire and drove local people to put an increasingly strong emphasis on the different dialects spoken by the various communities.

7. House of Commons, *Accounts and Papers* (London, 1878), p. ii.

8. Middle East Centre Archives, St Antony's College (MECA), JBGP. John Bagot Glubb (1897–1986), n.a.

9. R. Storrs, *Lawrence of Arabia: Zionism and Palestine* (New York: Penguin, 1943), p. 39.

10. B. Tuchman, *Bible and Sword* (New York: New York University Press, 1956), p. 161.

11. BLMC, Cecil Papers, Add. 51094, British orientalist Thomas Walker Arnold, 7 November 1918.

12. Sultan Abdul-Hamid II gifted Bismarck with a three-volume set of photographic albums. The latter, commissioned by the sultan in 1886 to document the early Ottoman settlements, were aimed at capturing the Turkish essence of Ottoman identity through a proto-nationalist understanding of Ottoman history. The albums made their way into the Ömer M. Koç Collection in 2017.

13. M. A. Ubicini, *Lettres sur la Turquie* (Paris: Dumaine, 1854), vol. 2, p. 113.

14. One of the most common difficulties among historians focused on the Tanẓīmāt is that of establishing a shared definition regarding the nature of the changes triggered by the reforms. This debate is directly connected to the concepts of modernisation and Westernisation, often used as synonyms. On top of this, it should be noted that rather than focusing on the process of Westernisation of the Ottoman Empire, a number of studies emphasise the importance of paying attention to the internal dynamics of the early modern Ottoman society, as well as to intrinsic transformations that local societies implemented in order to cope with or adapt to the new circumstances. See A. Schölch (ed.), *Palestinians over the Green Line* (London: Ithaca Press, 1983), p. 10 and J. Berque in the introduction of W. Polk and R. Chambers (eds), *Beginnings of Modernization in the Middle East* (Chicago: University of Chicago Press, 1969), p. 24.

15. Quataert, *The Ottoman Empire*, p. 66.

16. ISA RG 160/2881-P. Finn, Jerusalem, 7 January 1856. In the same dispatch, Finn noted that the 'old prejudices are abating and liberality of sentiment greatly increased in Jerusalem also, which has been ever since I know of, in advance of other places with respect to toleration of non-Moslem religions'.

17. The Palestinian historian 'Āref al-'Āref (1891–1973) underlined that, when the Ottoman authorities regained possession of Jerusalem in 1840, it had around 22,000 inhabitants. Twenty-one years later, in 1861, the city was inhabited by around 68,000: Ā. al-'Āref, *Tārīkh al-Quds* [The History of Jerusalem] (Cairo: Dār al- Ma'ārif, 1951), p. 118. Other cities in the region witnessed significant expansion. On 29 November 1851, the consul Finn noted for example that, following the previous twelve months, Jaffa 'is greatly enlarged, and some of the most expensive dwelling houses in all Palestine have been erected there by native merchants': ISA RG 160/2881-P.

18. Hajjar pointed out that the *Hatt-ı Hümayun* and its international recognition 'are responsible for the regeneration of contemporary Eastern Christianity': J. Hajjar, *Le Christianisme en Orient* [Christianity in the East] (Beirut: Librairie du Liban, 1971), p. 105.

19. Ö. C. Sarç, 'Tanẓīmāt ve Sanayimiz' [The Tanẓīmāt and our Industry], in *Tanẓīmāt* (Istanbul: Maarif Vekaleti Neşriyatı, 1941), vol. 1, pp. 423–40, included also in C. Issawi (ed.), *The Economic History of the Middle East 1800–1914* (Chicago: University of Chicago Press, 1966), p. 58.

20. The Ottoman Empire registered other 'reformist eras' in previous historical periods (the Janissaries, for instance, were introduced to meet certain specific needs encountered in the fourteenth century). Such reforms often failed, due to the fact that the new governmental departments' military corps did not replace the pre-existing ones but rather functioned alongside them, creating a partial stall in the form of internal conflict.

21. Conder notes: 'In 1882 I saw only too plainly the change that had come over the land. The Palestine of the early years of the Survey [of the PEF] hardly now exists. The country is a Levantine land, where Western fabrics, Western ideas, and even Western languages, meet the traveler at every point': C. R. Conder, *Palestine* (London: Dodd, 1889), p. 21. On the Lebanese context see A. Tarbīn, *Lubnān Mundhu 'Ahd al-Muteṣarrīfiyah ilá Bedāyat al-Intidāb, 1860–1920* [Lebanon from the Time of the Muteṣarrīfiyah to the Beginning Mandate, 1860–1920] (Cairo: Ma'had al-Buhūth wa al-Dirasāt al-'Arabiyya, 1968).

22. TNA FO 195/1067, James H. Skene (1812–86) to the British ambassador in Istanbul Henry Elliot, 9 August 1875. The document is from Sultan Abdülaziz I's

times. The latter tried to modernise the Ottoman Empire, but was evaluated in negative terms by London. 'His temper is violent', Edmund Hornby (1825–96) wrote in 1864 to the then Foreign Minister John Russell (1792–1878), 'and his prejudices are thoroughly Mahomedan': TNA FO 78/1851, Hornby to Russel. Istanbul, 26 July 1864.

23. D. R. Divine, *Politics and Society in Ottoman Palestine* (London: Lynne Rienner, 1994), p. 81.

24. TNA FO 881/1177, Gawler (former British governor of Southern Australia from 1838 to 1841) to the then British Secretary of State Lord Palmerston, London, 9 November 1849.

25. J. C. D. Clark, 'Protestantism, Nationalism, and National Identity, 1660–1832', *The Historical Journal* 43(1) (2000): 249–76.

26. From a British travel guide published in the 1850s: 'The patriotism of the Syrian is confined to the four walls of his own house; anything beyond them does not concern him': J. L. Porter, *A Handbook for Travellers in Syria and Palestine* (London: John Murray, 1858), vol. 1, p. xlvi.

27. E. Finn, 'The fellaheen of Palestine', in *The Committee of the PEF, The Surveys of Western Palestine: Special Papers on Topography, Archaeology, Manners and Customs* (London: PEF, 1881), p. 333.

28. Cit. in R. Hyam, *Britain's Imperial Century, 1815–1914* (London: Batsford, 1976), p. 256.

29. John Dickson, British consul to Jerusalem, 23 November 1905. ISA RG 160/2881-P.

30. Thomas E. Lawrence (1888–1935), better known as 'Lawrence of Arabia', expressed an opinion that was not uncommon among British officials for most of the nineteenth and early twentieth centuries: 'The Semites [Lawrence was referring to Arab speakers] have no middle ground of seeing things [. . .]. they don't understand our metaphysical problems, our introspective questions. They only understand true and false, faith and no faith, without our hesitating result of subtle nuances [. . .]. They were limited people [and] of limited vision, whose inert intellect remains arid in careless resignation. Their imaginations were vivid, but not creative. There was so little Arab art in Asia that one could almost say that there was no art whatsoever [. . .]. They didn't invent any philosophical system, no complex mythology': T. E. Lawrence, *Seven Pillars of Wisdom* (Harmondsworth: Penguin, 1962), pp. 36–7.

31. E. Warburton, *The Crescent and the Cross* (New York: Wiley, 1845), pp. 1, 5. Warburton's book was reprinted in eighteen editions.

32. PEF/MINS, 22 June 1865.

33. Writing about Mark Twain and other Western writers, Klazner noted that 'it appears that travel writers were not expected to discover anything new, only to confirm what was already known': D. Klazner, 'Sacred Journeys: Jerusalem in the Eyes of American Travelers before 1948', in Y. Ben-Arieh, M. Davis (eds), *Jerusalem in the Mind of the Western World, 1800–1948* (Westport: Praeger, 1997), p. 48.

34. TNA FO 371/3395, Weizmann to Balfour, 30 May 1918.

35. See al-Qaraḍāwī, *Al-Hulūl al-Mustawrada*, p. 1.

36. It was indeed the awareness, developed in the first century of Islam, of being part of an 'Arab nation' – a new unified polity with its ideological and religious coherence – that contributed to triggering the first Muslim military and political action against the outside world.

37. For an analysis of al-Ṭahṭāwī's conceptualisation of Egyptian nationhood (*al-Ummah al Misriyyah*) largely focused on the conversation internal to the debates of the Islamic tradition, see A. Warren, 'For the Good of the Nation: The New Horizon of Expectations in Rifaʿa al-Tahtawi's Reading of the Islamic Political Tradition', *American Journal of Islamic Social Sciences* 34(4) (Autumn 2017): 30–55.

38. J. Carmichael, 'Islam and Arab Nationalism: The Role of Religion in Middle Eastern Politics', *Commentary*, 1 July 1957. Available at: https://www.commentarymagazine.com/articles/islam-and-arab-nationalismthe-role-of-religion-in-middle-eastern-politics.

39. J. Hajjar, *Le Christianisme en Orient* [Christianity in the Orient] (Beirut: Librairie du Liban, 1971), p. 3. The first capitulation goes back to February 1535 and was agreed between King François I of France (1494–1547) and Ottoman sultan Suleyman I (1494–1566). At first, the capitulations were concessions that the sultan granted to foreigners as a guarantee of religious tolerance and legal protection. In the eighteenth and nineteenth centuries, however, they became equivalent to treaties whose conditions were imposed by external powers, which took much advantage of the concessions. A meaningful example of this attitude can be found in the 'right to import luxury weapons, hunting rifles, guns and a small amount of gunpowder for private use', ratified by article 11 of the treaty agreed between Great Britain and the Ottoman authorities in 1861: Archivio Storico-Diplomatico del Ministero degli Affari Esteri (ASDMAE), AP 1946–50, Palestine, b. 9. For a long time, the French pretence of representing all Catholics in the Middle East was perceived by many, particularly in Rome, as 'arrogant and artificial'. See for instance Italian diplomat Antonio Rosset

Desandré, Tehran, 11 October 1933. ASV, Arch. Deleg. Apostolica in Iran, fasc. 43, b. 24, f. 3.

40. J. Bicheno, *The Restoration of the Jews* (London: Barfield, 1807), p. 201.

41. TNA FO 78/368, Young to Palmerston. Jaffa, 14 March 1839.

42. In 1853, the Ottoman authorities issued a *firman* acknowledging the right of the Protestant communities in the Ottoman Empire to vote their representatives in the local *Majālis* (assembly). This, however, occurred in a very fragmented way, to the point that, in the years to follow, the Prussian consul Georg Rosen (1821–91) made a hint as to the 'systematical exclusion of the Protestants from the Majālis of Palestine': ISA RG 67/439/10.

43. Y. Ben-Arieh, *Jerusalem in the 19th Century. The Old City* (Jerusalem: St Martin's, 1984), p. 194.

44. The LJS was the last of the four major British missionary societies to be established in the two decades in between the end of the nineteenth and beginning of the twentieth centuries. The first was the Baptist Missionary Society, established in London in 1792. It followed the London Missionary Society (1795) and the Church Missionary Society (1799).

45. ITAC, 1841–44, Letters, f. 4. Nicolayson to the LJS's Secretary William Ayerst, 31 March 1841.

46. 'The Jewish Expositor and friend of Israel' (London, 1819), vol. 4, p. 187. The cited quotation is included in a letter published on the 'The Jewish Expositor' (called 'Jewish Repository' until 1813), one of the two major publications of the LJS.

47. ITAC, 1809–14, Reports, p. 16.

48. J. S. Frey, *Judah and Israel* (New York: Fanshaw, 1812), p. 71.

49. In their missions in the region, the CMS, which was initially perceived with scepticism by the Anglican religious authorities, stood firstly in opposition to Catholic influence. It was, therefore, the 'rescuing' of 'Eastern Christians', more than the conversion of local 'pagans', that represented their main focus. The first missionary to be sent in the region by the CMS was William Jowett (1787–1855). He provided the following impressions: 'The professors of our most holy faith have, in Syria and Palestine, wandered very far indeed from the truth and simplicity of Gospel. Darkness and Discord share the dominion here [. . .] That professing Christians have departed from the purity of the faith': W. Jowett, *Christian Researches in Syria and the Holy Land* (London: Church Missionary Society, 1825), p. 5.

50. The report was sent to the Foreign Ministry, Arthur Balfour. The private secretary of the latter answered on 7 December 1917, pointing out that Balfour 'has

every appreciation of the admirable cultural and philantropic work which has been performed by these institutions in the past': LPL, DP, 400, f. 109.

51. LPL, DP, 400, ff. 86–94. Document signed by the presidents/secretaries of the mentioned churches and missions.

52. BOA CE 4860/5, folder containing letters of gratitude written by Christian Ottoman citizens about the permission for building new churches within the Empire.

53. Cit. in A. Carmel, in D. Kushner (ed.), *Palestine in the Late Ottoman Period* (Jerusalem: Ben-Zvi, 1986), p. 303. In 1836, the Reverend H. Stowell exclaimed the following: 'Palestine is freed from the bondage of Turkey: she is now literally, as Isaiah foretold she should be, "the third with Egypt and Assyria", destined to be "a blessing in the midst of the land"': ITAC, 1836, Report, pp. 23–4.

54. ITAC, Palestine Mission Journal, 1833–8, vol. 2, f. I. 24 October 1833.

55. Contrary to what has been argued by Philip Khoury, William Cleveland and several other scholars, a number of primary sources produced by Ottoman officials and Western consuls based in the region in the second half of the nineteenth century confirm that the influence exerted by nationalistic-inspired or 'proto-national' concepts was felt well beyond local elites. See CDM, file n. 2358 FO614312 T188.

56. Though a number of schools belonging to different Christian denominations were active well before Gobat's episcopate, the latter boasted of being the fore-runner of the educational system in Palestine and the broader region: 'There was not a single Christian school in the whole of Palestine [. . .] now we have in Judea, Samaria, and Galilee thirty-six or thirty-seven Protestant Bible Schools, not to speak of nearly as many Roman Catholic and Greek schools established at first with a view of counteracting ours. Again, there was then only one native Protestant in the country: and now we have twelve native Protestant communities': Gobat to Tait, 21 November 1877, LPL, TP, 234, ff. 280–3.

57. BOL, CMJ, D62/1, Hastings Kerk (1835–1908; head of the LJS in Jerusalem from 1879 to 1901), 2 March 1885.

58. In the late nineteenth and the early twentieth centuries the French authorities worked hard to establish new French schools, often at the expense of Vatican institutions. On 28 January 1902, friar Eugenio da Modica, of the Catholic mission in Trabzon (north-eastern Turkey), wrote to Pope Pius X complaining that the French consuls were calling for the renaming of local Catholic schools. They wanted to transform them into 'French schools, with all the consequences that are easy to foresee [*scuole francesi, con tutte le conseguenze facili a prevedersi*]': ASV, Segr. Stato, rubricella 543 – 'Pilgrimages', 1902, rubr. 280, fasc. 9.

59. Between 1876 and 1908, Sultan Abdul-Hamid II tried to reinforce a feeling of loyalty to the Empire, countering at the same time the rising of Arab nationalism, by also developing or improving the communication system. Similar efforts had been made in previous times. For instance, a railway from Varna to the Danube was begun in 1856 (in later years it started to serve also the harbour of Smyrna). Yet, it was under Abdul-Hamid II that such attempts became more systematic and organised. A powerful example of this can still be seen in Bal'a, a Palestinian village near Ṭūlkarem, where a railway and a train tunnel were built (remaining in use until the First World War) with the double purpose of better linking the region with the capital (Istanbul) and connecting the latter to Medina and Mecca. Yet, despite these 'futuristic' attempts, it should be noted that at the beginning of the First World War, when German and British cartographers were able to produce highly precise maps, the Ottoman authorities continued to measure the distances between various areas of a region in terms of hours of travel: BOA DH.ID, 59/72, 20 May 1914. The document, which included the distances in travel hours, was written at the conclusion of a tour made by the governor Ahmed Mecid in Syria and Palestine. On the increasing concerns expressed by Ottoman administrators in relation to roads see BOA DH.ID, 25/11, 18 April 1912.

60. See R. al-Ṭahṭāwī and M. 'Imārah (eds), *al-'Amāl al-Kāmilah li al-Ṭahṭāwī* [The Full Works of al-Ṭahṭāwī] (Beirut: al-Mu'assasat al-Arabīyya, 1973), vol. 1, p. 123.

61. Ibid., vol. 2, p. 4.

62. See R. al-Ṭahṭāwī, *Kitab Takhlīs al-Ibrīz fi Talkhīs Bārīs* [The Book of the Extraction of Pure Gold in the Compendium of Paris] (Cairo: al-Haya al-Misrīya al-'Amma li al-Kitāb, 1993 [1834]), pp. 195–200.

63. R. al-Ṭahṭāwī, *al-Murshid al-Amīn li al-Banāt wa al-Banīn* [The Trustworthy Guide for the Education of Guys and Girls] (Cairo: al-Majlis al-A'lā lil-Thaqāfah, 2002).

64. On the rich yet often-neglected perception of Europe in the Medieval Arabic literature, and for an external perspective on the formation of Europe, see N. F. Hermes, *The [European] Other in Medieval Arabic Literature and Culture* (New York: Palgrave, 2012), B. A. Catlos, *Infidel Kings and Unholy Warriors* (New York: Farrar, Straus and Giroux, 2015), and D. G. König, *Arab-Islamic Views of the Latin West* (Oxford: Oxford University Press, 2015). As noted by König, 'distinguished international scholars have had no qualms to reduce a large and differentiated range of Arabic-Islamic perceptions to a single basic pattern which is often subsumed under the keywords "ignorance", "indifference", and "arrogance"': ibid., p. 16.

65. See al-Ṭahṭāwī, *Kitab Takhlīs al-Ibrīz*.

66. E. Dawn, 'Ottomanism to Arabism: The Origin of an Ideology', in A. Hourani, P. Khoury and M. Wilson (eds), *Modern Middle East: A Reader* (Berkeley: University of California Press, 1993), p. 377.

67. In 1847, al-Bustānī, together with Greek Catholic philologist Nāṣif al-Yāzigī (1800–71) and a few American missionaries, established the first literary society in the Arab world: Jamiyyat al-ādāb wal-'Ulūm (The Scientific and Literary Society). The latter, whose members were Arab Christians and figures belonging to missionary or diplomatic Western institutions, was replaced by al-Jam'iyya al-'Ilmiyya al-Sūriyya (The Syrian Scientific Society) in 1857, which included also a few Druzes and Western-educated Muslims.

68. Dawn argued that 'the conflict between Arab nationalist and Ottomanist in pre-1914 Syria was a conflict between rival members of the Arab elite': Dawn, *From Ottomanism*, p. 173.

69. Khālidī noted that 'a significant problem with the work of many historians who have downplayed the extent of Arabist feeling before 1914 is that they seem to be arguing in the face of several important categories of primary evidence': R. Khālidī, 'Ottomanism and Arabism in Syria Before 1914: A Reassessment', in R. Khālidī, L. Anderson, M. Muslih and R. S. Simon (eds), *The Origins of Arab Nationalism* (New York: Columbia University Press, 1991), p. 52.

70. J. Carmichael, 'Islam and Arab Nationalism: The Role of Religion in Middle Eastern Politics', *Commentary*, 1 July 1957.

71. See J. Hannsen, '"Malhamé–Malfamé": Levantine Elites and Transimperial Networks on the Eve of the Young Turk Revolution', *International Journal of Middle East Studies* 43(1) (February 2011): 25–48.

72. During the entire Ottoman rule, the expression 'Turkish Empire' was very popular in the West. This is explained by the fact that the Osmanlı family was ethnically Turkish. Yet, both the Osmanlı dynasty and its empire very soon lost their 'purity', both through intermarriage and inclusion of other ethnicities and religions.

73. Tamarī noted that, during the First World War, Ottomanism 'was no longer primarily an ideology of common citizenship and legal equality. Under the strain of ethnic nationalism and the threat of secession, the Young Turks began to utilize the Ottoman bond in order to mobilize the Arab and other non-Turkish population in the defense of the homeland against European colonial ambitions': S. Tamarī, *The Great War* (Oakland: University of California Press, 2017), p. 11.

74. BOA YEE 136/63. The document reports the proceedings of a meeting organised by a number of Ottoman ministers at the Yıldız Palace in Istanbul on 22 May 1898.

75. Cit. in H. M. Sachar. *Farewell Espana: The World of the Sephardim Remembered* (New York: Vintage Books, 1994), p. 75.

76. Cit. in D. P. Bell, *Jews in the Early Modern World* (Lanham MD: Rowman & Littlefield, 2008), p. 211.

77. CAMS, KP 379, Farasa (Cappadocia), p. 3. Undated testimonianal by Ath. Prodromidis: 'With Turkish we were like siblings'.

78. On the risks connected to an 'idealized Ottoman coexistence', see R. M. Hayden and S. Naumović, 'Imagined Commonalities: The Invention of a Late Ottoman "Tradition" of Coexistence', *American Anthropologist* 115(2) (June 2013): 324–34.

79. U. Makdisi, 'The Problem of Sectarianism in the Middle East in an Age of Western Hegemony', in N. Hashemi and D. Postel (eds), *Sectarianization* (London: Hurst, 2017), p. 26. Regarding a very consequential case that had much influence on the 'emancipation of Jews', Sharkey noted that 'the complete non-involvement of Muslims in the Mortara Affair in Bologna [a *cause célèbre*, in the 1850s, concerning Papal States' seizure from a Jewish family of one of their children] – the affair that set the AIU [Alliance Israélite Universelle] into motion – shows how the Islamic world was becoming drawn, inextricably, unwittingly, and unavoidably, into deep currents of European history that involved relations between Christians and Jews': Sharkey, *A History*, p. 160.

80. Walker Arnold noted that the *jizya* was paid by those 'whose religion precluded them from serving in the army, in return for the protection secured for them by the arms of the Muslims': T. W. Arnold, *The Preaching of Islam* (Lahore: Ashraf, 1961), p. 61.

81. ISA RG 160/2881-P. Johann Schmidt (British vice-consul in Haifa) to the Foreign Minister Granville, 19 June 1883. Schmidt was referring to abuses committed by Ottoman authorities against Russian Jews.

82. M. Brenner, *A Short History of the Jews* (Princeton NJ: Princeton University Press, 2010), p. 74. Lewis pointed out that 'tolerance is by modern standards an essentially intolerant idea': B. Lewis, 'The New Anti-Semitism', *The American Scholar* 75 (1) (Winter 2006): 25–36.

83. Ma'oz noted that 'even under the conservative Muslim Sultan Abdul Hamid (1876–1908) the Ottoman government continued to protect Jews against anti-Semitic eruptions in Christian provinces [. . .] Jews in Ottoman provinces

continued to be treated fairly well, certainly better than Christians, also during the Young Turks' rule (1908–1918)': M. Ma'oz, *Muslim Attitudes to Jews and Israel* (Eastbourne: Sussex University Press, 2010), p. 6. It should be added that a number of Turkish officials, including diplomat Selahattin Ülkümen (1914–2003), played a significant role in saving Jews during the Holocaust.

84. Cit. in Hyamson, *The British*, p. 6. In the same period, Young pointed out to Palmerston that: 'A strong proof that the Jews in Jerusalem are on the increase, rather than the decrease is that numerous families are to be found living out of their own quarter, this would not be the case if they could find room among their brethren [. . .] The Jews in Jerusalem are in general very poor [. . .] The Pasha has much more consideration for the Jews than his people have. I have heard several acknowledge that they enjoy more peace and tranquility under this government than ever they have enjoyed here before': Young to Palmerston, 25 May 1839, TNA FO 78/368.

85. Ibid.

86. ISA RG 160/2881-P. Finn, Jerusalem, 1 January 1857.

87. Cit. in Campos, *Ottoman Brothers*, p. 210.

88. There are of course also many other sources. For instance, the Cairo Geniza, a treasure of thousands of medieval Jewish documents from the eleventh to the nineteenth centuries housed in the Ben Ezra Synagogue in Old Cairo, further confirm that different communities played a constructive and inclusive role. According to Princeton historian Mark R. Cohen: 'The Geniza reveals Jews integrated into a single world, living and working side-by-side with Muslims. This appears particularly, but not only, in the economic sphere. In the marketplace, Jews had complete freedom of commerce. There was no restriction on their economic activity': J. Preville, 'Interview with Mark Cohen on Muslim-Jewish Relations: History and Relevance Today', *ISLAMICommentary*, 26 January 2015. Available at: http://www.worldreligionnews.com/religion-news/islam/interview-mark-cohen-muslim-jewish-relations-history-relevance-today. Particularly meaningful, from today's perspective, is also the Iranian case, where Jews have been 'an active factor in the development of Iranian history, society, and culture': H. M. Sarshar (ed.), *The Jews of Iran* (London: I. B. Tauris, 2014), p. i.

89. A. Cohen, *A World Within: Jewish Life as Reflected in Muslim Court Documents from the Sijill of Jerusalem (XVIth Century)* (Philadelphia: Center for Judaic Studies, University of Pennsylvania, 1994), vol. 1, pp. 22–3.

90. See F. Braudel, *Civilization and Capitalism, 15th–18th Century: The Structure of Everyday Life* (Berkeley: University of California Press, 1992).

91. M. Couroucli, 'Introduction', in D. Albera and M. Couroucli (eds), *Sharing Sacred Spaces in the Mediterranean* (Bloomington: Indiana University Press, 2012), p. 3. It should be noted that the concurrence of Jewish and Muslim holidays, like for instance the Yom Kippur and the 'Āshūrā', is hardly a casual coincidence.

92. P. Girard, 'Historical Foundations of Antisemitism', in Joel E. Dinsdale (ed.), *Survivors, Victims and Prepetrators: Essays on the Nazi Holocaust* (Washington DC: Hemisphere Publishing, 1980), pp. 70–1.

93. A. de Benoist, *Identità e comunità* (Naples: Guida, 2005), p. 11.

94. K. H. Karpat, 'Historical Continuity and Identity Change or How to be Modern Muslim, Ottoman, and Turk', in K. H. Karpat (ed.), *Ottoman Past and Today's Turkey* (Boston MA: Brill, 2000), pp. 1–28.

4

The Third Moment – From Ethnocentric Drives to a New Millet System

The period between the declaration of the 1908 constitution and the commencement of World War I [. . .] was a period of fluidity in the formation and recasting of local identities in Bilad al-Sham.[1]

Salīm Tamarī

I don't think there was a national movement anywhere in the Arab world until 1908, not even in Lebanon. [. . .] We have to differentiate between some people who have a national consciousness and a national movement.[2]

'Ādil Mannā

The months between 1907 and 1908 mark one of the major turning points in the history of the late modern Middle East. This was the inception of the Iranian Constitutional Revolution – which led to the establishment of a parliament in the country – and the discovery (1908) of oil reserves by the Anglo-Persian Oil Company (APOC) in Masjed Soleyman (Iran), the first big petroleum find in the region, which set off a wave of exploration, extraction and exploitation destined to change global history.

The same historical phase also marks, to a large extent, the ideological beginnings of the Israeli-Palestinian conflict. In 1907, a few months before the Jaffa clashes,[3] and just after the 'Denshaway incident' in Egypt,[4] the eighth Zionist Congress created a Palestine Office ('Agricultural Colonisation Department') in Jaffa, under the direction of Arthur Ruppin (1876–1943), whose goal was the creation of 'a Jewish milieu and of a closed Jewish economy, in which producers, consumers and middlemen shall all be Jewish';[5]

these kinds of approach and policy had a long-lasting impact both on the Holy Land and the broader region.[6] Yet, and despite the practical and ideological relevance of these and other watershed moments, it was the outbreak of 1908's Young Turk Revolution that was perhaps the seminal moment in the framework of the passage from multifaceted to sealed identities.[7]

This chapter starts by analysing the rise to power of the Young Turks and the related process of 'alienation' witnessed among a large percentage of Muslims and others in the region; this prompted many to embrace the nationalist discourse that their Christian counterparts had been advocating for some time. In the same period (the focus of the section that follows), the British authorities developed various policies aimed at enshrining religious differences and at promoting a Muslim communal identity, through the establishment of a new 'millet system'. Taking the Supreme Muslim Council as a case study, the final part of the chapter investigates the establishment of communal institutions, perceived by a number of Western policymakers as a stabilising element and a useful tool of control.

'Turkification': Embracing the National Discourse

The 1908 Young Turk Revolution started in the Balkans and resulted in the restoration of the 1876 constitution and the reconvening of parliament in July 1908. Once in power, the Young Turks – an expression coined by European observers – implemented a number of policies aimed at the centralisation and 'Turkification' of different areas within the Empire, Anatolia first and foremost.[8] Yet despite the fact that the 'Unionists' – the term used within the Ottoman context to refer to the Young Turks – played a major role in the historical chain leading to the establishment of the Turkish Republic, it would be incorrect to claim that they were ready to accomplish what Atatürk did fourteen years later (establishing a Turkish nation-state).[9] On the contrary, they were firmly committed to the idea of preserving the Empire and its institutions.

Their policies were largely rooted in the failures of Ottomanism as well as in the mounting deterioration in Turkish–Arab relations,[10] with tensions resting to a large extent in the 'issue of centralisation versus decentralisation'.[11] They were also a result of the increasingly nationalist-oriented political agendas adopted by a number of 'minorities' – a process further fostered by the discriminatory policies implemented by the Young Turks with the aim of promoting full assimilation for 'all branches of our [Ottoman] race'.[12] These included the removal of a number of Arab public figures from prominent positions and the imposition of Turkish as the sole language allowed in courts and government offices located in the Arab provinces.[13]

The ethnocentric drives that resulted from these processes came into increasing conflict with pan-Islamist calls and set afoot political and social changes destined to clash with all efforts aimed at providing political freedom and equality in exchange for loyalty to the Empire from all its citizens. A significant individual in regard to this process was Mehmed Ziya Gökalp (1876–1924), the leading ideologue behind the doctrines promoted by the Young Turks. Gökalp, who adopted his pen name (Gökalp means 'sky hero') after the 1908 revolution, published a number of highly influential works advocating the 're-Turkification' of the Ottoman Empire, the marginalisation of Turkey's Arab neighbours and the rejection of Ottomanism and Islamism as ideological and cultural identifiers.

When Muslims and others in the region felt alienated by these ideologies and policies, they further embraced the nationalist discourse promoted by their Christian counterparts. The heavy loss suffered by the Ottomans during the 1911–12 Italo-Turkish war in Libya – when Italian forces secured a rapid and easy victory, conquering Ottoman Tripolitania and the Dodecanese islands in the Aegean Sea – played a key role in convincing a growing number of Arabs of the inability of the Ottoman authorities to address the concerns, and protect the integrity, of non-Turkish areas. These perceptions were further strengthened by the First Balkan War of 1912–13, when Balkan states, galvanised by the quick results of the Italian campaign in Tripolitania, attacked the numerically and strategically disadvantaged Ottoman armies.

A number of secret and open societies were formed by Arab activists and intellectuals in the seven years that followed; all of them rejected assimilation and promoted a new Arab ethnic consciousness as well as unity among all Arabs and equal rights and opportunities for all the different components that comprised the Empire.

The first such society, Jam'īyat al-Ikhā' al-'Arabī al-'Uthmānī (the 'Society for Arab-Ottoman Brotherhood'), was established in August 1908 by a number of former functionaries of the Ottoman regime. Unlike some of the other societies that followed, it aimed at promoting the Arab cause within the framework of the Ottoman constitution, enhancing the status of Arabs and Arabic through the establishment of new schools, books, newspapers and trade organisations. From a more practical perspective, its founders were committed to retaining the positions that they held before the rise of the Young Turks and their 'pan-Turkish' policies.

This first attempt did not last long. The society, which had local branches in Beirut, Jerusalem, Tripoli, Damascus and a number of other cities across the region, was shut down by the Ottoman authorities in the Spring of 1909 due to its alleged ties with Ittihad-i Muhammed ('Mohammadan Union'), a counter-revolutionary party. In the minds of several Ottoman Arab activists, it was soon replaced by al-Muntada al-Adabi ('The Literary Club'), a semi-clandestine organisation founded in 1910 by Istanbul-based Arab students. Headed by ʿAbd al-Karīm al-Khalīl (1884–1916), a Shiʿa political activist from southern Lebanon, it soon emerged as a prominent meeting point for Lebanese, Syrian and Palestinian intellectuals, many of them accused, a few years later, of planning an Arab revolt against the Ottoman Empire.[14]

It might be an irony of history that al-Khalīl's fate was ultimately decided by one of the two main protagonists of the Sykes–Picot Agreement. Before the outbreak of the First World War, al-Khalīl and others – Muslims and Christian alike – in fact appealed to the French consul in Beirut, François Georges-Picot himself, sending a number of secret letters in which was requested French support or protection in their attempt to gain independence from the Ottomans. When the war started, Picot, who was soon after transferred to Cairo, left these letters in the abandoned French consulate in Beirut. Not much time passed before the Ottoman security agents discovered them, provoking a harsh reaction from the commander of the Turkish Fourth Army in Syria, Ahmed Jemal Pasha. Ten days before the signing of the Sykes–Picot Agreement (10 May 1916), ʿAbd al-Karīm al-Khalīl and a number of his collaborators were tortured and hanged in downtown Beirut, a few metres away from where the grave of Lebanon's former Prime Minister, Rafīq al-Harīrī (1944–2005), lies today.

A similar agenda – the promotion of Arab nationalism – was shared by the founders of al-Jam'iyya al-Qahtaniyya ('The Qahtan Society'), a secret society established in Istanbul in late 1909. Among them was Amīn al-Ḥāfiẓ, a high-ranking Arab officer who held the command of the Turkish 136th Regiment at Antioch during the Dardanelles campaign. In view of an expected (but not forthcoming) British invasion of the Syrian coast, al-Ḥāfiẓ tried to organise a revolt among the Arab soldiers and carried out extensive sabotage operations against the Turkish defences at Alexandretta in anticipation of the British landing.[15] He was executed for treason in May 1916, together with 'Arif al-Shihabi, 'Abd al-Karīm al-Khalīl and a number of other leaders of the organisation.

Relatively more successful moves were made by Ahmad Qadrī (from Damascus), 'Awnī 'Abd al-Hadī (from Jenin), Rafīq al-Tamīmī (from Nāblus), and Rustum Haydar (from Ba'albek), some of the leading figures credited with the establishment of Jam'iyat al-'Arabiya al-Fatat ('The Young Arab Society'), the first fully clandestine Arab nationalist organisation. Formed in the aftermath of the 1908 Young Turk Revoluton, this organisation, headquartered first in Paris and then in Beirut, aimed at opposing the Turkish nationalist agenda and at fostering unity and independence for Arab territories that were under Ottoman authority. With this purpose in mind, in June 1913 some of the leading figures of the organisation convened an 'Arab National Congress' in Paris, where twenty-five official delegates met to debate on reforms and political tools to gain autonomy from the Ottoman Empire. Largely due to the outbreak of the First World War, these intentions remained little more than abstract theoretical wishes, with a marginal impact both in and outside of the region.

The largely negative, at times tragic, results of the efforts from these organisations did not deter a number of other Arab thinkers and activists from pursuing similar goals. Several other secret organisations were established in the two years preceding the First World War, including Hezb al-lamarkaziyya al-Idariyya al-'Uthmaniyya (The Ottoman Administrative Decentralisation Party). Established in early 1913 by the future Syrian Prime Minister Haqqi al-Azm (1864–1955) and other prominent Syrian thinkers, it aimed at granting decentralisation for the Arab provinces and represented the last attempt to bridge the gap between the long-established Ottoman and emergent Arab loyalties.[16]

Figure 4.1   Some of the al-Fatat's members at a resort near Damascus. Bottom row (left to right): Tawfiq al-Hayyani, Fayez al-Shihabi, Rafic al-Tamimi, Awni Abd al-Hadi, Ahmad Qadri, Mu'in al-Madi, Tawfiq al-Yazagi and Sa'id Talab. Middle row (L to R): Wasfi al-Atassi, Ahmad Muraywed, Shukri al-Quwatli, Bahjat al-Shihabi, Saleem al-Attar, Zaki al-Tamimi, Husni al-Barazi. Top row (L to R): Adil al-Azma, Rushdi al-Husami, Riyad al-Solh, Saadallah al-Jabiri, Afif al-Sulh, Izzat Darwaza. (Source: https://www.pinterest.co.uk/pin/446700856760078176/?lp=true)

Yet the gap was already too wide: increasing divisions, broken trust and the outbreak of the First World War confirmed once and for all the impossibility of bringing about a process of reconciliation from within the Empire. Moreover, the media, and more specifically the post-1908 reduction of restrictions imposed by the Ottoman censure, played a leading role in the process. The partial lifting of restrictions resulted in the establishment of a large number of new journals, many of them – such as Lebanese journals *Abābīl* and *al-Balagh* – directly linked to, and subsidised by, Istanbul; others were more independent and committed to tackling and/or spreading nationalist agendas.[17] In the context of what, in official Ottoman correspondence,[18] was referred to as *Arz-i Filasṭīn ve Surīye* (Land of Palestine and Syria),[19] dozens of new journals were set up within just five years, including *al-Karmil* (founded in 1908 in Haifa by Najib Nassar), followed by *al-Quds* (which began in Jerusalem in 1908 and shut down three years later), *Al-Munādi* (first published in 1912), *Filasṭīn* (which went to press from 1911 to 1948) and *al-Dustūr* (printed by Khalīl Sakānīnī [1878–1939] between 1910 and 1913).[20] This brief phase, when most people in the region were reported to be eager to achieve 'peace at any price without regard to its political consequences',[21] was ultimately interrupted by the outbreak of the First World War, when the Porte gagged all press agencies.[22] Yet the many competing, often uncompromising, ideologies and concepts developed at the time continued to exert significant influence well beyond 'the war that will end all wars'.[23]

Crafting a New 'Millet System'

Constantin Iordachi noted that, in order to inspire new political loyalties and to forge a unified and homogeneous community, 'Young Turks had to dismantle the Ottoman communal traditions centred on the millets and based on communal rights and privileges'.[24]

When, at midday on 11 December 1917, six weeks after the publication of the Balfour Declaration, General Edmund Allenby and his soldiers made their triumphant entry through Jerusalem's Jaffa gate, Britain's approach towards the millets and the various 'souls' of the Ottoman Empire was still unclear.[25] In order to respect the solemnity of the place and not inflame the resentment of the local people, Allenby and his troops decided to get off their horses and continue on foot. They stopped a short distance before the historic Phasael Tower (rebaptised the Tower of David, as a result of a misunderstanding, many centuries later) where Allenby read out an emphatic declaration:

> The object of the war in the East on the part of Great Britain was the complete and final liberation *of all peoples* formerly oppressed by the Turks and the establishment of national governments and administrations in those countries deriving authority from the initiative and free will of the people themselves. [emphasis added][26]

Despite the caution showed by Allenby, all those involved were aware that, for better or worse, nothing would ever be the same again.[27] 'We felt', noted

Figure 4.2   The surrender of Jerusalem to the British, 9 December 1917. The Mayor of Jerusalem Hussein al-Husaynī with Sergeants Sedgwick and Hurcomb. (Source: Hol Lars [Lewis] Larsson, American Colony Photo Dept photographers. G. Eric and Edith Matson Photograph Collection, Library of Congress, Washington DC)

Bertha Vester, head of the American Colony in Jerusalem, that 'we were witnessing what we thought then was the climax of the last Crusade'.[28] In the press release that reached the Turkish Foreign Minister Ahmed Nessimy Bey on 3 January 1918, it was argued that 'the entrance of the "infidels" in Jerusalem will weaken the prestige of the Turkish Caliph'.[29] The most direct consequences, however, were felt by local and regional actors. The 'fall' of Jerusalem was perceived by a significant percentage of Zionist sympathisers as a 'glorious victory for the Jewish nation [. . .] We feel that our race is entering in a new era'.[30] This reflected a deeply felt optimism which, over the decades to follow, would transform, for many, into profound disillusionment.[31] Less profound (due to minor expectations), but in many ways more traumatic, was the frustration felt by a large percentage of Ottoman Arabs, both in and outside of Palestine. After an initial phase in which London's assurances seemed to prevail, at least regarding the inviolability of the holy places,[32] an increasing number of Arabs in the region became persuaded that the British establishment aimed 'to transform the Holy Land into an Anglo-Zionist colony, no more no less'.[33] It was a prospect that, in the months and years to follow, according to the Bishop of Jerusalem Rennie MacInnes (1870–1931), pushed many citizens into fantasising about the return of the Ottomans to power.[34]

Yet an Ottoman return was then more unrealistic than ever, and the British authorities were swift in understanding the necessity of developing a new approach that would take on board the Wilsonian rhetoric of self-determination. The direct control of large areas of the Middle East and the following granting of the relevant mandates by the League of Nations took place within the frame of a new epoch in which empires were losing their legitimacy, as well as their grasp on power and ability to respond to the social complexity of the post-First World War era.

The proposed solution, believed by British authorities to provide new answers to the pressing challenges of the time had, once again, much to do with religious factors. In this regard, the Holy Land represents possibly the most significant microcosm within which to assess and approach the dynamics of these broader impacts. In the months following Allenby's entrance at Jaffa Gate, London implemented a number of policies with the aim of turning Muslim, Jewish and Christian religious identities into legal categories. This process, that was also aiming at stymieing any form of local nationalism, relied primarily on a spatial-confessional understanding of local contexts. In Jerusalem, any attempt at shaping a supra-religious sense of citizenship was curtailed through a number of pervasive policies. These included the hardening the Old City's division into four sealed-off quarters (Armenian, Muslim, Jewish, Christian), and the changing of street names according to religious criteria (each district was associated with religious figures or spaces linked to a specific religion). Benedict Anderson would have defined these kinds of practice as 'the seeds of a territorialization of faiths'.[35] Roberto Mazza goes a step further and contends that through the agency of the first British governor of Jerusalem, Ronald Storrs (1881–1955), London 'set in motion a social and spatial process that aimed at the division and homogenisation of the Old City and the city outside the walls according to religion'.[36]

Figure 4.3   The Ottoman Clock Tower of Jerusalem's Jaffa Gate, built by the Ottomans in 1908 and destroyed by the British in 1922. (Source: American Colony Photo Dept photographers. G. Eric and Edith Matson Photograph Collection, Library of Congress, Washington DC)

No less relevant from a symbolic point of view was the decision taken by Storrs to demolish the Ottoman clock tower that stood near the Jaffa Gate between 1908 and 1922. In Ottoman eyes, the new clock,[37] like electric lighting and civic buildings, was symbolic of a new modern-oriented empire based on a sense of common citizenship. It mirrored, in other words, the vision promoted by the Young Turks in the last part of the nineteenth century (and until the Revolution of 1908).

Beyond the specific, yet paradigmatic, case of Jerusalem and the Holy Land, London policies in former Ottoman lands were based on the principle of rethinking and reshaping what it perceived as a 'millet system', that is, the pillars of the existing legal system inherited by London in 1917. British authorities did not only maintain this system, perceived as a stabilising element and a useful instrument of control, but opted also to broaden its scope. Muslims of the former Ottoman Empire were then included in a new millet and controlled through a number of newly established communal institutions.

The decision to extend the scope of the millet system – through the redefinition of the Muslim community as the largest and most influential millet, and by separating it from Arab Christians (perceived as inherently divided by ancestral theological quarrels) – was hardly a feature confined only to the Middle East. The necessity of relying on a 'system' was in fact common in a number of other imperial contexts. In British Empire's the 'jewel in the crown' (India), for instance, the 'caste system' was, to a great extent, shaped through the integration of a number of useful elements, with the aim of providing order and stability to the European understanding of Indian culture and society. This cluster of elements included:

> the claims about the nation of the Hindus as a variant of that of the Jews; conception of the Brahmin priesthood and its practices as an instance of false religion similar to the institutions of Catholicism and Judaism; the idea that such institutions deceived the believers into following a set of human fabrications as though these were divine commandments; the claim that the Hindu religion revolved around external ceremonies and concerns about purity and pollution.[38]

In this sense, both the millet and the caste systems can largely be traced back to an ancestral inclination very common among human beings: the assumption that local customs are equivalent to laws of nature. Indeed, the tendency to standardise the complexity of the 'other' – not uncommonly induced by an intellectual arrogance unable to grasp realities that were anything but static – generated similar misunderstandings even within very different contexts.[39] When, for example, American anthropologist Harold Conklin began to analyse the way in which the Hanunóo of the Philippines classify colours, he was at first surprised at the apparent confusion and contradictions; however, this subsided as soon as the informants were asked to define oppositions within contrasting pairs of colours, rather than separate samples. Even within such a framework, there was, then, a more complex logic at work but one which had no way of standing out in terms of 'our system' and that would have remained unknown had Conklin not been equipped with the tools necessary to interpret that particular reality;[40] or if, as often used to happen in anthropological studies, the temptation to erase all that resisted the colonial map imposed by the 'authorised observer' had had the upper hand.[41]

Returning to the context of the Middle East and the new millet system imagined by London: it was developed and implemented in the early stage of the post-First World War, when empires were in decline and Woodrow Wilson's rhetoric of national self-determination was at its climax. The policies implemented in this transitional phase aimed primarily at enshrining religious differences and succeeded at defining any form of dissent as the expression of ancient religious disputes. In practical terms, the promotion of a Muslim communal identity was perceived as a tool for achieving three main goals: confining Muslim political expression to religious issues; pre-empting the creation of multireligious nationalist movements and thus the rising of a potential pan-Islamic rebellion – in Malaysia, Egypt, India, Palestine and elsewhere – against London; and, finally, appeasing Muslim opinion throughout the British Empire, particularly in India, where influential intellectual Muhammad Iqbal worked and was establishing strong ties with Muslim communities in Palestine and elsewhere.[42]

Marginalising 'Minorities': The Supreme Muslim Council as a Case Study

One of the most potent examples of the new approach based on the creation of new communal institutions can be found in the establishment of the Supreme Muslim Council (al-Majlis al-Islāmī al-A'alā; SMC), a body with no precedent in the history of the region or, because of its numerous ramifications, in that of Islam. It was established by Herbert Samuel (1870–1963) – the first, controversial,[43] British High Commissioner for Palestine – at the end of twelve months' 'incubation', on 20 December 1921.[44]

The new body was to provide a degree of representational autonomy to the local Muslim majority, so as to balance the institutions accorded by London to the Zionist counterpart, as well as to staunch the growing discontent.[45] 'We have no means', protested 'Abdallāh Sa'īd al-Danaf and 'Abdel Raḥmān el-Danaf in August 1921, 'to obtain our rights as long as the Justice of the British Government rules'.[46] In addition to this, the British authorities needed an 'imperium in imperio',[47] that is, a sort of 'government within

Figure 4.4   Herbert Samuel reading his proclamation at the inauguration of Emir Abdullah in Transjordan, 17 April 1921. (Source: American Colony Photo Dept photographers. Visual materials from the papers of John D. Whiting Library of Congress, Washington DC)

the government' with which to interact. However, as was predictable in a context marked by power vacuums and the absence of any sort of legitimate representation, it soon acquired an all-encompassing role. The results of this did not take long to make themselves felt. 'The present administration of Palestine', lamented the representatives of the Palestine Arab Delegation in a letter to British public opinion in 1930, 'is appointed by His Majesty's Government and governs the country through an autocratic system in which the population has no say'.[48]

The SMC, legally bound to the mandatory power, allowed the person appointed by Samuel, Ḥajj Amīn al-Ḥusaynī, to preside over it,[49] and to oversee for good the control of the enormous flows of funds from Islamic public donations (the public *awqāf*).[50] The latter, which were quantifiable, when

Figure 4.5   Delegation of Arab women protesting against the British policy in Palestine, Government House, Jerusalem, 1920s. (Source: American Colony Photo Dept photographers. G. Eric and Edith Matson Photograph Collection, Library of Congress, Washington DC)

Ḥajj Amīn took office, to £100,000 per year, had previously been supervised by Istanbul. As clarified in 1935 by the London scholar Beatrice Erskine (1860–1948), who was based in Ḥaifā during the years of the mandate, with the introduction of the new body, the deployment of those resources went completely out of control:

> The head office of the *Wakf*, or Religious Bequests, was in Istanbul in Turkish times, and the great wealth attached to it was administrated there under Government supervision. After the [First World] War the British Government handed over the funds to the Moslems free of all control, and instituted the Moslem Supreme Council [. . .] [It] manages eighteen religious courts, with a staff of two hundred and fifty assistants; superintends six *wakf* departments, in which five hundred and ninety-two men are employed; controls ten schools and a theological college, having a total of one thousand six hundred and fifty students.[51]

Besides being able to dispose of enormous sums of money at his own discretion, the new office enabled al-Ḥusaynī to propose and elect judges, local muftīs and the administrators of the *waqf* (singular of *awqāf*), and to lay off and hire functionaries in the Sharī'ah Court.[52] All these positions were distributed by the neo-*ra'īs al-'ulamā'* (neo-head of Muslim scholars) to people he deemed unconditionally loyal.[53] According to an official protest sent from Hebron and signed by several local sheiks:

> Many petitions and complaints were submitted by the inhabitants of Palestine to the [British] Secretariat against the President of the Supreme Muslim Council [Ḥajj Amīn al-Ḥusaynī] and the improper manner in which he administers the Awqaf, Orphan funds and the Sharia Courts. [The British] Government's reply to the majority of such petitions was that it cannot interfere with Waqf and Sharia affairs. Such policy cannot be concealed from ignorant people (shepherds) as Government has actually interfered with the Supreme Moslem Council, by appointing the members of the Council. Such an attitude is, indeed, inconsistent with the terms of the Palestine Mandate and casts reflection on the administration of a civilized power, such as Great Britain.[54]

The new Supreme Muslim Council – whose influence helped, between 1921 and 1929, to maintain a period of relative calm in Palestine – became a mere tool used to strengthen the status of the 'Grand Muftī'.[55] To the religious power he wielded, Ḥajj Amīn could, in this way, add an unchallenged political role within Palestinian society, preventing it from forming its own representational and inclusive institutions. Furthermore, the new council also played a decisive part in shaking up the status quo between Christian and Muslim Palestinians.

The local Muslim demographic component paid a price for the decision to centralise all the Islamic institutions in the hands of one person; the Christian component of the population did as well. Although the latter had always been a marginalised minority, it had gradually acquired a more central role in the last years of the First World War. It was considered a 'natural bridge' to Europe in an era in which the 'Old Continent' was the political centre for all decisions concerning Palestine. As evidence of the renewed focus on the Arab Christians and the desire to concentrate on a 'balance' between the two religions, the first of a long series of Muslim–Christian associations, al-Jam'īya al-Ahlīya ('Local Association'), was created in Jaffa. In June 1918, it was renamed in Jerusalem as al-Jam'īya al-Islāmīya al-Masīḥīya ('Muslim–Christian Association'), and adopted as its symbol a flag with the cross and the half-moon held by a woman wearing the traditional black veil (*hijāb*). The purpose was to underline that the Palestinian struggle in those years was not limited solely to the efforts of Muslims, or just to men.[56] This movement, deemed essential in order to oppose the Zionist threat effectively, immediately became so popular that organisations with the same name were formed in Nāblus and many other cities. Most of the leaders of this movement, one of whom was the Greek Orthodox intellectual Khalīl Sakānīnī, were careful to avoid any explicit definition of Arab nationalism in Islamic terms. The SMC and the powers awarded to Ḥajj Amīn al-Ḥusaynī were a deciding factor that relegated Christians once again to a marginalised position; it was no coincidence that, from 1922 onwards, local leaders appealed increasingly frequently to the religious feelings of ordinary people.

Notes

1. Tamarī, *The Great War*, p. 89.
2. 'Ādil Mannā in a roundtable transcribed in Scham, Salem and Pogrund (eds), *Shared Histories*, p. 57.
3. On the 1908 clashes and the impact of Zionist immigration on the agricultural lands around Jaffa, see M. LeVine, *Overthrowing Geography: Jaffa, Tel Aviv and Struggle for Palestine* (Berkeley: University of California Press, 2005), p. 45. According to LeVine, 'For Tel Aviv's founders, the attempt to separate physically as well as ideologically and espistemologically their new neighborhood from Jaffa and its existing Arab and Jewish quarters was a primary concern': ibid., p. 156. On the desire of the Zionist pioneers to mark out a distinction also between the old Jewish neighbourhoods of Jaffa and embryonic Tel Aviv, see T. Meroz, *Tel Aviv-Yafo: Sipur Ha'Ir* [Tel Aviv-Jaffa: History of a City] (Tel Aviv: Ben-Zion, 1978), p. 35.
4. In Denshaway, a small village in the Nile delta, a number of Egyptian peasants were executed as a consequence of an altercation over the shooting of the villagers' pigeons, part of the livelihood of local inhabitants. Mansfield defined the 'Denshaway accident' as a 'turning-point in the British occupation of Egypt comparable to the Amritsar massacre of 1919 in India': P. Mansfield, *The British in Egypt* (London: Holt, 1972), p. 167.

5. A. Ruppin, *Three Decades of Palestine* (Westport, CT: Greenwood, 1936), p. 62. The same year (1907), the future first President of the State of Israel, Chaim Weizmann (1874–1952), overtly favourable, like many other Zionist leaders, to more or less extreme forms of boycotting of the Arab workforce, expressed the following thoughts to his wife in Jaffa: 'If our Jewish capitalists, say even only the Zionist capitalists, were to invest their capital in Palestine, if only in part, there is no doubt that the lifeline of Palestine – all the coastal strip – would be in Jewish hands within twenty-five years [. . .] The Arab retains his primitive attachment to the land, the soil-instinct is strong in him, and by being continuously employed on it there is a danger that he might feel himself indispensable to it, with a moral right to it': C. Weizmann [B. Litvinoff (ed.)], *The Essential Chaim Weizmann* (London: Weidenfeld, 1982), pp. 11 and 208. Weizmann held that the fears of the fellaḥīn were the result of misinformation: 'The poor ignorant fellah does not worry about politics, but when he is told repeatedly by people in whom he has confidence that his livelihood is in danger of being taken away from him by us, he becomes our mortal enemy': Weizmann to the London offices of the Zionist Organization. Central Zionist Archive (CZA) Z3/526, Cairo, 7 November 1919. On the other hand, Yitzhak Epstein (1862–1943) emphasised in the same period that 'in our beloved land lives a whole people which has lived there for many centuries and has never considered the idea of leaving it': Y. Epstein, 'A Hidden Question', in *Ha-Shilo'ah* 17 (July–December 1907): 193–206.

6. Nationalist leader Rafik Bey Hakim explained in the newspaper *Cheriot el-Moquattam* the process by which Arab public opinion moved from viewing Jewish immigration as a possible resource to it being a cause of apprehension. In his opinion, it was primarily the result of the fact that the Zionists 'cut themselves off completely' from the rest of the local population: MDC, 'El-Moqattam', 14 April 1914.

7. In a matter of just a few years, in fact, new identities were crafted, and others experienced an unprecedented 'hardening process'. This was mirrored, for instance, in the ethnographic map included in *Filastin Risalesi* ('The Epistle of Palestine') – a manual released (1915) for wartime intelligence to the benefit of Ottoman officials serving in the Syrian-Palestinian context – in which local inhabitants appear for the first time 'X-rayed and vivisected' according to ethnic and religious criteria.

8. As noted by Erol Ülker, 'at the time when the Turkification measures were being carried out in Anatolia, [. . .] in the Arab provinces, the Young Turks appealed

to Islamic unity under the Caliph': Erol Ülker, 'Contextualising "Turkification": Nation-Building in the Late Ottoman Empire, 1908–18', *Nations and Nationalism* 11(4) (2005): 623.

9. C. E. Black and L. C. Brown, *Modernization in the Middle East* (Princeton NJ: Darwin Press, 1992), p. 160. The period of the Young Turk Revolution has been perceived and described in very different ways by scholars and observers. This includes also anti-Semitic claims. On 19 May 1910, British ambassador in Istanbul Gerald Lowther (1858–1916) wrote, for instance, that the revolution of 1908 was the outcome of an international conspiracy orchestrated by 'Jews, Freemasons and Zionists'. It is believed that the source used by Lowther was Gerald Fitzmaurice (1865–1939), Istanbul embassy's dragoman from 1907 to 1914. See M. Kemal Oke, 'Jews and the Question of Zionism in the Ottoman Empire, 1908–1913', *Studies in Zionism* 7(2) (Autumn 1986): 199–208.

10. See S. al-Husri, *Al-Bilād al-ʿArabiyya wa al-Dawla al-ʿUtmāniyya* [The Arab Countries and the Ottoman State] (Beirut: Dār al-ʿIlm li-al-Malāyīn, 1960).

11. See H. Kayalı, *Arabs and Young Turks: Ottomanism, Arabism and Islamism in the Ottoman Empire, 1908–1918* (Berkeley: University of California Press, 1997).

12. Excerpt from the declaration issued by the Young Turks the day the Ottoman Empire officially entered the First World War. Cit. in H. Luke, *The Making of Modern Turkey* (London: Macmillan, 1936), p. 161.

13. A number of Ottoman documents show that only Turkish-speaking representatives were selected by the Porte to sit in local assemblies: BOA DH.MUI 103/2/1, 14 June 1910.

14. M. Al-Shihābī, *Al-Qawmīya al-ʿArabīya* [Arab Nationalism] (Cairo: Muhādarāt, 1961), pp. 71–2.

15. P. A. Mohs, *Military Intelligence and the Arab Revolt: The First Modern Intelligence War* (London: Routledge, 2008), p. 21.

16. T. Philip, 'From Rule of Law to Constitutionalism: The Ottoman Context of Arab Political Thought', in J. Hanssen and M. Weiss (eds), *Arabic Thought beyond the Liberal Age* (Cambridge: Cambridge University Press, 2016), p. 260.

17. Even if most journals were able to print only a few hundred copies each, most of them were available in public places and libraries; they were also often sent free of charge to the *mukhtār* (village chiefs) of various inhabited areas. On the specific Palestinian context, see J. Yehoshua, *Tārīkh al-Ṣaḥāfa al-ʿArabīya fī Filasṭīn fī al-ʿAhd al-ʿUthmānī, 1909–1918* [The History of the Arabic Press in Palestine during the Ottoman Era] (Jerusalem: Maṭbaʿat al-Maʿārif, 1974), pp. 17–18 and 44.

18. BOA I.HUS 140/43, 12 February 1906.

19. '*Arz-i Filasṭīn ve Surīye*' was also used in the maps printed in 1729 in Istanbul by Ibrahim Müteferrika (1674–1745). For a reproduction of the map, see N. Matar, *Turks, Moors, and Englishmen in the Age of Discovery* (New York: Columbia University Press, 1999), p. 134.

20. See Y. Khuri, *Al-Sahāfa al-'Arabyya fi Filastīn* [The Arabic Press in Palestine] (Beirut: Institute for Palestine Studies, 1976).

21. TNA FO 195/2453, British Consul in Jerusalem, Peter J. C. McGregor (1865–1936), to British ambassador in Istanbul, Gerard Lowther (1858–1916), 29 January 1913.

22. At the end of the war, local newspapers began to reorganise; in 1919/20 a new phase began, that of the censorship imposed by London. Almost twenty years later (February 1937), British authorities registered the presence of eight political dailies, four Arabic (*al Liwa'*, *Filastīn*, *al Difa'a*, *al Jamia al Islamiya*) and four Jewish (*Palestine Post*, *Haboker*, *Ha'aretz*, *Davar*). In six months, between 19 April and 12 October 1937, that is immediately following the years of the Great Arab Revolt of 1936–9, the 'Arab newspapers were suspended on thirty-four occasions and Hebrew papers on thirteen occasions': TNA CO 733/346/10.

23. Expression used by British author H. G. Wells (1866–1946) in 1914 to refer to the First World War. See H. G. Wells, *The War that Will End War* (London: Palmer, 1914).

24. C. Iordachi, *The Ottoman Empire*, in T. Baycroft and M. Hewitson (eds), *What Is a Nation? Europe 1789–1914* (Oxford: Oxford University Press, 2006), pp. 132–3.

25. See L. Kamel, *Imperial Perceptions of Palestine: British Influence and Power in Late Ottoman Times* (London: I. B. Tauris, 2015).

26. In *Journal of the Parliaments of the Empire* (London: Empire Parliamentary Association, 1922), vol. 3, p. 486.

27. Robert Cecil (1864–1958), Balfour's nephew and undersecretary to the Foreign Office, noted that the entry into Jerusalem coincided with 'the final termination of the infidel possession of the Holy City': Cecil, 26 November 1917, LPL, DP, 400, f. 206. 27–30.

28. ACAC, Scrapbook of articles, 1922–6. Bertha Vester recalled her impressions during Allenby's entrance at Jaffa Gate in a lecture held in 1949. She added that: 'A renaissance will come, of course, but it will take a long time to forget the suffering which the Jews, who have suffered so much themselves, have brought upon the non-Jewish inhabitants of Palestine'.

29. BOA HR.SYS 2446/9, press release, Office of the Turkish Foreign Minister Ahmed Nessimy Bey, 3 January 1918.

30. Ibid.

31. In a memorandum entitled 'The Palestine Problem and proposals for a solution' drawn up in August 1947 by the Irgun group for the attention of UNSCOP (United Nations Special Committee on Palestine) it was emphasised that 'the history of the mandate as such can be described as a trick perpetrated by Great Britain at the expense of the Jewish people', ASDMAE, AP 1946–50, Palestine, b. 2.

32. BOA HR.SYS 2456/9.

33. BOA HR.SYS 2334/45. Text drawn up by a Palestinian delegation made up of Muslims and Christians. It was sent to the second general assembly of the League of Nations and printed in 'La Tribune d'Orient' on 20 May 1922.

34. LPL, DP, 400, f. 187. MacInnes to the Archbishop of Canterbury, 28 February 1920. 'British prestige, which was so high after the liberation of Jerusalem, has suffered grievously [. . .] [the people] would far prefer to have the Turks back again.'

35. B. Anderson, *Imagined Communities* (New York: Verso, 1991), p. 17.

36. R. Mazza, 'Transforming the Holy City: From Communal Clashes to Urban Violence, the Nebi Musa Riots in 1920', in U. Freitag, N. Fuccaro, C. Ghrawi and N. Lafi (eds), *Urban Violence in the Middle East* (New York: Berghahn, 2015), pp. 179–96.

37. On how the very notion of modernity is directly linked to the conceptualisation of time as a timeline see A. Wishnitzer, *Reading Clocks, Alla Turca: Time and Society in the Late Ottoman Empire* (Chicago: University of Chicago Press, 2015), pp. 1–16.

38. J. De Roover, *A Nation of Tribes and Priests*, in M. Fárek, D. Jalki, S. Pathan and P. Shah (eds), *Western Foundations of the Caste System* (London: Palgrave, 2017), p. 203.

39. Elémire Zolla (1926–2002) argued that 'in many traditions it is customary to expose supreme archetypes in a domestic, childish way. Thus, the European did not understand the depth of the fables retold among the tribes of Africa and America [ ] It is a marvelous trick because it is the greatest obstacle to real understanding [ ] The proud shall never bow to studying with love a modest reality, nor shall it ever be able to suspect that it might be discussed, like the miserly dress of the caliph Hārūn ar-Rashīd in the *Thousand and one nights*'. E. Zolla, *Uscite dal mondo* [Out of this World] (Milan: Adelphi, 1992), p. 433.

40. C. Lévi-Strauss, *Le pensée sauvage* [The Savage Mind] (Paris: Plon, 1969), p. 75.

41. Anthropology, in Hamid Dabashi's words, 'was as instrumental in the European colonial conquest of multiple worlds as the soldier who carried the gun. The anthropologist's pen was, and remains, mightier than the colonial officer's sword': H. Dabashi, *The Arab Spring* (New York: Zed Books, 2012), p. 52.

42. Robson, *Colonialism and Christianity*, pp. 45–6.

43. 'The appointment of Sir Herbert Samuel [. . .] as High Commissioner for Palestine has an humiliating effect [ta'sīr mohīn] in all Arab nations': ISA, 5040/16-M, letter signed by the 'General Secretary of the Palestine Committee', 25 September 1920.

44. On 9 November 1920, a meeting was organised at the British headquarters in Jerusalem to discuss the matter. Kāmil al-Ḥusaynī and seven other Muslim representatives were invited to participate. Samuel, Storrs and six other British officials were also present. The British authorities decided who these eight representatives would be. But Samuel had no doubts '[t]hat the members of the Conference fully represented Moslem opinion is unquestionable': ISA, 649/7-P, Samuel to Curzon (1859–1925), 14 November 1920.

45. According to Ghandour, 'the Mandatory authorities chose to deal with the Palestinian Arabs not as Arabs but as Muslims [. . .] the 'Muslims' did not so much want a Supreme Muslim Council as much as they wanted a representative government'. Z. B. Ghandour, *A Discourse on Domination in Mandate Palestine: Imperialism, Property and Insurgency* (New York: Routledge, 2010), p. 131.

46. CHIR, 13/21/6,1/40, Abdallah Sa'id El-Danaf and Abdel Rahman Rashid El-Danaf ('servants of the Holy Rock' of Jerusalem) to Wyndham Deedes. Jerusalem, 10 August 1921.

47. An expression used by the Peel Commission in 1937 to refer to the Jewish Agency and the SMC.

48. ISA, RG65 1054/1-P, protest signed by the Palestine Arab Delegation, 19 May 1930.

49. The term 'appointment' should be preferred to 'election', although Ḥajj Amīn never missed an opportunity to remind that 'the President [he himself] was elected by Muslim representatives and was not appointed' (ISA 195/18M. 26 May 1936). Ḥajj Amīn was appointed on 9 January 1922 – following the wishes of Herbert Samuel – by fifty-six former grand electors of the last Ottoman parliament. It is noteworthy that as early as 24 August 1921, when those same fifty-six local notables were invited by Samuel to discuss the issue at Government House, 'Hajj Amīn was named as their leader'. T. Jabārah, *Palestinian*

Leader, Hajj Amin al-Husayni, Mufti of Jerusalem (Princeton NJ: Kingston Press, 1985), p. 47. This confirms that, as Uri Kupferschmidt remarked, 'Hajj Amīn al-Husaynī's election as *Ra'īs al-'Ulamā* was a foregone conclusion since he already held the position of *al-Muftī al-Akbar*': U. Kupferschmidt, *The Supreme Muslim Council* (Leiden: Brill, 1987), p. 20.

50. From the dispatches of British functionaries, it appears that they believed it possible, if not probable, that Ḥajj Amīn would be chosen for president of the SMC: ISA—RGW 10/12-M.

51. S. Erskine, *Palestine of the Arabs* (London: Harrap, 1935), p. 160.

52. The attempt to deprive Ḥajj Amīn of the control of the Sharī'a Court became the main focus of the efforts of the Nashāshībī clan over time: TNA CO 733/222/7, A. G. Wauchope to P. Culiffe-Lister, 30 January 1932.

53. This was an additional title 'granted' to Ḥajj Amīn al-Ḥusaynī. Although it is true that, starting from the seventeenth century, various *'ulamā* were called – due to their acknowledged authority – '*ra'īs al-'ulamā*', it is also true that such a 'title' never obtained official recognition. See M. al-Muḥibbī, *Khulāṣat al-Athār fī A'yān al-Qarn al-hādī 'Ashar* [Compendium of the Notables of the Eleventh Century] (Cairo: al-Maṭba'a al-Wahbīya, 1867), vol. 4, pp. 43–4.

54. ISA, 293/3-M. Hebron, 5 February 1934. The dispatch, sent to the then High Commissioner Wauchope, was signed by Tawfiq Tahbub, Haj Mohammad Badr and others. Two years earlier, seventeen local notables wrote to the British authorities denouncing that Ḥajj Amīn 'had appointed 25 persons, all members of his family, at different posts, thus putting at their disposal the revenues of the Moslem Wakfs as well as our own ones which they conjointly spent for their personal upkeep': ISA, 293/3-M. Jerusalem, 11 August 1932.

55. I. Pappé, *The Rise and Fall of a Palestinian Dynasty: The Husaynis, 1700–1948* (Berkeley: University of California Press, 2011), p. 222.

56. See A. Mukhlis, *Al-Muslimūn wa al-Naṣāra* [Muslims and Christians] (Ḥaifa: n.a., 1929). On the general atmosphere of that specific period see R. Mazza, 'Transforming the Holy City', in U. Freitag, N. Fuccaro, N. Lafi and C. Ghrawi (eds), *Urban Violence in the Middle East* (New York: Berghahn, 2014), pp. 214–29.

5

Balfour's 'Pattern'

If the Turks are left ostensibly in control of Palestine, the country is likely to fall, in course of time, under German influence. If Germany, or any other continental Power, is dominant there, Egypt would be exposed to constant menace. The best safeguard would be the establishment of a large Jewish population, preferably under British protection.[1]

Herbert Samuel (1870–1963), first British High Commissioner for Palestine, 3 October 1917

I notice that the Arab population are spoken of, or included in, 'the non-Jewish communities', which sounds as if there were a few Arab villages in a country full of Jews.[2]

John Tilley (1869–1952), commenting on a draft of the British mandate in Palestine, 19 March 1920

It is for the people to determine the destiny of the territory and not the territory the destiny of the people.[3]

Judge Hardy Cross Dillard (1902–82) in an advisory opinion (1975) on the Western Sahara context

James Renton remarks that the Balfour Declaration was the result of the misplaced decision of the British authorities to refer to 'ethnic groups in racial and nationalistic terms'.[4] Roberto Mazza further notes that 'the war and the British support to Zionism through the Balfour Declaration also proved to be a strong impetus to nationalist mobilization'.[5]

Notwithstanding the different opinions on the matter, it is certain that the Balfour's 'pattern' provided a powerful boost to the gradual and cumulative processes of ascribing ethnic or racial identities to the peoples of the region. In other words, Britain's 'fixation on segregating and categorising the Ottomans into racial hierarchies' found in the Balfour Declaration its most notorious and potent expression.[6] This assumes a particular relevance if considering the use of the 'distinct race' paradigm adopted by Balfour himself on occasion of his refusal to intercede with the Russian government to request the ceasing of the discrimination suffered by Jews:

> It was also to be remembered that the persecutors had a case of their own. They were afraid of the Jews, who were an exceedingly clever people [. . .] wherever one went in Eastern Europe, one found that, by some way or other, the Jew got on, and when to this was added the fact that he belonged to a distinct race, and that he professed a religion which to the people about him was an object of inherited hatred, and that, moreover, he was [. . .] numbered in millions, one could perhaps understand the desire to keep him down [. . .] He [Balfour] did not say that this justified the persecution, but all these things had to be considered.[7]

It should be noted, within the framework of these words and before focusing on the details one of the most debated documents of modern history,[8] that the general attitude shown by a significant percentage of the British authorities and British public opinion in the years preceding the First World War was influenced by the age-old attitude of considering Jews, including those converted to Christianity, as 'alien entities'.[9] Even where Jews were completely assimilated or employed in prestigious jobs, they were often considered as mysterious figures to be avoided.[10] When referring to Disraeli, Lord Salisbury, his direct superior in Parliament, branded him as an 'unprincipled Jew who had no right to be in the House of Commons'.[11] Lord Derby (1826–93), foreign secretary in the Disraeli government, underlined that the latter believed 'thoroughly in prestige – as all foreigners do'.[12] Herbert Henry Asquith (1852–1928), prime minister from 1908 to 1916, was accustomed to adopting first names when addressing his colleagues; the exception to this approach was embodied by Edwin Montagu (1879–1924), the only Jewish member of the British Cabinet at the time of the Balfour Declaration, for whom he used epithets such as 'the Assyrian', 'the Hebrew' or 'Mr Wu'.[13] Herbert Samuel, another eminent Jew, was dismissed by Prime Minister Lloyd George as 'a greedy, ambitious and grasping Jew with all the worst characteristics of his race'.[14] Not surprisingly, Montagu, a fierce opponent of the Balfour Declaration, on 23 August 1917 published a memorandum entitled 'The Anti-Semitism of the Present Government'.[15]

These examples represent only the tip of the iceberg. At the very time that the British establishment was laying the foundations for a 'Jewish national home' in Palestine, some of the most common facets of anti-Semitism found one of their most solid bastions in Britain itself. 'Anti-Semites', predicted Herzl in 1895,[16] 'will become our surest friends'.[17]

When the Aliens Act was approved on 11 August 1905, Arthur Balfour was serving as prime minister. He had come to power three years earlier and emerged immediately as a front-rank figure in the parliamentary process aiming to curtail what a *Manchester Evening Chronicle* editorial referred to as the 'dirty, destitute, diseased, verminous and criminal foreigner [mainly Jews[18]] who dumps himself on our soil'.[19] Just a month before the implementation of the law – approved with 211 votes for and 59 against – Balfour confirmed to the House of Commons the reasons for his distrust of Jews. One of the aspects that worried him the most was their 'damaging habit' of intermarriage:

> The right hon. Baronet [Charles Dilke] had condemned the anti-Semitic spirit which disgraced a great deal of modern politics in other countries of Europe, and declared that the Jews of this country were a valuable element in the community [. . .] But he undoubtedly thought that a state of things could easily be imagined in which it would not be to the advantage of the civilisation of the country that there should be an immense body of persons who, however patriotic, able, and industrious, however much they threw themselves into the national life, still, by their own action, remained a people apart, and not merely held a religion differing from the vast majority of their fellow-countrymen, but only inter-married among themselves.[20]

A comparative study based on an analysis of the literary and journalistic writings of the day shows that the most common racial stereotypes in Central Europe had Jews as their main targets. In Britain, on the other hand, black people represented the most common victims. In Britain as well, however, anti-Semitism was a tolerated and, in some cases, an actively encouraged practice. A significant amount of nineteenth-century British literature favoured the popularisation of the image of the Aryan as opposed to the Semite. Robert

Knox (1791–1862), Francis Galton (1822–1911), Karl Pearson (1857–1936) and, *mutatis mutandis*, Hilaire Belloc (1870–1953) and G. K. Chesterton (1874–1936) played, in this respect, particularly important roles.[21]

Well before the alleged tendency for self-exclusion to which Balfour also referred, the main issue that fed anti-Semitic propaganda of the time was linked to the myth of an 'international Jewish conspiracy'. It was popularised by two famous literary fakes – *Biarritz* (1868) and the *Protocols of the Elders of Zion* (1903) – and found 'valuable' support in Britain thanks to Arnold White's (1848–1925) *The Modern Jew* (1899) and Joseph Bannister's *England under the Jews* (1901).

At the end of the First World War, 'British anti-Semitism' was channelled by focusing on the hypothetical 'Jewish factor' that was believed to have triggered the 1917 Bolshevik Revolution. 'We must not lose sight of the fact', wrote H. Pearson in a dispatch on 2 January 1919, 'that this movement is engineered and managed by astute Jews, many of the criminals, and nearly every commissary in Russia is a Jew'.[22] In the years preceding the revolution, a variant of this anti-Semitic attitude could be detected in what was described as 'the international influence exercised by the Jewish race'.[23] The thesis of the 'world domination by the Jews' was not infrequently proposed, for political reasons, also by a certain number of Zionists. 'Her Majesty', argued Philipp Newlinski (1841–99) in 1897 to the Ottoman authorities in an attempt to convince them to accept economic support, 'could suddenly count on the biggest capitalists in the world as well as on the support of all the major newspapers of Europe, which are in Jewish hands [*qui se trouvent entre les mains juives*]'.[24]

Several studies on postcards in the Edwardian era (1901–10) have confirmed how common anti-Semitism was in early twentieth-century England.[25] But it was between 1917 and 1920 that anti-Semitic theories in Britain and elsewhere gained an 'exceptionally receptive and uncritical atmosphere'.[26] Lloyd George, prime minister in the year of the Balfour Declaration, was convinced that Jews would determine the outcome of the First World War and that they were the hidden forces behind the Russian Revolution.[27]

Lloyd George's opinions were also influenced by books, letters and reports produced by various members of his cabinet, or figures linked to it. In a clear allusion to Jews, John Buchan (1875–1940), director of information under his government, wrote that 'away behind all the governments and the armies there was a big subterranean movement going on, engineered by very dangerous people'.[28] In an introduction to Nahum Sokolow's (1859–1936) *History of Zionism*, Balfour claimed that Zionism represented 'a serious endeavour to mitigate the age-long miseries created for Western civilisation by the presence in its midst of a body which it too long regarded as alien and even hostile, but which it was equally unable to expel or to absorb'.[29] Robert Cecil (1864–1958), Balfour's nephew and undersecretary to the Foreign Office, clarified in March 1916 that he did not think it was easy 'to exaggerate the international power of the Jews'.[30] Mark Sykes (1879–1919), the figure who perhaps more than any other shaped the British pro-Zionist approach in the years preceding the mandate for Palestine, declared that 'with "Great Jewry" against us' there would be no chance of winning the war. Zionism was, in his eyes, a powerful force hidden in the shadows, a phenomenon that he defined as 'atmospheric, international, cosmopolitan, subconscious and unwritten – nay often unspoken – it is not possible to work and think on ordinary lines'.[31] Those same Jews whom Sykes had depicted as fat men 'with big noses' just a few years earlier were now perceived in a different light.[32] 'Jews', explained Sykes in June 1918, 'could be found in the councils of every state, in every business, in every enterprise'.[33]

The opinions expressed by Sykes and other leading figures are useful in order to throw light on some of the main motives that prompted the London establishment to express its support for a 'Jewish national home' in Palestine. The principal reason for this was not to promote British interests in the Ottoman context. Instead, it was mainly motivated by a desire to set in motion a global Zionist propaganda campaign that might attract the support of 'world Jewry' to the British war effort.[34]

To such considerations can be added a further element that can be summarised in three words: the Old Testament. If, on the one hand, the attitude of figures such as Balfour, Lloyd George and Churchill towards the Jews and Zionism was often based on more or less covert forms of anti-Semitism, on the other hand, this was expressed in the form of a deep-rooted philo-Semitism of evangelical and puritan memory.[35] This was the very same sentiment that prompted Balfour to state that the Jews were 'the most gifted race that mankind has seen since the Greeks of the 5th century',[36] and Churchill to argue that they were 'beyond all question the most formidable and the most remarkable race which has ever appeared in the world'.[37] Hate and love, philo-Semitism and anti-Semitism were, yet again, two sides of the same coin.

Framing the Balfour Declaration

In February 1919, Balfour wrote to Lloyd George to underline the 'weak point of our position' in Palestine. He noted, 'We deliberately and rightly decline to accept the principle of self-determination'.[38] In his opinion, Arab-Palestinians were to be considered a minority as compared to Jews. 'In any Palestine Plebiscite', Balfour argued, 'the Jews of the world must be consulted'.[39] This point of view was based on three assumptions: (1) that the majority of the Jews scattered around the world identified with Zionism; (2) that the Jews had been expelled by force from their 'ancestral lands'; (3) that a Jew born in another part of the world could, by their very nature, claim equal or superior rights to these lands as compared to a Palestinian Arab born and raised in Palestine.

The first of these assumptions can be regarded as possible if not, in later times, probable. The second has been rejected by various authoritative historians and intellectuals, including the doyen of Israeli writers, Abraham Yehoshua.[40] Doubts have indirectly been thrown on the third point. Albert Hourani explained them in the following terms:

> The Palestinian question is not one of two factions placed on the same level, both on the lookout for something more than they deserve, unwilling to understand the other side's point of view and incapable of opening up to dialogue without the attentive services of a third party. It is an issue between an indigenous population claiming the ordinary and inalienable democratic right to decide issues of general interest such as immigration for itself and, on the other hand, a minority of immigrants seeking to become a majority and to establish a state with the assistance of foreign powers to restrain the indigenous inhabitants until such time as they will be in a position to put their aims into practice.[41]

Balfour, as Weizmann confirmed, had only marginal knowledge of the elements underlying the Zionist movement.[42] And this was even truer as far as the Palestinian situation and its local majority was concerned. The bulk of his assumptions on this issue were linked to Weizmann's influence. The future first president of the State of Israel worked hard to implement the ethno-religious aspirations of millions of Jews and to explain Zionism's efforts to create the conditions so that 'Jews and Arabs can live in mutual peace'.[43] At the same time, however, he was committed to a strongly denigratory campaign against Palestinian Arabs, perceived as an inferior 'race'. One of his main aims was to persuade the British establishment that the 'so-called Arab question in Palestine' was not regarded 'as a serious factor by all those who know the local situation fully'.[44] A wealth of documents exists that confirm this attitude. What follows is a dispatch sent to Balfour by Weizmann on 4 May 1918:

> The Arabs who are superficially clever and quick witted, worship one thing, and one thing only – power and success [. . .] The British Authorities [. . .] knowing as they do the treacherous nature of the Arab, they have to watch carefully and constantly that nothing should happen which might give the Arabs the slightest grievance or ground of complaint [. . .] The present state of affairs would necessarily tend towards the creation of an Arab Palestine, if there were an Arab people in Palestine. It will not in fact produce that result because the fellah is at least four centuries behind the times, and the effendi (who, by the way, is the real gainer from the present system) is dishonest, uneducated, greedy, and as unpatriotic as he is inefficient.[45]

Balfour was not indifferent to these words, all the more so because the then foreign secretary, like Shaftesbury more than half a century earlier, had not ever seen the lands he talked about nor met the people he referred to so frequently. He visited Palestine for the first time in 1925. On that occasion, he presided over the opening of Jerusalem's Hebrew University, accompanied by Vera (1881–1966) and Chaim Weizmann (1874–1952).[46]

Despite Balfour's very limited knowledge of the situation in the ground, his actions were based on the rock-solid conviction that Zionist ambitions were, in his opinion, 'rooted in age-long traditions, in present needs, in future hopes of far profounder import than the desires and prejudices of the 700,000 Arabs who now inhabit that ancient land'.[47] He was fully aware that in Palestine 'we are dealing not with the wishes of an existing community but are consciously seeking to reconstitute a new community and definitely building for a numerical majority in the future'.[48]

Figure 5.1   Lord Balfour arrived at Jaffa on 25 March 1925. Hailed by crowds at Tel Aviv on the following day. (Source: American Colony Photo Dept photographers. Visual materials from the papers of John D. Whiting, Library of Congress, Washington DC)

That nearly 90 per cent of the people living in Palestine at the time of the First World War – Gilbert Clayton (1875–1929) reported on 5 February 1918 that the population in Palestine was composed by 573,000 'non-Jews' and 66,000 'Jews'[49] – were not considered a priority by London was further confirmed in the weeks preceding the publication of the Balfour Declaration. In the three main meetings in which Lloyd George's War Cabinet discussed the decision, the possibility of an Arab opposition was 'not discussed or even mentioned'.[50] The idea of consulting the exponents of the local 'majority' was ignored. In the three meetings referred to, it was instead the anti-Zionist positions expressed by numerous Jews of the time that attracted attention. There were essentially, from London's perspective, two opposing camps (Zionist versus anti-Zionist Jews), a mediator (Britain) and a considerable number of more or less passive spectators (Arab-Palestinians). The latter were officially informed of the Balfour Declaration on 1 May 1920, by General Louis Bols (1867–1930), almost three years after it was issued.

Furthermore, a significant percentage of the most authoritative British political figures who were not part of the War Cabinet considered it best to look beyond the problems that might potentially emerge in the area. Balfour himself, convinced that the Arabs owed a debt of gratitude to Britain,[51] was sure that 'the Arab problem could not be regarded as a serious hindrance in the way of the development of a Jewish national home in Dr Weizmann['s] sense'.[52] This was despite the fact that Nahum Sokolow (1859–1936)[53] – the future president of the Zionist Organization and the figure in pre-First World War Britain who held the highest rank among Zionists – and, to an even greater extent, Weizmann himself, had been very clear: their objective was to bring to Palestine 'about four to five million Jews within a generation and so make Palestine a Jewish country'[54] – that is, to make Palestine 'as Jewish as England is English'.[55]

How such an ambitious plan could be implemented without encountering the opposition and fears of most of the local population was an issue that the British establishment approached only in vague terms. It was, in fact, only with the white paper of 1922, a month before the approval of the mandate for Palestine by the League of Nations, that the British authorities took an official position on these issues.

Indeed, two first-rank figures, George Curzon (1859–1925) and Montagu tried – motivated by their own personal interests and opinions – to draw general attention to the expectations of a large part of the local population. Curzon, the only member of the Lloyd George cabinet who made a visit to Palestine, pointed out that 'Arabs are only allowed to look through the keyhole as a non-Jewish community'.[56] Furthermore, several British officials serving in Palestine[57] – in some cases motivated by age-old anti-Semitic feelings – made clear that the situation on the ground was extremely different to that perceived in London.[58] Despite these few cases, most of the concerns were considered in simplistic terms, or using an approach aiming to emphasise the 'inferiority' of the local majority.[59] 'I cannot conceal from myself', wrote Meinertzhagen to Curzon, 'that Arab fears regarding Zionism are not groundless [. . .] only one motive prompts anti-Zionist feeling in Palestine. It is the general and very real fear of superior Jewish brains and money.'[60]

Without fully assessing the consequences, in some specific but symbolic circumstances, the British authorities went so far as to refer to Palestine in terms of a 'Judae for the Jews' and to mock the wishes of the Arab majority.[61] 'If the Arabs', Alfred Milner clarified to Weizmann, 'think that Palestine will become an Arab country, they are very much mistaken'.[62] In certain private conversations, they went even further, supporting the idea that Palestine should become a 'Jewish homeland and not merely that there be a Jewish homeland in Palestine'.[63]

Only in the years to follow, when these ideas had been subjected to the most varied interpretations and had created unreasonable expectations, did the British authorities feel the necessity to officially clarify their position and to slow the immigratory waves that they themselves had contributed to triggering. Zionism, which until just a few years earlier had been the phenomenon on which London had based the bulk of its expectations in relation to Palestine, was now becoming something to be managed with caution. 'The pro-Zionists of 1917', in David Fromkin's words, 'turn into the anti-Zionists of 1921 and 1922'.[64]

The Two Sides of the Tunnel

Commenting on the process that culminated in the Balfour Declaration, Nahum Sokolow wrote that it 'resembled the construction of a tunnel begun at two sides at once'.[65] The first side was composed by the Zionist exponents active in England, with Weizmann and Sokolow in the front ranks. The second comprised the British authorities who were in favour of the Zionist ambitions.

While the beginning of what Isaiah Berlin (1909–97) referred to as a 'long and fascinated flirtation' between Balfour and Weizmann goes back to 1905, it was only with the outbreak of the First World War that the conditions for the construction of the 'tunnel' were created.[66] In the decade before the war, contact between the Zionist leadership and the British establishment declined drastically. This was not because of a reduced interest in Palestine. Quite the opposite: the Aqaba incident of 1906 – when British rule in Egypt was challenged by Ottoman authority – confirmed that Palestine was considered by the Foreign Office as an indispensable bastion in defence of Egypt. This 'cooling off' was rather a result of the departure from the political scene of the main exponents of the 'Uganda proposal' – Chamberlain resigned in September 1903, followed three months later by Prime Minister Balfour; Herzl died in July 1904 – and the subsequent advent of a new phase characterised by general apathy regarding Zionist aspirations. This was also the case for British Jews: among the around 300,000 Jews present in Britain in 1913, fewer than 10,000 considered themselves as Zionists.

Alongside this apathy, a certain measure of diffidence also developed. The fact that the Zionist establishment had chosen to build most of its offices in Berlin was interpreted in London, and in Paris too, as a dangerous sign of its intentions. At the same time, the British government had nothing to gain from an open confrontation with the Ottoman authorities: the Young Turks' rise to power in Istanbul following the 1908 Revolution had shown as much intransigence as the sultan had in denying the Jews a 'national home' in Palestine.[67]

The decision to approve the Balfour Declaration was taken by a small, elite group of men on the basis of a mixture of political, military and religious factors. The latter, in particular, played a crucial role. Weizmann himself, however, aware of the importance of practical aspects, noted that Lloyd George, Balfour, Churchill and others were 'deeply religious [. . .] to them the return of the Jewish People to Palestine was a reality, so that we Zionists represented to them a great tradition for which they had enormous respect'.[68]

A comparison with Germany's approach to the issue can throw much light on how 'unusual' the modus operandi of the British establishment was. For the Germans, Arabs, Jews, Turks, Afghans and Persians were means through which to impose a German hegemony. Berlin's foreign policy was inspired by a genuine interest in preserving and strengthening an ideal – which subsequently proved fatal – which has gone down in history by the name of *Deutschtum*, or 'German-ness'. Thus, and contrary to Britain's policies, German strategies in the Middle East were generally not inspired by suggestions linked to the Old Testament.[69]

The extent to which religious considerations affected the decisions taken at the time is still a matter of debate. What is certain is that the 'biblical predisposition' showed by the British policymakers of the time was anything but a secondary aspect. 'Biblical prophecy', as David Fromkin and others have observed, 'was the first and most enduring of the many motives that led Britons to want to restore the Jews to Zion'.[70]

As many as seven of the ten figures who at different periods composed the War Cabinet responsible for the decision to issue the Balfour Declaration had grown up in Nonconformist families, and one was from a strongly evangelical background. The reference to the War Cabinet, sometimes confused with the Ministry of War, is noteworthy. The decision to establish a 'national home' – a loosely defined expression, which for some was to be intended as a non-statual entity,[71] while for others it echoed the concept of a 'Jewish state' – in Palestine was not taken or discussed in the House of Commons or in the House of Lords.[72] As occurred with other measures taken during the First World War, such a decision was adopted behind closed doors by a small War Cabinet created in the wake of the uncertainties of the period. In June 1917, six months after Lloyd George took up residence in Downing Street, he created a small council with the purpose of concentrating power in a few hands in order to strengthen the war effort. It was a particularly radical decision, considering the traditional British system of parliamentary checks and balances. Liberalism, as highlighted by John Turner, was the first victim of the war.[73]

Between 1916 and 1922, Lloyd George was thus the key figure behind the British strategy in the Eastern Mediterranean. His role was so important that more than one historian has wondered if the Balfour Declaration should not be renamed the 'Lloyd George Declaration'.[74] His interest in Palestine was evident to the extent that he confided that it was 'the one really interesting part of the War'.[75] His connection with the Old Testament was profound. In a famous historic declaration, he claimed to have learnt the names of the mountains, rivers and valleys of the Holy Land before those of Wales (where he was born) and England.[76] This declaration was made during his first meeting with Weizmann, the same one that, in April 1919, defined the Balfour Declaration as 'our guide',[77] and that, thirty years later, recalled that the then British Foreign Secretary Ernest Bevin (1881–1951) had not succeeded in 'destroying what Balfour had created'.[78]

Messianic Times

One of the first to comprehend the possible consequences of the First World War for the Middle East, Palestine included, was Herbert Samuel. In previous years, the 'first member of the Jewish community ever to sit in a British

Cabinet',[79] as he called himself, had taken a benevolent approach to Zionist ideals. This, however, was not followed by any concrete steps. He belonged to a family that was well integrated into British society of the day and many, including Weizmann, believed that he had no particular interest in the Zionist cause. Despite all this, Samuel himself suffered repeated anti-Semitic attacks. In 1912, for instance, he was accused of insider trading in the context of the 'Marconi scandal': the mere fact of being Jewish, it seemed, was sufficient to implicate him in such a scandal.

Beyond the 'scars' left by anti-Semitism, it was Turkey's entry into the war (October 1914) that pushed Samuel's latent proto-Zionism into a progressively more direct commitment.[80] On 9 November that same year, only four days after Britain and France declared war on Turkey, Samuel met with the then Foreign Secretary Edward Grey (1862–1933). In contrast to what had occurred in March of the previous year, when Sokolow (1859–1936) had been received at the Foreign Office by second-rank figures, Zionist interests were now being promoted by one of the most influential members of the government. 'Perhaps', Samuel explained to Grey on that occasion, 'the opportunity might arise for the fulfillment of the ancient aspiration of the Jewish people and the restoration [in Palestine] of a Jewish state'.[81] The support for this plan would have attracted Jewish public opinion in favour of the Allied cause, facilitating, at the same time, British imperial ambitions. 'The geographical situation of Palestine', Samuel emphasised, 'and especially its proximity to Egypt would render its goodwill to England a matter of importance to the British Empire'.[82]

Istanbul was now perceived as an enemy that London no longer had an interest in protecting. Zionism, on the other hand, appeared to Grey as a tool to weaken Turkish influence in the Eastern Mediterranean. 'The [Zionist] idea', wrote Samuel reporting Grey's opinion, 'had always had a strong sentimental attraction for him'.[83] Grey's cautious enthusiasm – in early 1916, he seriously considered the idea of drawing up a document in favour of the creation of an 'autonomous Jewish settlement' in Palestine – induced Samuel to sound out the opinions of the then Chancellor of the Exchequer Lloyd George.[84] Samuel knew that Lloyd George had already worked together with the Zionist movement in 1903. The law firm he led at the time had prepared the draft that should have made Chamberlain's 'Uganda proposal' concrete. Lloyd George, as the *Jewish Chronicle* reported two years later, was already 'an ardent believer in the Zionist Movement'.[85]

The reaction of the future prime minister to Samuel's words was thus largely foreseeable. Lloyd George expressed himself 'very keen to see a Jewish State established there [Palestine]' and asked Samuel to prepare a memorandum on the subject to be forwarded to the other cabinet members.[86] In one of those coincidences that rarely happens in history, in the same days in which Samuel was working on drawing up his memorandum, Charles Prestwich Scott (1846–1932), 'the soul of the Manchester Guardian', managed to put him in direct contact with Weizmann. In a meeting between the two on 10 December 1915, Samuel made a reference to the memorandum about the possible creation of a Jewish state in Palestine that he was preparing for Prime Minister Asquith. He went further, declaring his hope to 'rebuild the Temple [of Jerusalem], as a symbol of Jewish unity'.[87] A mixture of incredulity and emotion overwhelmed Weizmann. 'Messianic times', he wrote to his wife, 'have really come'.[88]

These and other factors convinced Weizmann that the situation was potentially an epoch-defining one – a sensation that was heightened by his firm conviction that Palestine would soon pass under London's direct control.[89] After making contact with Samuel, as well as with Scott and various members of Rothschild's entourage, Weizmann decided to turn to Arthur Balfour, foreign secretary from December 1916, with whom he had talked about Zionism eight years earlier in Manchester, shortly before the 1905/6 general elections.

Balfour, like many influential people of his generation, believed that 'subaltern races' had existed from time immemorial and that it was reasonable to expect that 'different and unequal they are destined to remain'.[90] Furthermore, he was convinced that Jews had been an enduring source of misfortune for 'Western civilization' and that Zionism could become an 'instrument of Providence'.[91] The coexistence of these three factors – a 'subaltern race' (Arab-Palestinians), an 'instrument of Providence' (Zionism) and empathy with the history of 'God's ancient people' (the Jews) – made Balfour, from Weizmann's point of view, an ideal point of reference. This feeling was reinforced on 12 December 1914, when, two days after meeting Samuel, Weizmann crossed the threshold of Balfour's private residence for an hour and a half of discussions. 'Balfour', Weizmann wrote, 'remembered everything we discussed eight years ago'.[92] When the Zionist leader complained about the slowdown that the war had apparently imposed on Zionist plans, the future foreign secretary confidently replied: 'You may get your things done much quicker after the war'.[93]

While the outcome could not, in any sense, have been taken for granted, the process that only two years later would culminate in the Balfour Declaration had begun to take shape. On 15 January 1915, Weizmann met Lloyd George at Downing Street. 'When Dr Weizmann was talking of Palestine', Lloyd George confessed to Dorothy Rothschild, 'he kept bringing up place names which were more familiar to me than those of the Western Front'.[94] Less than two weeks later, Samuel was ready to present his first memorandum to the cabinet:

> The course of events opens a prospect of change, at the end of the war, in the status of Palestine. Already there is a stirring among the twelve million Jews scattered throughout the countries of the world. A feeling is spreading with great rapidity that now, at last, some advance may be made, in some way, towards the fulfilment of the hope and desire, held with unshakable tenacity for eighteen hundred years, for the restoration of the Jews to the land to which they are attached by ties almost as ancient as history itself [. . .] I am assured that the solution of the problem of Palestine which would be much the most welcome to the leaders and supporters of the Zionist movement throughout the world would be the annexation of the country to the British Empire [. . .] It is hoped that under British rule facilities would be given to Jewish organisations to purchase land, to found colonies, to establish educational and religious institutions, and to spend usefully the funds that would be freely contributed for promoting the economic development of the country.[95]

Samuel's words provoked a mixed reaction, but the most influential response, that of Prime Minister Asquith, left no room for doubt: 'I am not attracted', he wrote to his confidante Venetia Stanley (1887–1948), 'by this proposed addition to our responsibilities'.[96] Asquith considered Samuel's pronouncements as a 'lyrical outburst' and Zionism as an unattainable fantasy;[97] he declared himself willing to consider a new memorandum on the subject on condition that it was less 'dithyrambic' and more practicable.[98]

On 13 March 1915, Asquith's cabinet gathered to discuss the future of Palestine from the perspective of the new memorandum outlined by Samuel. It was a highly symbolic meeting. In the new memorandum, which borrowed from the earlier one to a considerable extent, the author was careful to underline the need to guarantee the rights of the 'non-Jewish population'. He also erased the word 'annexation' and reiterated the need to create a British protectorate in Palestine. For greater clarity, right from his opening comments, Samuel outlined five possible scenarios: (1) the inclusion of Palestine in the French sphere of influence; (2) the retention of Turkish power there; (3) an internationalisation of the region; (4) its annexation to Egypt; and (5) the creation of a British protectorate to safeguard the incorporation of the Jews. The latter alternative was, in Samuel's eyes, the only one worthy of real consideration. 'The establishment of a great European Power so close to the Suez Canal', he wrote, 'would be a continual and a formidable menace to the essential lines of communication of the British Empire'.[99]

Such a formula was adopted by Samuel after careful consultation with several prominent figures. Among them were the head rabbi of the English Sephardic community, Moses Gaster (1856–1939), Grey and Weizmann, who already and with good reason considered him as the backbone of Zionist ambitions.[100] 'You were good enough', wrote Weizmann to Samuel on 21 March 1915, 'to guide us up to now, and I am sure you will continue to help us. We look to you and to your historical rôle which you are playing and will play in the redemption of Israel'.[101]

Samuel's second memorandum attracted the unconditional, and in many ways predictable, support of Lloyd George,[102] to whom the *Zionist Review* assigned 'the foremost place inside the Cabinet among the architects of this great decision [the Balfour Declaration]'.[103] Despite having such an authoritative supporter, the majority of Samuel's colleagues – with a few important exceptions embodied by Lord Haldane (1856–1928) and the Marquis of Crewe (1858–1945) – received Samuel's proposals with hostility. Edwin Montagu, Chancellor of the Duchy of Lancaster, in particular, accused him of having overemphasised the strategic importance of the region and downplayed the issue of 'racial homogeneity'.[104] 'Palestine in itself', wrote Montagu to Asquith on 16 March 1915, 'offers little or no attraction to Great Britain from a strategical or material point of view'.[105] He also pointed out that there was no 'Jewish race now as a homogeneous whole'.[106] Like many other Jews, English or otherwise,[107] Montagu considered 'the Jews as a religious community and himself as a Jewish Englishman';[108] the rift between assimilationist Jews and Zionists had reached the point of no return.[109]

In the weeks and months that followed the presentation of the new memorandum, Samuel, despite the paltry results, kept up his personal mission. Many years later, Edwin 'Nebi' Samuel (1898–1978) noted that his father understood the dynamics and complexity of the issue earlier, and more comprehensively, than anyone else, Weizmann included.[110] While he could not count on the support of authoritative figures such as Asquith, Montagu and Kitchener, Samuel managed, nonetheless, to place Zionism at the heart of Britain's political agenda.

Mark Sykes's 'Door of Hope'

The 'door of hope' was Sokolow's way to refer to the door of Mark Sykes's office. Sokolow considered him as 'one of the most valiant champions of Zionism'.[111] Over the years, in fact, Sykes made himself into a vital *trait d'union* between the Zionist leaders and the Foreign Office. 'It was he', Weizmann wrote later about Sykes, 'who guided our work into more official channels'.[112]

There was nothing inevitable about the process that moved Sykes towards Zionism. His first writings on the matter confirm that he had a low opinion of Jews, comparable only to his opinion of Armenians. 'Even Jews', noted Sykes at the turn of the century, 'have their good points, but Armenians have none.'[113] According to Fromkin, from his earliest schooldays, Sykes developed an 'almost excessive fear' of Jews.[114] Particular targets of his disdain were 'assimilationist Jews'. He supplemented his dislike of Armenians and Jews with a powerful aversion to Arabs, with whom he had come into contact since childhood during the travels that he made in the region with his father, Tatton Sykes (1826–1913). In his writings, Arabs of cities such as Mosul, Hama, Homs and Damascus were described as 'insolent yet despicable' and 'one of the most deplorable pictures one can see in the East',[115] while the Bedouins – specifically the vast Shammar tribe – were considered on a par with 'animals', 'rapacious, greedy'.[116]

The hostility Sykes reserved for Jews, Armenians and Arabs is worthy of particular note if only because, with the onset of the First World War, the causes espoused by these peoples actually found in him a powerful champion. In taking on this new role, Sykes – who maintained considerable prejudices regarding Arabs – was not inspired by a 'Guevarian approach'.[117] It was practical considerations that mattered to him. He aimed, in particular, to halt the German advance towards the East and to create a sort of Arab–Jewish–Armenian 'buffer zone' between the Turko-German front and that was made up by Iran (Persia), Egypt and India.[118]

The Zionist cause quickly became a priority towards which Sykes channelled most of his energies. It was Samuel's memorandum that instilled in him the idea that this movement could be a suitable tool to reinforce British ambitions in Palestine and elsewhere. 'I read the memorandum', clarified Sykes to Samuel shortly before departing for Russia, 'and have committed it to memory'.[119] These words were written in February 1916, when Sykes was fresh from the negotiations with Georges-Picot (1870–1951), from which the secret Sykes–Picot agreement to divide up the region into spheres of influence developed. The strategic and symbolic importance of Palestine made it an area of considerable significance for both powers. It was decided to place it under international supervision, although both London and Paris considered the decision a provisional measure. The ambiguous contents of the Ḥusayn–McMahon correspondence and the equally evasive Balfour Declaration demonstrate, with the benefit of hindsight, that the decisions made at the time were not the upshot of clear strategies and, in quite a few cases, did not involve binding commitments. 'It is not unthinkable', commented the founder of the Hebrew University, Judah Leon Magnes (1877–1948), a few years later, 'that governments in war time should, unfortunately, make contradictory promises and declarations'.[120]

Sykes was aware of the connection that bound many of the Zionist leaders to London. As pointed out by Clayton, the 'Zionists who follow Dr Weizmann are strongly pro-British'.[121] It was only at the beginning of 1917 – when Sykes, through an Armenian anti-Semite by the name of James Aratoon Malcolm (1865–1952), met Weizmann and Sokolow for the first time and established daily contact with them – that he was able to ascertain the reliability of his contacts.[122] It was then that Sykes realised the extent to which Zionist plans coincided with British strategies. On the one hand, both Weizmann and Sokolow had declared themselves opposed to an Anglo-French 'cohabitation' in Palestine. On the other, they supported the implementation of a British trusteeship. London could now demonstrate to France that it enjoyed the full support of one of the two main actors in the region. Zionism was thus becoming a formidable instrument in strengthening Britain's position, freeing London from the provisions of the Sykes–Picot agreement. In Sykes's own words:

> if the French agree to recognize Jewish Nationalism and all that carries with it as a Palestine political factor, I think it will prove a step in the right direction, and will tend to pave the way to Great Britain being the appointed Patron of Palestine.[123]

In the space of a few months – thanks also to the role played by James Aratoon Malcolm and Aaron Aaronsohn (1876–1919),[124] a Zionist spy in Britain's service – Sykes transformed himself into an indefatigable champion of Zionism, going so far as to declare that Zionists embodied 'now the key of the situation',[125] and that those Jews who opposed the movement were nothing more than ill-concealed supporters of Turko-German ambitions.[126] Sokolow believed that Sykes was born 'to work with us Hebrews for Zionism'.[127] Indeed, more than ever, Sykes was committed to serve 'the chaotic pluralism of British interests'.[128] It was thanks to him that the creation of a 'buffer Jewish State' in Palestine as 'strategically desirable for Great Britain' came to be perceived as an increasingly established fact.[129] Years later, Leo Amery (1873–1955) – a Zionist stalwart in Lloyd George's new cabinet secretariat – described Sykes's role in the following terms:

> Sykes soon persuaded me that from the purely British point of view a prosperous Jewish population in Palestine owing its inception and its opportunity of development to British policy, might be an invaluable asset as a defence of the Suez Canal against attack from the North and as a station on the future air-routes to the East.[130]

Garden Suburb, the Turning Point

On the morning of 26 January 1917, Neil Primrose (1882–1917) – parliamentary secretary to the Treasury who died in action in Palestine eleven months later – participated in a work lunch together with Lloyd George. '"What about Palestine?", asked Primrose. "Oh!" replied Lloyd George, "We must grab that; we have made a beginning."'[131]

Lloyd George had taken up service in Downing Street just fifty days earlier. Nonetheless, in comparison to the previous government, the changes that had occurred were already huge. A powerful image to mark this transitional period was published by the weekly *Punch* magazine: Lloyd George was portrayed dressed as an orchestra conductor working on the 'Opening of the 1917 Overture'.[132]

The 'orchestra' created by the new prime minister was soon embodied by a small War Cabinet. Its members met 200 times in the first 235 days of its existence alone. Since their first meetings, they expressed the firm belief that the war could only be won if 'the willingness of the German government and people to continue the war had been extinguished'.[133]

The need to mark a turning point in British strategy was dictated by the dispiriting results of Allied efforts in the first two years of the war. The Asquith government, in particular, had shown worrying weakness. This was even more evident considering Asquith's playing-for-time approach and the surfeit of members (as many as twenty-two) making up his cabinet. In order to summarise the change of pace that occurred with the arrival of Lloyd George's new cabinet, it is enough to point out that, just a few days after he took up his post, General Archibald Murray (1860–1945), head of the British Army in Egypt, was asked to supply his proposals in light of a possible intervention in Palestine.

The fall of Asquith's government on 5 December 1916 coincided with Herbert Samuel's resignation. This could have represented a major blow for Zionist ambitions. Very soon, however, the new government offered new opportunities for the relaunching of Zionist aims. Asquith never met Weizmann and was consistently cold to Zionist expectations. The new prime minister, Lloyd George, and his foreign minister, Balfour, showed, on the contrary, a long-standing interest in Zionist ambitions and had long been in contact with its leaders.

It was, however, the composition of the War Cabinet and the mechanisms at its disposal that contributed the most to revolutionising the British approach to Palestine. The cabinet was initially made up of the four ministers most directly involved in the war effort – Alfred Milner, George Curzon, Andrew Bonar Law (1858–1923) and Arthur Henderson (1863–1935). Five other influential figures were added between 1917 and 1919, including

Edward Carson (1854–1935), George Barnes (1859–1940) and Jan Christiaan Smuts.[134]

Two further bodies were set up to support the War Cabinet. The Garden Suburb (its name taken from the courtyard garden within the prime minister's residence where the meetings took place) was a sort of prime-ministerial think tank; and the Cabinet Secretariat, with Maurice Hankey (1877–1963) at its head, which could count on the contributions of Sykes, Amery and William Ormsby-Gore (1885–1964), the last two appointed on the initiative of Milner and destined to play important parts in support of Zionism. Philip Kerr (1882–1940), Lloyd George's private secretary, was also part of the group and shared the opinion that, in Weizmann's words, 'a reconstructed Palestine [or a Jewish Palestine] will become a very great asset to the British Empire'.[135]

The first tangible consequence of the government change was the new role played by Sykes, whom Ormsby-Gore called 'the chief motive force in London behind the British Government's Near Eastern policy in the war'.[136] From this point onwards, Sykes counted on greater room for manoeuvre and direct, ongoing access to the most influential ministers. A second, and in many ways even more momentous, turn of events took place with the rise of Alfred Milner who quickly established himself as the most influential member of Lloyd George's War Cabinet.

Milner, who at the beginning of the century was heavily involved in setting up the concentration camps in which no fewer than 26,000 Boer women and children and 14,000 black South Africans died, had demonstrated since Herzl's time a genuine interest in the fortunes of the Jews.[137] Nonetheless, his conversion to the 'Zionist creed' took place only after reading Samuel's 'Memorandum on the future of Palestine'. 'It contains suggestions', wrote Milner to Samuel in January 1917, 'which are new to me'.[138] He added that, of the various alternatives proposed by Samuel, 'the one which you yourself favour certainly appears to me the most attractive'.[139] The memorandum advocated creating a British protectorate in Palestine, and Milner was referring to this option. However, there was little room for idealistic gestures. Milner, clarified the British ambassador in Paris Francis Bertie (1844–1919), 'is not a Zionist engagé; he only hopes that the adoption of Zionism will benefit us'.[140] In Milner's eyes, Zionism did not imply the establishment of a Jewish state in

Palestine but rather the creation there of a vaguely defined 'Jewish home', or an 'autonomous Jewish community'.[141] Similarly vague concepts were later used in the Balfour Declaration – whose terminology was largely dictated by Milner himself – which in 1922 was interpreted in fifty-two different ways by the League of Nations.[142]

Once again, then, imperial interests and the requirements of war took precedence in dictating London's agenda. Washington's entrance into the war (2 April 1917) encouraged the British authorities to support a massive pro-Zionist propaganda campaign in the USA.[143] Furthermore, the rise to power of the Bolsheviks in Russia – perceived by Berlin as a chance to get St Petersburg out of the war – compelled the British government to consider Sykes's strategy with growing urgency. Zionism thus became a crucial factor in supporting the British war effort and a tool to keep Paris out of Palestine.

London's gradual movement from a generally favourable position to an increasingly official encouragement of Zionist strategies was also bolstered, in this period, by the events unfolding in the region. The failures of the British Army during the First (26 March 1917) and the Second (19 April) War of Gaza campaigns convinced London of the need to reformulate the Palestine campaign and make it more incisive. There existed a growing risk of losing contact with the Palestinian front, particularly now that the Russian collapse would have allowed Constantinople to redeploy a considerable number of its troops. In April 1917, then, the War Cabinet took the decision to advocate the intensification of its efforts to capture Jerusalem and expel the Turks from Palestine once and for all. 'We realized', recalled Lloyd George about a meeting that took place on 2 April 1917, 'the moral and political advantages to be expected from an advance on this front, and particularly from the occupation of Jerusalem'.[144] This aim required a more resolute leadership but also a clearer stance on the approach to be taken towards Zionism and its leaders.[145]

Both aspects were taken on by the War Cabinet in the months that followed. On 27 June, General Allenby was appointed to replace Murray as head of the British forces in Egypt. The new chief of staff quickly earned the respect of his soldiers by regularly visiting the troops at the front and moving his army headquarters from Cairo to the 'less reassuring' Rafah. At the same time, over the weeks to follow, the British authorities, after requesting

Zionist leaders to publicly display their support, began to discuss the possibility of issuing an official declaration supporting the creation of a Jewish 'national home' in Palestine.

Already, on 13 June 1917, Ronald Graham (1870–1949), head of the Foreign Office's Middle-Eastern affairs section, intimated to Balfour the need to 'secure all the political advantage we can out of our connection with Zionism',[146] adding that this would have Russia.[147] Moreover, Graham declared that the moment had come to satisfy the ambitions of the Zionists and that it was thus desirable to supply them with 'an assurance that His Majesty's Government are in general sympathy with their aspirations'.[148] More than simply desirable, Graham's recommendation seemed, in many ways, a pressing necessity. As Zionist leaders made every effort to demonstrate, Berlin's authorities were committed 'to work upon the Zionists in Germany' in order to match the interests of the two parties. 'Further delay', clarified Cecil to Balfour, 'may [. . .] throw the Zionists into the arms of the Germans who would only be too ready to welcome this opportunity'.[149]

Balfour reacted to these solicitations by asking Rothschild and Weizmann to put forward a formula that the then foreign minister intended to present to the War Cabinet. Increasingly detailed proposals followed over the next few weeks. Rothschild, after a month of talks with Sokolow and Sykes, asked for an explicit declaration in which the British government officially declared its acceptance of 'the principle that Palestine should be reconstituted as the National Home for the Jewish people'.[150] This formula was positively received by Balfour, while Milner, opposing the use of the term 'reconstituted',[151] supplied two alternative drafts. In the first one, submitted to the attention of the War Cabinet in August 1917, the expression 'Palestine as a National home' was substituted with the less binding and more realistic prospect of a 'home in Palestine'.[152] The second, presented two months later, referred to the setting up 'in Palestine of a National Home for the Jewish Race'.[153]

The heated debates that followed – Lord Curzon asked how it was proposed to free Palestine 'of the existing majority of Mussulman inhabitants' and introduce 'the Jews in their place'[154] – convinced the members of the War Cabinet to submit the second Milner proposal to the attention of President Wilson (whom Balfour described as being 'extremely favourable to the

[Zionist] Movement'[155]) as well as to the leaders of the Zionist movement and to some anti-Zionist representatives of the British Jewish community. Ten individuals were consulted, six of whom – Rothschild, Weizmann, H. Samuel, Sokolow, Joseph H. Herz (1872–1946), the chief rabbi of Great Britain, and Stuart Samuel (1856–1926), the head of the Jewish Board of Deputies – were in favour of the declaration, while four others – C. G. Montefiore, Montagu, Leonard L. Cohen (1888–1973), the head of the Jewish Board of Guardians, and MP Philip Magnus (1842–1933) – were against it.

Rabbi Herz, in particular, expressed 'the profoundest gratification' with the intentions shown by the cabinet. Rothschild emphasised that the draft constituted 'a slur on Zionism' in that it posited a possible 'danger to non-Zionists'.[156] Cohen objected that it implied 'that the Jews are a nation, which I deny'.[157] Weizmann expressed his gratitude but asked for the term 'establishment' to be replaced with 're-establishment'.[158]

After evaluating the different points of views expressed by pro- or anti-Zionist Jews, Balfour declared that there was no time to be lost. Despite the various stances, the opinion was now widespread that 'from a purely diplomatic and political point of view', it was desirable to move towards issuing a declaration 'favourable to the aspirations of the Jewish nationalists'.[159] A formula was found, thanks, in particular, to the efforts of Amery and Milner, which appeared to take into account the various objections without 'impairing the substance of the proposed declaration'.[160] On the morning of 31 October 1917 – the same day on which Allenby launched the military operation that, one week later and thanks also to the use of asphyxiating gas against enemy positions,[161] led to Gaza falling into British hands – Chaim Weizmann sat in the waiting room in front of the War Cabinet. A few hours later, his companion in a thousand battles, Mark Sykes, came to the door. 'Dr Weizmann', he exclaimed with no attempt to conceal his emotion, 'it's a boy!'

His Majesty's government view with favour the establishment in Palestine of a national home for the Jewish people, and will use their best endeavours to facilitate the achievement of this object, it being clearly understood that nothing shall be done which may prejudice the civil and religious rights of existing non-Jewish communities in Palestine, or the rights and political status enjoyed by Jews in any other country.[162]

Figure 5.2   Regimental standard presented to defenders of Gaza for repulsing the first British attack, 1917. (Source: American Colony Photo Dept photographers. Visual materials from the papers of John D. Whiting, Library of Congress, Washington DC)

Weizmann immediately expressed his opposition to this formula. The trouble was, it referred to the creation of a 'Jewish national home' *in* Palestine. Thus, if the 'national home' was to become a state at some point in the future, it would have to be 'either a binational state or a state in only a part of Palestine'.[163] Furthermore, the declaration recognised the civil and religious rights of the local 'non-Jewish communities'. This clarification, added to the draft on explicit request of Curzon and Montagu, together with an awareness that the declaration did not permit to the Zionists to claim the whole of Palestine, was commented on by Weizmann in the following terms:

A comparison of the two texts – the one approved by the Foreign Office and the Prime Minister, and the one adopted on 4 October, after Montagu's attack – shows a painful recession from what the Government itself was prepared to offer. The first declares that 'Palestine should be reconstituted as the national home of the Jewish people.' The second speaks of 'the establishment in Palestine of a national home for the Jewish race'. The first adds only that the 'Government will use its best endeavours to secure the achievement of this object and will discuss the necessary methods with the Zionist Organization'; the second introduced the subject of the 'civil and religious rights of the existing non-Jewish communities' in such a fashion as to impute possible oppressive intentions to the Jews, and can be interpreted to mean such limitations on our work as completely to cripple it.[164]

In the space of little more than a month, in order to bring to practical fruition and optimise the expectations contained in the Balfour Declaration, the Foreign Office set up a special section within the Department of Information with the task of producing and distributing Anglo-Zionist propaganda material. Albert Hyamson, a Zionist Jew who later, after serving in Mandatory Palestine as head of the Immigration Department, became an anti-Zionist, was called in as head of the new section. Thanks to the tireless work of the new team led by Hyamson, thousands of leaflets, films and books were circulated among the Jewish communities scattered around the world. Furthermore, countless pamphlets and booklets were dropped into Austrian and German cities in order to attract the sympathies of Jewish soldiers fighting on the front line. 'Palestine', promised the leaflets, 'must be the national home of the Jewish people once more [. . .] Remember! An Allied victory means the Jewish people's return to Zion.'[165]

Beyond its more practical political and geostrategical effects, the 'Balfour's pattern' powerfully accelerated the process of homogenisation of the region and the ethnocentric drives of most of the nation-states that replaced the Ottoman Empire. This enabled a further 'process of familiarisation' of the region and its inhabitants, that is, the tendency to translate the other into terms more 'familiar' and comprehensible to the self. Such dynamics developed hand in hand with the increasing Western penetration in the region and reached its apex in the five years immediately following the end of the First World War, on which the next two chapters will focus.

Notes

1. TNA CAB 21/58, Herbert Samuel, 3 October 1917.

2. Cit. in A. L. Ṭībāwī, *Anglo-Arab Relations and the Question of Palestine, 1914–1921* (London: Luzac, 1977), p. 427.

3. Cit. in International Court of Justice (ICJ), *Reports of Judgments, Advisory Opinions, and Orders* (Leiden: A. W. Sijthoff, 1975), p. 122.

4. J. Renton, *The Zionist Masquerade: The Birth of the Anglo-Zionist Alliance 1914–1918* (New York: Palgrave, 2007), p. 149.

5. Mazza, *Transforming the Holy City*, p. 186.

6. G. Nash, 'Politics, Aesthetics and Quest in British Travel Writing on the Middle East', in T. Youngs (ed.), *Travel Writing in the Nineteenth Century* (London: Anthem Press, 2006), p. 66.

7. TNA FO 800/210, conversation between Lucien Wolf and Balfour, 21 January 1917. Wolf reported the contents of the conversation he had with Balfour on the subject on 31 January 1917.

8. This section partially relies on content that I covered in L. Kamel, *Imperial Perceptions of Palestine: British Influence and Power in Late Ottoman Times* (London: I. B. Tauris, 2015), ch. 6.

9. Kimche underlined that neither the Germans nor the French or the Americans 'could conceive of conceding a Jewish nationality to the Jews of their countries. Only the British could do it because of the deeply-rooted English (rather than British) attitude that Jews [. . .] always remained Jews, some kind of foreigner': J. Kimche, *The Unromantics, The Great Powers and the Balfour Declaration* (Liverpool: Tinling, 1968), p. 70.

10. Henry Mayhew (1812–87) recorded that, in the first half of the nineteenth century, the Jews of London were seen as 'an entire people of misers, usurers, extortioners, receivers of stolen goods': H. Mayhew, *London Labour and the London Poor* (London: Griffin, 1864), vol. 2, p. 129. A guide drawn up in February 1919 by the president of the Council of Deputies of British Jews, David L. Alexander, and the then president of the Anglo-Jewish Association, Claude G. Montefiore, highlighted that, for reasons that were certainly not entirely religious, 'the British public was intensely sympathetic to the idea of Palestine for the Jews' in the first half of the nineteenth century: TNA FO 373/7/36.

11. A. L. Kennedy, *Salisbury, 1830–1903: Portrait of a Statesman* (New York: Kraus, 1971), p. 51.

12. Ibid., p. 109.

13. M. and E. Broch (eds), *H.H. Asquith, Letters to Venetia Stanley* (Oxford: Oxford University Press, 1982), p. 99.

14. Cited in J. M. McEwen (ed.), *The Riddell Diaries, 1908–1923* (London: Athlone, 1986), p. 82. Lloyd George's phrase dates to April 1914.

15. Montagu clarified the following: 'As the one Jewish Minister in the Government I may be allowed by my colleagues an opportunity of expressing views which may be peculiar to myself [. . .] When the Jews are told that Palestine is their national home, every country will immediately desire to get rid of its Jewish citizens, and you will find a population in Palestine driving out its present inhabitants, taking all the best in the country': TNA CAB 24/24. Montagu's memorandum submitted to the British cabinet on 23 August 1917.

16. Herzl himself was motivated by a certain distrust of the Jews until a few years earlier. Schorske noted: 'Another tie linking Herzl to his enemies, even though he drew different conclusions from it, was his distaste for the Jews': C. E. Schorske, *Fin-de-Siècle Vienna* (New York: Vintage Books, 1981), p. 160.

17. T. Herzl, *The Complete Diaries of Theodor Herzl* (New York: Herzl Press, 1960), vol. 1, p. 84.

18. Brustein clarified that 'though the Aliens Act did not mention Jews outright, it was clear to most observers that the purpose of the act was to halt the flow of Eastern European Jews into Great Britain': W. Brustein, *Roots of Hate* (Cambridge: Cambridge University Press, 2003), p. 149.

19. In the *Manchester Evening Chronicle*, 12 May 1905. Similar practices and feelings had been recorded in the last two decades of the nineteenth century in relation to Polish workers in Germany and the Chinese in the United States. In Britain, the 1905 measures were made even harsher in 1914 and 1919.

20. *The Parliamentary Debates* (London: His Majesty's Stationery Office, 1905), 4th series, vol. 149, p. ccvi.

21. Belloc and Chesterton, anything but marginal figures in early twentieth-century England, worked for the implementation of harsh civil limitations on British Jews and favoured their mass emigration to Palestine. See H. Belloc, *The Jews* (London: Constable, 1922) and G. K. Chesterton, *The New Jerusalem* (London: Hodder, 1920).

22. TNA CAB 24/73. Pearson's letter to the head of a textile business active in Russia was circulated by the Secretary of State for War, Alfred Milner, to his cabinet colleagues in a memorandum dated 8 January 1919. Both the Foreign Office and the press of the day focused with a certain constancy on a supposed 'Jewish factor'.

'Whoever is in power in Downing Street', wrote Leopold Maxse (1864–1932), director of the *National Review* and brother of Violet Milner (1872–1958), Alfred Milner's future wife, 'whether Conservatives, Liberals, Radicals, Coalitionists, or pseudo-Bolsheviks – the International Jew rules the roost': L. Maxse, 'The Second Treaty of Versailles', *National Review* 73 (1919): 819.

23. Already, on 19 May 1910, British ambassador in Istanbul Gerald Lowther (1858–1916) wrote that the Young Turks revolution of 1908 was the outcome of an international conspiracy orchestrated by 'Jews, Freemasons and Zionists'. It is believed that the source used by Lowther was Gerald Fitzmaurice (1865–1939), the Istanbul embassy's dragoman from 1907 to 1914. See M. Kemal Oke, 'Jews and the Question of Zionism', pp. 199–208.

24. BOA Y.PRK.TKM 38/51, Newlinski (who was working at the time in Istanbul as Herzl's diplomatic agent) to the Porte. Vienna, 23 March 1897.

25. E. Pearlman, 'The Representation of Jews on Edwardian Postcards', in B. Cheyette and N. Valman (eds), *The Image of the Jew in European Liberal Culture, 1789–1914* (London: Vallentine Mitchell, 2004), pp. 217–42.

26. B. Wasserstein, 'British Officials and the Arab-Jewish Conflict in Palestine, 1917–1929', PhD thesis (Oxford, 1974), p. 16.

27. D. Lloyd George, *Memoirs of the Peace Conference* (New Haven CT: Yale University Press, 1939), vol. 2, p. 721. Even Churchill, in a speech in Sunderland on 2 January 1920, described Bolshevism as a 'Jewish movement'. Many sources report that Balfour mentioned to Felix Frankfurter (1882–1965) and Louis Brandeis (1856–1941) that he knew that Lenin's (1870–1924) mother was Jewish: CZA Z4/16009, 24 June 1918. See also Z. Szajkowski, *Jews, Wars, and Communism* (New York: Ktav, 1972), vol. 2, p. 174.

28. J. Buchan, *The Thirty-Nine Steps* (New York: Doran, 1915), p. 6.

29. N. Sokolow, *History of Zionism* (London: Longmans, Green, 1919), vol. 1, p. xxxiv.

30. Cited in K. Robbins, *Sir Edward Grey* (London: Cassell, 1971), p. 332.

31. Sykes, 18 March 1916. Cit. in R. Adelson, *Mark Sykes: Portrait of an Amateur* (London: Cape, 1975), p. 207.

32. Schneer noted that Sykes 'was an anti-Semite – during his travels he sketched grotesque cartoons of fat Jews with big noses': J. Schneer, *The Balfour Declaration* (London: Bloomsbury, 2010), p. 44. According to Schneer, 'Sykes's exposure to Zionism at a crucial moment in the war led him to adapt, but hardly to relinquish, his prewar prejudices and stereotypical thinking about Jews. He continued to believe in their enormous if subterranean power', p. 168.

33. Cited in M. J. Cohen, *Britain's Moment in Palestine: Retrospect and Perspectives, 1917–1948* (London: Routledge, 2014), p. 10.

34. Eric Hobsbawm argued that 'the British government, anxious for international Jewish support during the war, had incautiously and ambiguously promised to establish "a national home" for the Jews. This was to be another problematic and unforgotten relic of the First World War': E. Hobsbawm, *The Age of Extremes* (New York: Vintage, 1996), p. 32.

35. Projected to our day, it can be noted, as Uri Avnery wrote in a newsletter dated 12 April 2012, that 'this extreme kind of pro-Semitism is just disguised anti-Semitism. Both have a basic belief in common: that Jews – and therefore Israel – are something apart, not to be measured by the standards applied to everybody else': A. Avnery, 'Günter the Terrible', in *Uri Avnery's Column*, 14 April 2012. Available at: http://zope.gush-shalom.org/home/en/channels/avnery/1334242715.

36. R. F. Mackay, *Balfour, Intellectual Statesman* (Oxford: Oxford University Press, 1985), p. 317. Balfour made this declaration in 1917 to Harold Nicolson (1886–1968).

37. *Illustrated Sunday Herald*, 8 February 1920.

38. TNA FO 371/4179, Balfour to Lloyd George, 19 February 1919. Balfour justified his position by arguing 'that we regard Palestine as being absolutely exceptional', in that he thought 'the question of the Jews outside Palestine as one of world importance': Ibid.

39. R. Meinertzhagen, *Middle East Diary, 1917–1956* (London: Cresset, 1959), p. 25.

40. A. B. Yehoshua has written that 'history teaches us a cruel thing in the relationship of the Jewish people with the land of Israel. The Jewish population was not expelled by force from its home country but rather expelled itself (and continues to ignore this). In the Second Temple period, half of the Jewish people lived outside the borders of Eretz Israel by its own choice! The Roman exile, and there is much historical evidence on this, was not a mass movement but concerned only small numbers of people. The land of Israel lost its Jewish inhabitants because these did not retain their ties with it and preferred to move to lands both near and far': A. B. Yehoshua, *Bizkhut ha-normaliut* [In Defence of Normality] (Tel Aviv: Schocken, 1980). The passage has been translated from the Italian edition: A. B. Yehoshua, *Elogio della normalità* [Praising of Normality] (Florence: Giuntina, 1991), pp. 89–90.

41. NARA, RG59, Palestine-Israel 1945-49, LM 163, Roll 7. Hourani, 31 May 1946.

42. Forty years after the event, Weizmann confirmed that Balfour 'had only the most naive and rudimentary notion of the [Zionist] movement'. He did not even know Theodor Herzl's real name, calling him, in his closest approximation, "Dr. Herz"'. Weizmann, *Trial*, p. 111.

43. BOA HR.SYS 2334/40, report drawn up by the Ottoman authorities about a speech given by Weizmann at an official dinner on 2 April 1918, at Jerusalem's 'Government House'. Weizmann expressed the wish that Palestine would remain 'undivided and have only one fair and responsible government'.

44. CZA Z4/16055, Weizmann to Balfour, 17 July 1918.

45. TNA FO 371/3395, Weizmann to Balfour, 30 May 1918.

46. 'Lord Balfour', noted Humphrey Bowman (1879–1965), 'was here [in Palestine] for 10 days and was surrounded by Jews the whole time, so that he never had a chance of hearing the Arab point of view. Indeed, he did not seem to wish to do so': from Bowman's diaries, 13 April 1925. Cited in S. S. Boyle, *Betrayal of Palestine* (Boulder CO: Westview, 2001), p. 129.

47. TNA FO 371/4185, Balfour to Curzon, 11 August 1919. Balfour added: 'In Palestine we do not propose even to go through the form of consulting the wishes of the present inhabitants of the country.'

48. Balfour to Curzon, 20 January 1919. British Foreign Office, *Documents on British Foreign Policy, 1919–1939* (London, 1952), p. 1277. George Kidston, Foreign Office official, warned that Balfour's strategy did not respect the wishes of the large majority of the local population. In Kidston's opinion, the idea that such a strategy 'will entail bloodshed and military repression never seems to have occurred to him [Balfour]': TNA FO 371/4183. Kidston, 22 September 1919. Cit. also in A. Ṭībāwī, *A Modern History of Syria, Including Lebanon and Palestine* (New York: Macmillan, 1969), p. 300.

49. TNA FO 608/98. According to Howard M. Sachar, there were more than 17,000 Jews in Palestine in 1856. Sixty-two years later, at the end of the First World War, there were 55,000 as opposed to 560,000 Arabs (the war years saw a rise in the number of Jews as a result of the conflict). H. M. Sachar, *A History of Israel: From the Rise of Zionism to Our Time* (New York: Knopf, 2006), p. 118.

50. L. Stein, *The Balfour Declaration* (New York: Simon & Schuster, 1961), p. 550.

51. 'I hope', wrote Balfour in July 1920, 'the Arabs will remember that Great Britain has freed them from the tyranny of their brutal conqueror': NARA, RG 59, Palestine-Israel 1945–9, LM 163, Roll 8.

52. Cited in C. Weizmann, *The Letters and Papers of Chaim Weizmann* (New Brunswick NJ: Transaction Publishers, 1983), vol. 1, p. 216.

53. Sokolow underlined that the day that London took control of Palestine, 'she would clearly and obviously take such necessary steps as to secure that the Jews should be the predominant people in Palestine [and] that it should be *their* country': cit. in Schneer, *The Balfour*, p. 149.

54. TNA FO 371/3385, Weizmann to Balfour, 4 December 1918.

55. Weizmann to the Paris Peace Conference in 1919. Palestine Royal Commission Report (London: HMSO 1937), p. 301. A telegram sent a few months earlier (27 October 1918) by Zionist leader Victor Jacobson (1869–1935) to Zionist headquarters around the world highlighted the need that the peace negotiations support the establishment of Palestine 'as a national homeland for the Jewish people'. BOA HR.SYS 2334/43.

56. TNA FO 371/5199, Curzon, 20 March 1920. Curzon argued that the vague promises made to the Zionists could generate false expectations. 'Their [Zionists's] program is expanding from day to day. They now talk about a Jewish State. The Arab portion of the population is well-nigh forgotten and is to be ignored. They not only claim the boundaries of the old Palestine, but they claim to spread across the Jordan': TNA CAB 27/24. Curzon to the Eastern Committee, 5 December 1918.

57. For Major-General H. Watson, the opposition to Zionism 'of the majority of the population is deep rooted – it is fast leading to hatred of the British – and will result, if the Zionist programme is forced upon them, in an outbreak of a very serious character': TNA FO 371/1051. Watson to Allenby, 16 August 1919.

58. Vladimir Jabotinsky (1880–1940), leader of the revisionist Zionist right-wing, stressed that 'Palestine has become the theatre of an undisguised anti-semitic policy. [. . .] high officials, guilty of acts which any Court would qualify as instigation to anti-Jewish pogroms, not only go unpunished, but retain their official positions': JIA, Mictavim [letters], n. 3, 1919–21. Jabotinsky, Lydda, 6 July 1919.

59. According to Sykes, 'Arabs could be managed, particularly if they receive Jewish support in other matters'. Cit. in M. Gilbert, *Exile and Return* (Philadelphia PA: Lippincott, 1978), p. 93.

60. TNA FO 371/5034, Meinertzhagen to Curzon, 31 March 1920. Meinertzhagen, Allenby's political adviser, was described by Weizmann as 'an ardent Zionist': C. Weizmann, *Trial and Error: The Autobiography of Chaim Weizmann* (Westport CT: Greenwood, 1972), p. 181. However, Meinertzhagen himself admitted that he was 'imbued with anti-semitic feelings': R. Meinertzhagen, *Middle East Diary, 1917–1956* (London: Cresset, 1959), p. 67. More nuanced were the

opinions expressed by several Zionist leaders and members. American historian Hans Kohn (1891–1971), who worked with Zionist organisations since 1909, wrote the following: 'Lately I have become increasingly aware that the official policy of the Zionist Organization and the opinion of the vast majority of Zionists are quite incompatible with my own convictions. I, therefore, feel that I can no longer remain a leading official within the Zionist Organization. [. . .] We pretend to be innocent victims. Of course the Arabs attacked us in August [1929]. Since they have no armies, they could not obey the rules of war. They perpetrated all the barbaric acts that are characteristic of a colonial revolt. But we are obliged to look into the deeper cause of this revolt. We have been in Palestine for twelve years [since the British mandate] without having even once made a serious attempt at seeking through negotiations the consent of the indigenous people. We have been relying exclusively upon Great Britain's military might. We have set ourselves goals which by their very nature had to lead to conflict with Arabs. [. . .] for twelve years we pretended that the Arabs did not exist and were glad when we were not reminded of their existence': JNUL 376/224, Kohn to Berthold Feiwel (1875–1937). Jerusalem, 21 November 1929. In the same historical phase, Arthur Ruppin expressed similar views: see A. Ruppin, *Pirqei hayai, be-binyan ha'aretz ve-ha'am 1920–1942* [Chapters of My Life Building Land and People, 1920–1942] (Tel Aviv: Am Oved, 1968), p. 33.

61. 'The Arabian lands for the Arabs', exclaimed, among many others, Robert Cecil at the London Opera House on the occasion of the publication of the Balfour Declaration, 'Armenia for the Armenians, and Judaea for the Jews': cit. in P. Goodman (ed.), *The Jewish National Home* (London: Dent, 1943), p. 28.

62. Cit. in Weizmann, *Trial*, p. 179. The future of Palestine, pointed out Alfred Milner in a House of Lords debate in 1923, 'cannot possibly be left to be determined by the temporary impressions and feelings of the Arab majority of the present day', cited in Palestine Royal Commission (London, 1937), p. 30.

63. TNA FO 800/217, Brandeis to Balfour, 24 June 1919. Balfour expressed his 'entire agreement' with this position. Ibid.

64. D. Fromkin, *A Peace to End all Peace* (New York: Holt, 1989), p. 19.

65. Sokolow, *History*, vol. 2, p. xxvi.

66. I. Berlin, *Personal Impressions* (Oxford: Oxford University Press, 1982), p. 53.

67. Immediately after their rise to power, the Young Turks abolished the limits on Jewish immigration to Palestine, creating considerable expectations in Zionist ranks. In August 1909, the previous limits were reimposed: BOA YEE 136/63.

68. Weizmann, *Trial*, p. 157.

69. J. Kimche, *The Second Arab Awakening* (London: Thames & Hudson, 1970), p. 37.

70. Fromkin, *A Peace*, p. 298.

71. The first Attorney General of Palestine, 'lifelong Zionist' Norman Bentwitch (1883–1971), contended that 'a national home, as distinguished from a state, is a country where a people are acknowledged as having a recognized legal position and the opportunity of developing their cultural, social and intellectual ideals without receiving political rights': cit. J. N. Moore, *The Arab-Israeli Conflict: Readings* (Princeton NJ: Princeton University Press, 1975), p. 206. This position was also consistent with the one expressed a few years earlier by Nahum Sokolow. The latter represented the Zionist Organization at the 1919 Paris Peace Conference, where he made it clear that the 'object of Zionism is to establish for the Jewish people a home in Palestine secured by public law [. . .] It has been said and is still being obstinately repeated by anti-Zionists again and again, that Zionism aims at the creation of an independent "Jewish State". But this is wholly fallacious. The "Jewish State" was never part of the Zionist programme. The Jewish State was the title of Herzl's first pamphlet, which had the supreme merit of forcing people to think. This pamphlet was followed by the first Zionist Congress, which accepted the Basle programme – the only programme in existence': N. Sokolow, A *History of Zionism 1600–1918* (London: Longmans, 1919), vol. 1, p. xxv. See also S. H. H. Nadvi, *Filasṭīn Aur Bain Al-Aqvaīmiī Siyaīsiyaīt* [Palestine and International Politics] (Karachi: Academia, 1976), p. 439 (in Urdu).

72. 'I did my best', Zionist leader Max Nordau (1849–1923) clarified, 'to persuade the claimants of the Jewish State in Palestine that we might find a circumlocution that would express all we meant': cit. in C. Sykes, *Crossroads to Israel* (Bloomington: Indiana University Press, 1973), p. 10. Speaking to UNSCOP's (United Nations Special Committee on Palestine) members, David Ben-Gurion noted, on 7 July 1947, that thanks to the direct intervention of the United Nations 'there will be a clear-cut, unequivocal decision that Palestine is becoming a Jewish State. The fact – and this has been admitted by many – the fact that this was not quite clear in the Mandate has led to contradictions'. Available at: http://unispal.un.org/UNISPAL.NSF/0/C6723C052629426085256E 8B007092DF. Speaking in front of the Peel Commission in 1937, Winston Churchill made it clear that there was nothing in the definition of the 'National Home' that might have precluded 'the establishment of a Jewish State'. (Palestine Royal Commission: Command Paper 5479 of 1937.) As noted by Isaiah Friedman: 'Whether [the first British High Commissioner for Palestine

Herbert] Samuel had this ultimate aim in mind when conceiving his policy is dubious. But Churchill, as his response of the Peel Commission shows, did favour it. Throughout his career as Colonial Secretary, he adhered to his Zionist convictions': I. Friedman, *British Pan-Arab Policy, 1915–1922* (New Brunswick NJ: Transaction Publishers, 2011), p. 389.

73. J. Turner, *Britain and the First World War* (London: Unwin Hyman, 1988), p. 117.

74. H. Purcell, *Lloyd George* (London: Haus, 2006), p. 69.

75. C. P. Scott, *The Political Diaries of C. P. Scott, 1911–1928* (London: Collins, 1970), p. 274.

76. The fact that Lloyd George was born in a small country that had always striven to protect its identity seems to have influenced his approach to Zionism. Josif Trumpeldor (1880–1920), icon of Socialist Zionism, proposed to him to create a Jewish regiment, emphasising that 'we ask for the Jew the privilege the Welshman and Scotsman enjoy – to fight for their country; to fight like the Welsh and Scotch do – in regiments of their own, not scattered and nameless': Jabotinsky Institute Archive (JIA), Mictavim [letters], n. 2, 1914–19, Trumpeldor, 24 January 1917. Lloyd George himself elaborated in 1925 on the role of Jewish history in the Welsh education of the time: 'On five days a week in the day school, and on Sunday in our Sunday schools, we were thoroughly versed in the history of the Hebrews': cit. in G. Davies (ed.), *The Chosen People: Wales & the Jews* (Bridgend: Seren, 2002), p. 92.

77. TNA FO 800/216, Weizmann to Balfour, 9 April 1919.

78. ASDMAE, AP 1948–50, Israele, b. 1. Italy's general consulate ('Ufficio di Caifa') to the ministry for Foreign Affairs in Rome, 10 November 1948. The document, signed by the consul, contains excerpts of a speech given by Weizmann during his first official visit to Haifa. According to Bevin, the Balfour Declaration possessed 'the congenital ill of being unilateral. Neither its British authors nor its British and American supporters have taken account of the Arabs. Such a unilateral policy should be abandoned in order to avoid asking the Arabs to bear the weight of the Jewish problem alone': ASDMAE, AP 1946–50, Palestine, b. 1.

79. H. Samuel, *Mémoirs* (London: Cresset Press, 1945), p. 139.

80. Samuel wrote that 'the moment Turkey entered the war' his position 'was entirely changed': ibid.

81. Ibid., p. 140.

82. H. Samuel, *Great Britain and Palestine* (London: The Jewish Historical Society of England, 1935), p. 13.

83. Ibid. Samuel reported that Grey had expressed himself 'quite favourable to the proposal' and that he would have been 'prepared to work for it if the opportunity arose'.

84. In March 1916, Lucien Wolf proposed to the Foreign Office to issue a declaration in order to clarify that the Allied powers would have taken into account 'the historic interest that country [Palestine] possesses for the Jewish community': TNA FO 371/2817, Wolf to Lancelot Oliphant (1881–1965), 3 March 1916.

85. *Jewish Chronicle*, 15 October 1905.

86. Samuel, *Mémoirs*, p. 142.

87. C. Weizmann, *The Letters and Papers of Chaim Weizmann* (Oxford: Oxford University Press, 1973), vol. 6, p. 112. Samuel did not clarify whether the Temple would be built on the Dome of the Rock or elsewhere.

88. Ibid., p. 77.

89. In a conversation with Zangwill on 19 October 1914, Weizmann confirmed that he had no doubt 'that Palestine will fall within the sphere of England. Palestine is a natural continuation of Egypt and the barrier separating the Suez Canal from Constantinople, the Black Sea and any hostility which may come from this side': F. Hardie and I. Herrmann, *Britain and Zion: The Fateful Entanglement* (Belfast: Blackstaff, 1980), p. 33.

90. A. Balfour, *Henry Sidgwick Memorial Lecture* (Cambridge: Cambridge University Press, 1908), p. 47. 'Parliamentary institutions', clarified Balfour, 'have rarely been a great success, except amongst the English-speaking peoples': cit. in D. Judd, *Balfour and the British Empire* (London: Macmillan, 1968), p. 261.

91. Balfour wrote that if Zionism 'succeeds, it will do a great spiritual and material work for the Jews, but not for them alone. [. . .] it is [. . .] a serious endeavour to mitigate the age-long miseries created for Western civilization by the presence in its midst of a Body which it too long regarded as alien and even hostile, but which it was equally unable to expel or to absorb': Balfour in the preface to Sokolow, *History*, vol. 1, p. xxxiv.

92. Weizmann, *The Letters*, p. 81.

93. Ibid. According to Weizmann, Balfour 'listened for a long time and was very moved – I assure you to *tears* – and he took me by the hand and said I had illuminated for him the road followed by a great suffering nation': ibid., p. 82.

94. Weizmann, *Trial*, p. 152.

95. TNA CAB 37/123, Samuel, memorandum entitled 'The Future of Palestine', January 1915.

96. H. H. Asquith, *Memories and Reflections, 1852–1927* (Boston MA: Little, 1928), vol. 2, p. 71.

97. Ibid.

98. Ibid., p. 78.

99. J. Bowle, *Viscount Samuel, A Biography* (London: Gollancz, 1957), p. 172.

100. Already, in November 1915, Samuel had emphasised to Grey 'the danger of any other Power than England possessing Palestine'. Grey, according to Samuel, 'agreed that that was so'. Samuel, *Mémoirs*, p. 154.

101. Weizmann, *The Letters*, p. 181.

102. Despite their shared views, Lloyd George's opinion of Samuel was never positive. 'During the War', Lloyd George recalled in his memoirs, 'he [Samuel] had done nothing in particular, but he had done it very well': D. Lloyd George, *War Memoirs of David Lloyd George* (Boston MA: Little, 1937), p. 32.

103. *Zionist Review*, December 1917, p. 214.

104. See Khālidī, *al-Qaḍīya al-Filasṭīnīya*, p. 367.

105. Cited in Friedman, *The Question*, p. 22.

106. Cited in T. M. Endelman, *The Jews of Britain, 1656 to 2000* (Berkeley: University of California Press, 2002), p. 192.

107. Zionism was viewed by many Jews, and primarily by rabbis, as an anti-Jewish rebellion comparable to Luther's challenge to the Church of Rome. Luigi Luzzatti (1841–1927), Italy's second Jewish prime minister, declared, for instance, that Jews 'must acquire everywhere full religious liberty as existing in the United States and in Italy. In Palestine, delivered from Turks, Jews will live, not as sovereigns but as free citizens, to fertilise their fathers's land. Judaism is not a nationality, but a Religion': TNA CAB 21/58, Luzzatti, 18 May 1917.

108. TNA CAB 23/4, Balfour on Montagu, 2 October 1917.

109. Many anti-Zionist Jews were not against the creation of a Jewish state *tout court*. Lucien Wolf, for example, explained to Balfour (30 December 1917) that he was not opposed to the idea of creating 'a local Jewish nation and a Jewish State' in Palestine. Wolf, however, like Montefiore and others, was alarmed by the prospect that the Zionists might put the status of Jews in the rest of the world at risk.

110. 'Nebi' (prophet), Edwin Samuel's nickname, was given to him as a result of the battle he fought in November 1917 with the Jewish Legion around the village of Nabi Samwil/Nebi Samuel.

111. Sokolow, *History*, vol. 2, p. xvii. Sokolow wrote that 'sometimes I had to go there [Sykes's office] three times a day and to remain there till late at night': ibid., p. xxxii.

112. Weizmann, *Trial*, p. 182.

113. M. Sykes, *Through Five Turkish Provinces* (London: Bickers, 1900), p. 80.

114. Fromkin, *A Peace*, p. 181.

115. M. Sykes, J. H. Smith and E. G. Brown, *Dar-ul-Islam* (London: Bickers, 1904), p. 178.

116. M. Sykes, *The Caliphs' Last Heritage* (London: Macmillan, 1915), p. 441.

117. According to Sykes, 'from top to bottom, where Syrian Arabs are left to themselves, graft and rascality and ambitious designs are the only things one is able to see': TNA FO 608/105, Sykes, in a memorandum entitled 'Appreciations of the Situation in Syria, Palestine, and Lesser Armenia', 22 January 1919.

118. MECA, The Sledmere Papers, Sykes, 19 July 1917. On 11 February 1918, Shmuel Tolkowsky (1886–1965) Weizmann's secretary, wrote in his diary that the alliance between Armenians, Arabs and Jews 'is an artificial issue created by the Foreign Office which wants to use us as an instrument to achieve goals which are incomprehensible to me'. Cit. in Y. Auron, *The Banality of Indifference* (New Brunswick NJ: Transaction, 2009), p. 258.

119. Cited in Schneer, *The Balfour*, p. 155.

120. ISA RG72 695/4-P, J. L. Magnes, 12 November 1929.

121. TNA FO 371/3385, Clayton, 18 November 1918.

122. Malcolm, who worked during and after the war to represent Armenian interests in Europe, attempted to convince Sykes that the only way to attract the sympathy 'of certain politically-minded Jews everywhere' was to speak up to guarantee 'Palestine for them': J. A. Malcolm, *Origins of the Balfour Declaration: Dr. Weizmann's Contribution* (London: British Museum, 1944), pp. 2–3. Sokolow noted that Malcolm 'has great sympathy for Zionism (not for the Jews in general) [. . .] It is possible that he [. . .] believes that the Jewish *haute finance* will help the Armenians': cit. in R. Sanders, *The High Walls of Jerusalem* (New York: Holt, 1984), p. 507.

123. TNA FO 800/210, Sykes to Balfour, 8 April 1917.

124. Aaronsohn, renowned botanist and founder of Nili, a Jewish espionage organisation that worked in Palestine during the First World War to supply information to London, enjoyed Sykes's full trust. 'If Rabbi Gaster', wrote Sykes's biographer a few months before, 'had provided Sykes with the grace note of Zionism in Europe, here was Aaronsohn who had actually played the trumpet in Palestine': Adelson, *Mark Sykes*, p. 279.

125. TNA FO 800/381, Sykes to diplomat Arthur Nicolson (1849–1928), 18 March 1916.

126. MECA, TSP, Sykes, 29 July 1917.

127. Sokolow, *History*, vol. 2, p. xxii.

128. J. Darwin, *The Empire Project: The Rise and Fall of the British World-System, 1830–1970* (Cambridge: Cambridge Univerity Press, 2009), p. 3.

129. TNA 371/4178, memorandum entitled 'The Strategic Importance of Syria to the British Empire', drawn up by the War Cabinet on 9 December 1918.

130. L. Amery in the introduction to P. Goodman (ed.), *Chaim Weizmann: A Tribute on His Seventieth Birthday* (London: Gollancz, 1945), p. 11. In October 1918, Amery declared himself convinced that 'the Jewish settlement of Palestine is not likely in the long run to be confined to Palestine in the narrower sense. It is sure to spread not only into the trans-Jordan country, but to Egypt, Mesopotamia and the Near East generally': TNA FO 371/3384.

131. The episode was reported by C. P. Scott, who took part in the meeting. Scott, *The Political Diaries*, p. 255.

132. In *Punch*, 20 December 1916, p. 423.

133. TNA CAB 37/161/14, War Cabinet, 22 December 1916.

134. 'Smuts, Barnes [. . .] and Lord Milner', wrote Weizmann to Judge Louis Brandeis in October 1917, 'have advocated our cause very strongly': cit. in Weizmann, *The Letters*, p. 525.

135. Weizmann to Kerr, 7 October 1917. Stein, *The Balfour*, p. 519.

136. S. Leslie, *Mark Sykes: His Life and Letters* (New York: Cassell, 1923), p. 288.

137. In 1902, Milner wrote to the president of the South African Zionist Federation, Samuel Goldreich, that 'some of the best people I have ever known are Jews, some of the closest personal friends are Jews, and Jews intensely devoted to their race and religion': A. Milner, *The Milner Papers* (London: Cassell, 1931), vol. 2, p. 379.

138. Samuel, *Mémoirs*, p. 145.

139. Ibid.

140. F. Bertie, *The Diary of Lord Bertie of Thame, 1914–1918* (New York: Hodder, 1924), vol. 2, p. 168.

141. CZA AK 46/1, Claude Montefiore Papers, Montefiore's Milner interview, 16 May 1917.

142. Any intention of creating a Jewish state in Palestine continued to be denied on all sides. 'There is no idea whatever on the part of the British administration', declared Bentwich in August 1921, 'of creating a Jewish State. What they hope to do is to create a condition in which Jew and Arab in more or less equal numbers shall live and govern side by side': LPL, DP, 400, f. 206.

143. A memorandum drawn up in January 1923 by Ormsby-Gore pointed out that six years earlier the Foreign Office held that Washington could be 'favourably influenced if His Majesty's Government gave an assurance that the return of the Jews to Palestine had become a purpose of British policy': TNA CAB 24/158. C. P. Scott also noted that, in order to promote British control in Palestine, it was 'very important to obtain American Jews' support. It would be unanimous if they could be assured that in the event of a British occupation of Palestine the Zionist scheme would be considered favourably': Scott, *The Political Diaries*, p. 258.

144. D. Lloyd George, *War Memoirs*, cit., p. 89.

145. On 8 April 1917, Weizmann clarified that 'since the invasion of Palestine by the British army our problem has become much more tangible and "*actuel*". Everybody here realises the importance of the Palestinian campaign, and the press on the whole is extremely favourable to a Jewish Palestine under a British Protectorate': Weizmann, *The Letters*, pp. 357–8.

146. TNA FO 371/3058, Graham to the permanent undersecretary at the Foreign Office, Charles Hardinge (1858–1944), 13 June 1917.

147. Ibid.

148. TNA FO 371/3058, Graham to Hardinge, 13 June 1917.

149. TNA FO 371/3054, Cecil to Balfour, 24 October 1917.

150. TNA FO 371/3058, Rothschild to Balfour, 18 July 1917.

151. Milner 'thinks the word "reconstituted" is much too strong, and also the word "secure"': TNA CAB 21/58. Ormsby-Gore to Hankey, 23 August 1917.

152. TNA CAB 21/58, Milner to the War Cabinet, 5 August 1917.

153. TNA CAB 23/4, Milner to the War Cabinet, 4 October 1917.

154. TNA CAB 24/4, Curzon to the War Cabinet, 4 October 1917.

155. TNA CAB 23/4, Balfour to the War Cabinet, 4 October 1917. A year earlier, during a meeting with New York rabbi Stephen Samuel Wise (1874–1949), Wilson, a Presbyterian, declared: 'To think, that I, the son of the manse, should be able to help restore the Holy Land to its people': cit. in P. Grose, *Israel in the Mind of America* (New York: Knopf, 1983). p. 67.

156. These responses are set out in a document signed by Hankey: TNA CAB 24/4, 17 October 1917.

157. Ibid.

158. Ibid.

159. TNA CAB 23/4. Balfour to the War Cabinet. 31 October 1917.

160. L. Amery, *My Political Life* (London: Hutchinson, 1953), vol. 2, p. 116.

161. The first recorded use of smoke as a weapon of asphyxiation against civilians in the 'MENA region' dates back to the mid-nineteenth century, when French general Thomas Robert Bugeaud (1784–1849) adopted this method against thousands of people in Algeria: 'If these rogues [Algerians] retreat to their caverns', Bugeaud argued, 'then smoke them out like foxes [*renards*]' : cit. in L. Ouar, *Le procès de l'impérialisme et du colonialisme français: l'Algérie, bastion de la résistance* (Algiers: Entreprise Nationale du Livre, 1986), p. 39. Seventy years later, the region witnessed its first recorded use of chemical weapons. This occurred during 1917's Third Battle of Gaza, when the troops led by Allenby fired about 10,000 cans of asphyxiating gas. Their limited impact did not meet Allenby's expectations. However, the use of gas attracted much attention to the point that – right after the 1920 Iraqi Revolt against the proposed British Mandate of Mesopotamia – Secretary of State for the Colonies Winston Churchill asserted he was 'strongly in favour of using poisoned gas against the uncivilised tribes', clarifying that it 'would spread a lively terror': cit. in W. Dockter, *Churchill and the Islamic World* (London: I. B. Tauris, 2015), p. 113.

162. The declaration, whose final form included a few small amendments, was privately sent by Graham to Weizmann on 1 November 1917. The next day, Balfour forwarded it to Rothschild officially.

163. V. Kattan, *From Coexistence to Conquest* (New York: Pluto Press, 2009), pp. 60–1.

164. Weizmann, *Trial*, p. 207.

165. A. Cohen, *Israel and the Arab World* (New York: Funk, 1970), p. 124.

6

The Racialisation of Middle Eastern People

Whereas Ottomans presupposed that cultural difference within society was a given, Westerners tended to proceed from a diametrically opposite position, seeing societal homogeneity as normative and the Babel-like conditions in the Near East as symptomatic of societal degeneration.[1]

Nicholas Doumanis

We are getting reports that the Arabs in territory occupied by us are beginning to forget what they suffered under the Turks [. . .] Gratitude in the East is largely limited by what you get out of people in hard cash![2]

William Ormsby-Gore

The First World War claimed the lives of 9 million soldiers and around 7 million civilians. While American President Woodrow Wilson believed that the enormity of such a catastrophe required peace without conditions, Lloyd George was persuaded that a war of such magnitude demanded annexations and indemnities to an extent never seen before.

While the war was still underway, many people began to wonder what new instruments could be created to prevent such disasters from happening again.[3] In his 'Fourteen points', drafted in collaboration with Edward M. House and presented before the US Senate on 8 January 1918, Wilson expressed the intention to create an entity that would join various nations together in order to provide reciprocal guarantees 'of political independence and territorial integrity to great and small states alike' (point 14). The roots of this idea were not new in themselves. In the *Nouveau Cynée*, a pioneering work by the French monk Émeric Crucé (1590?–1648), the features of a 'Universal League of Nations' capable of refusing war as a means for resolving international disputes were outlined. However, Wilson's ideas were advanced at the end of a war of unprecedented scale. What is more, they were under-girded by the idea that 'all national aspirations shall be accorded the utmost satisfaction', as well as by the ambition to apply the 'Monroe Doctrine' ('America for Americans') globally.

In order to outline his programme in detail, Wilson followed the advice of The Inquiry, a research group, which he created in September 1917, chaired by House and with Walter Lippman (1889–1974) as research director. Far more definitive, however, was the input of Jan Christiaan Smuts, author of the 1918 memorandum 'The League of Nations: A Practical Suggestion'. Wilson himself confirmed having rewritten the founding draft of the League of Nations 'in the light of a paper by General Smuts, who seemed to have done some very clear thinking in regard to what was to be done to the pieces of the dismembered empires'.[4]

Despite being awarded the Nobel Peace Prize in 1919 and having gone down in history as the president who best represented the people's right to self-determination (a rather ambiguous concept), Wilson was a controversial figure.[5] His administration reinstated the practice of racial segregation, abolished by Abraham Lincoln (1809–65) in 1863, within the federal government.[6] It was under his two terms, moreover, that it became common practice to require photos for those looking for jobs, in order to determine their race. Wilson, in fact, was convinced that racial segregation was not humiliating and that it had been adopted to benefit black people.[7]

This aspect is important in that it provides a point of connection between the US president and the figure which, as noted, inspired the founding draft of the League of Nations. For most of his political life, Smuts was also an open supporter of racial segregation. In 1929, he endorsed the idea of creating separate institutions for whites and blacks, a prelude to the subsequent proposal of the practice of apartheid. Like many other figures of his era, Smuts was persuaded by the idea that 'these children of nature [Africans] have not the inner toughness and persistence of the European, not those social and moral incentives to progress which have built up European civilization in a comparatively short period'.[8]

In the country of John Locke (1632–1704) and John Stuart Mill (1806–73), the idea that freedom was a man's natural condition was quite widespread. It was held, however, that, as Mill had already clarified in *On Liberty* (1859), this criterion was to be applied selectively: only 'mature' human beings, in full possession of their faculties, could aspire to that status. The 'immature' included not only children but entire 'races' which were not completely civilised, lacking the necessary qualities of a democratic citizen. This was also a widespread conviction on the other side of the Atlantic, where ex-slaves and their descendants were considered, in Wilson's words, 'excited by a freedom they did not understand', and thus not ready to participate in the American public life.[9] The League of Nations was born with the backdrop of an era in which the presumed innate quality of a given 'race' was invoked in order to explain the tenor of life of various groups of workers. Furthermore, the idea that immigration weakened the fibre of American society – allowing 'inferior races' to outnumber the Anglo-Saxons, best fitted for national and worldwide hegemony – was widespread.[10]

The League of Nations, depicted in the Arab press of the time as 'a tool for the realisation of its [Britain] wickedest objects',[11] prevented the inclusion of a clause for 'racial equality', proposed by Japan, in its founding charter. Since the Meiji era (1868–1912), which was marked by deep political and social changes, the Japanese establishment demonstrated clear intolerance for the discriminatory treatment espoused by Western governments. While the founding charter of the League of Nations was being discussed, the Japanese delegates fought for the inclusion of a clause validating the principle of 'racial non-discrimination', the same idea which, at the end of the Second World War, became one of the pillars of the United Nations. Such a clause was intended to secure equality of Japanese nationals and egalitarianism among members of the League. It was, therefore, far from being considered by them as a universal principle. Nonetheless, it represented a meaningful step that the Japanese media of the time stressed on several occasions. In January 1919, the distinguished daily newspaper *Asahi* – followed by the *Nichi Nichi, Osaka Mainiki* and other national media – pointed out that the authorities in Tokyo were unmovable regarding the need to officially guarantee the 'equal international treatment of all races' and that if President Wilson was not able to tear down 'the wall of discrimination', he would have spoken of 'peace, justice and humanity in vain, demonstrating [himself] to be only a hypocrite'.[12]

Convinced, with good reason, that the US Senate would never have approved a treaty containing an article concerning racial equality,[13] Wilson ordered the commission for the League of Nations to reject the proposal in that it had not been approved unanimously. Eleven of the seventeen delegates on the committee were in favour of the insertion of the anti-discrimination clause. Furthermore, there was no law requiring unanimity. However, Wilson held it as essential given the delicacy of the subject.

The considerations discussed up to this point help us to understand why Washington, London and other European powers approached the 'Middle East chessboard' without considering the needs and wishes of the local populations, which were viewed as amorphous and incapable of taking decisions. The conference that set forth the final affirmation of this kind of approach began on 18 January 1919. The delegates of the five victorious powers of the war – United States,[14] Britain, France, Italy and Japan – and those of the defeated countries met in the clock room of Paris's Ministry of Foreign Affairs to convert the armistice of 1918 into a peace agreement, or, according to many, into new instruments of oppression. '*Ce n'est pas une paix* [This is not peace]', warned Ferdinand Foch (1851–1929), a French First World War hero, commenting on the peace imposed on Germany, '*c'est un armistice de vingt ans* [it is a twenty-year armistice]'.[15]

The decision to create the League of Nations and the approval of its charter became official during these months of negotiations. They ended on 21 January 1920, when the General Assembly of the League of Nations was inaugurated. Japan and the United States – Washington, despite the role played by Wilson, rejected the option to join the League – did not participate, adopting a more cautious, isolationist approach.

Article 22 of the charter, which, inspired by Smuts's report,[16] supported the introduction of the mandates system, was presented as a tool to realise 'the general interests of mankind'.[17] For this purpose, three distinct categories of mandate were created (classes A, B, C), depending on to what extent the population under examination was believed ready to 'stand on its own two feet', or, in the language of the time, 'able to stand by themselves under the strenuous conditions of the modern world' (Art. 22).

Beyond the different interpretations, a common denominator can be detected at the core of each of the three mandate categories: the 'white man's burden' – that is the self-assigned task to 'civilise' Africa, as well as a significant number of Asian populations.[18]

The official purpose of the mandate system was to prepare the various peoples for self-determination and self-government. In practical terms, however, the victorious powers used it to legitimise their own 'rights of conquest' in order to divide the spoils of former empires, or of areas belonging to the defeated nations. This aim was pursued through a paternalistic approach which, on the one hand, supported the idea that there was a hierarchy among the various 'races'[19] – Smuts described the African populations as 'barbarians' – and, on the other, put an exaggerated emphasis on the need to establish well-defined borders based on ethnic principles.[20] In other words, the mandate system represented – paraphrasing M. Cherif Bassiouni and Shlomo Ben-Ami – 'a new form of colonialism that had the appearance of international legitimacy'.[21]

Already by this time, such an appearance of legitimacy could be perceived by many as precarious, not least for the fact that – in Paris as well as in subsequent conferences organised in the same period – the opinions of virtually all representatives of the people subject to the mandate system were not taken into consideration. A symbolic example is represented by Ho Chi Minh (1890–1969), at the time a young Vietnamese nationalist. When he arrived in Paris in 1919 – for the occasion he had drafted eight programme points which, in line with the principle of self-determination promoted by Wilson, were aimed at freeing his country from French colonialism – the future Vietnamese president was pushed aside in a firm and hasty manner. Shortly afterwards, Ho Chi Minh decided to turn his attention to Bolshevik

Russia, welcoming a partnership with communism that Washington paid for dearly in the decades to follow.

A historical figure who would seem to support what was claimed by the British authorities,[22] and thus to partially contradict what has just been claimed, is Fayṣal, the son of the self-proclaimed 'King of Hijaz', Ḥusayn (1854–1931), in representation of whom he participated as the head of the 'Arab delegation' in the Paris Conference.[23] Quoting a report written by the British Foreign Office in March 1921:

> The Allied Powers took every opportunity of ascertaining the wishes of the Arabs before the mandates were actually allocated. The Emir Feisal, representatives of the Syrian Committee in Paris and of the Lebanon were heard by the Supreme Council in Paris in the early days of the Peace Conference.[24]

Figure 6.1   King Fayṣal of Iraq visiting his brother Emir Abdullah at 'Amman, Transjordan, 1922. (Source: Visual materials from the papers of John D. Whiting Library of Congress, Washington DC)

Following the Arab Revolt of 1916–18 Fayṣal and his father Ḥusayn – who was born in Istanbul and was the last member of the Hashemita family to be named *Sharīf* of Mecca by an Ottoman sultan – established a solid alliance with London. The strong ties between T. E. Lawrence, Gertrude Bell and Fayṣal – harshly condemned for this by Muhammad Iqbal (1877–1938) and numerous other Arab intellectuals – bear further witness to this.[25] The British authorities, which, between 1919 and 1922, looked condescendingly at the bleak outlook expressed by their officials serving in the region and at the suggestions provided by several Palestinian delegations,[26] then had an interest in choosing Fayṣal as their interlocutor and in using him as a tool for promoting British interests in the region.[27] This was even more the case given the fact that those interests were shared by the Zionist leadership. The letter written by Weizmann to his wife on 17 July 1918, a few days after the private meeting which took place in ʿAqaba between Zionist leaders and Fayṣal himself, is, in this sense, worth noting. Fayṣal's personal ambitions alone can hardly explain his 'contemptuous' attitude:

> I made the acquaintance of Fayṣal [. . .]. He is not interested in Palestine, but on the other hand he wants Damascus and the whole of Northern Syria. He talked with great animosity against the French, who want to get their hands on Syria. He expects a great deal from collaboration with the Jews. *He is contemptuous of the Palestinian Arabs whom he doesn't even regard as Arabs.* [emphasis added][28]

In the weeks prior to the Paris Conference, Fayṣal was 'summoned' to London for what was his first visit to the English capital. According to Tibawi, Fayṣal and his entourage – composed of convinced pan-Arabists – had no knowledge of English, and were fully dependent on T. E. Lawrence 'for interpreting and advice'.[29] In London, Weizmann and Fayṣal perfected an agreement, signed afterwards on 3 January 1919 in Paris, in which the two parties established that every effort was to be made to implement the Balfour Declaration (Article 3) and that all 'necessary measures shall be taken to encourage and stimulate immigration of Jews into Palestine on a large scale' (Article 4). Fayṣal added a handwritten footnote,[30] highlighting that he would 'not be then bound by a single word of the present Agreement' should the promises his family received from London during the war (correspondence Husayn–McMahon) not be kept.[31]

Some researchers claimed that the Fayṣal-Weizmann agreement legally bound the entire 'Arab national movement for which Fayṣal was the recognized spokesman at the Paris Peace conference' to accept the idea of transforming Palestine into a 'Jewish National Home'.[32] An alternative interpretation suggests, on the contrary, that the way in which Fayṣal and his father Husayn – both snubbed by the Arab-Palestinians during the 'Great Revolt' of 1916–18[33] and perceived in the region (and elsewhere) as mere instruments in the hands of London[34] – were handled, was further confirmation of the discriminatory approach of the Paris Conference.[35] The will to consider the Sharīf of Mecca and his sons as 'natural leaders' of the Arab-Palestinians was, not surprisingly, rooted in the idea that the local majority was composed of 'false Arabs'. 'The so-called Arabs of Palestine', Clayton wrote to Bell in 1918, 'are not to be compared with the real Arab of the Desert. [. . .] He is purely local and takes little or no interest in matters outside his immediate surroundings'.[36] This perception, which in various forms was also projected onto the Jewish component present in Palestine, was brought up again as a sort of mantra by dozens of His Majesty's representatives.[37] A symbolic example, among many available, may be found in Roger Courtney, a member of the Palestine Police Force at the time. He clarified that 'this particular kind of Arab-Palestinians' was not in any way composed by 'Arabs' but rather by degenerate 'Levantines', that is, individuals undeserving of being confused with 'the real Arabs of the desert'.[38] In his eyes, as well as of those who believed that Fayṣal was the 'legitimate spokesperson' for Arab-Palestinians, they were nothing more than 'a craven, cowardly lot'.[39] In claiming that the Fayṣal-Weizmann agreement in some way bound the entire 'Arab national movement' there is the risk of subscribing to the prejudices that transpire from such approaches.

San Remo: Whose Interests?

The San Remo Conference was called by the victorious powers in April 1920 with the specific purpose of deciding the future of Syria,

Palestine and Iraq. It was widely held that Britain would gain the mandate for Palestine, and France that of Syria (including Lebanon).[40] The meetings in Paris, however, ended without any official decision being made regarding the former Ottoman territories, and without a peace agreement being signed with Turkey. The decisions pertaining the mandates were confirmed officially by the Council of the League of Nations only on 24 July 1922. They became operative on 29 September of the following year, when Turkey renounced its rights and agreed to the terms imposed by the Treaty of Lausanne. The latter did not come into force until 6 August 1924.

The main limitations of the San Remo Conference were the same as those which had undermined the meetings in Paris, as well as the origin itself of the League of Nations: tens of millions of Arabs and hundreds of millions of Muslims did not have – at the moment in which the features and borders of their countries were being arbitrarily drawn – any state or representative body that could give voice to their aspirations.

The words written by the historian Elizabeth Monroe (1905–86) on the decisions taken in San Remo hold, in this sense, significant symbolic value:

> The decisions accorded neither with the wishes of the inhabitants nor with the unqualified end-of-war undertakings about freedom of choice. They were pieces of unabashed self-interest, suggesting to many onlookers that all talk of liberating small nations from oppression was so much cant.[41]

Besides British Prime Minister Lloyd George and his French counterpart Alexandre Millerand (1859–1943), the meetings in San Remo were also attended by Italian Prime Minister Francesco Nitti (1868–1953) and the Japanese Ambassador Matsui Keishiro (1868–1946). Rome and Tokyo played, in reality, purely representative roles. Italy was considered 'of very little importance',[42] while its leaders were viewed with disdain.[43] The historian Itagaki Yuzo described the subordinate role played by his country, highlighting that in order to protect 'the interests and rights acquired in Asia and the South Pacific, Japan's position at the San Remo conference was to leave the Middle East to Britain and France. She said in effect, please do whatever you like.'[44]

In San Remo, then, Paris and London – with Washington providing 'external support' – divided up the Eastern Mediterranean area, without for the moment establishing the exact wording of the agreement, or the specific borders.[45]

Indeed, the League of Nations – as well as the mandates with which it was entrusted at San Remo – was an instrument created by Western powers to carry out Western interests: referring to it as an *ex cathedra* source of legality means to apply a simplistic approach to an issue that is anything but simple.

Almost the only system at the disposal of a huge multitude of human beings at this time for the expression of their wishes and fears consisted in sending letters to the authorities who had taken it upon themselves to decide the fate of the masses. Nonetheless, there were some isolated exceptions. For instance, a Christian and Muslim Palestinian delegation was welcomed in London by His Majesty's authorities in August 1921; in the following months, the British Colonial Office engaged in consultations with Mūsā Kāẓim al-Ḥusaynī (1850–1934), president of the Palestine Arab delegation.[46] However, these exceptions were also more fantasy than reality. Most of the decisions regarding the future of the various peoples of the region had already been taken in the previous months and years. Furthermore, the petitions coming from the members of that delegation, which attempted, in broken English, to influence any outstanding resolutions in the subsequent months,[47] were not in any way taken into consideration:[48]

> We strongly object to any further steps being taken with regard to the Mandate while we are still negotiating with the British government about the future of Palestine. We again wish to inform you that the Arab people of Palestine can never accept the Mandate in its present form.[49]

There is today a consensus that the punishments imposed on Germany at Versailles, the same which facilitated the end of the Weimar Republic and the rise of Adolf Hitler (1889–1945), were counterproductive, as well as being dictated by interests that had much to do with ideas of the 'survival of the fittest' and concerned with the general present-day understanding of public international law. The solipsistic and paternalistic approach imposed by the League of Nations on millions of men and women in Asia and Africa requires an evaluation that applies, at the very least, a similar approach.[50] Even more so considering that local populations had no responsibility for the outbreak of the First World War, by many there perceived as 'someone else's war'.[51] They should not, therefore, have been required to pay the price for its outcome, nor to strive for the establishment of defined borders that might satisfy the expectations of the European powers. Thinking the opposite[52] – claiming, for example, that the mere fact that they had been victims of previous domination might justify such impositions – would mean endorsing, once more, the discriminatory approach of the time.

Fostering Ethno-sectarian Racialisation

The European discourse about 'race' – a concept that by the mid-nineteenth century was already embraced by some Arab (mainly Christian) scholars,[53] but that it is still not a frequently discussed topic in public discourse in the region – started in the last part of the eighteenth century. The racialisation of nationalisms, on the other hand, is a global feature of much of the nineteenth and twentieth centuries. Notwithstanding these considerations, it was only following the Balkan Wars (1912–13), the Armenian genocide (1915–16) and the Greco-Turkish Treaty signed at Lausanne (1922–3) that the *racialisation of identities* – that is, the tendency to ascribe a nonmutable, culturally genetic profile to a group – as well as the *ethno-sectarianisation of communal identities* – meaning the process of turning the affiliation to a given confession into a defining and exclusive element of ethnic consciousness – acquired legal validity. As noted by Hakem al-Rustom, 'post-ottoman societies witnessed the ruling in the name of a "sect" among the other sects within the larger religious tradition, and not merely ruling in the name of a religious affiliation or organization'.[54] In other words, Lausanne provided a decisive component needed for the transformation of Greece and Turkey – and, more generally, large parts of the Middle East – on the base of sectarian (Eastern Orthodoxy and Sunni Islam), rather than simply religious (Islam versus Christianity), criteria.[55]

More specifically, the Turkish delegation at the Treaty of Lausanne, headed by the future second President of Turkey İsmet İnönü (1884–1973), worked, under the auspices of Britain and France, towards a policy of selective racialisation and minoritising of local peoples, whilst promoting a sense of 'diversity' and tolerance:

> The Turkish delegation at the conference prevented the diverse Muslim populations in Anatolia such as the Kurds, Alevis, Laz, and Circassians from being racialized and recognized in the international system as 'minorities' because they were made to constitute the demographic majority of the newly founded Turkish state. If they were divided on ethnic and sectarian terms similar to the non-Muslim, it would have been hard for the Turkish delegation to argue that it was a representative of the 'majority' on the territory that would become the republic of Turkey. The residual non-Muslim population in Turkey – the Armenians, the Roman-Orthodox, and the Jews – were consequently prevented from becoming full Turkish citizens because their sectarian affiliation rendered them non-Turks.[56]

Historically speaking, the exchange of populations was hardly unknown: unofficial transfers, that is, 'demographic warfare' partially resembling consensual exchange of populations, were, for instance, tacitly agreed between the Russian and Ottoman empires in the latter part of the eighteenth century.[57] Furthermore, it should be noted that between the early 1820s and 1922 about 5 million Muslims had been expelled from their lands: the present-day map of the Balkans and the southern Caucasus is composed of countries whose broad ethnic and religious homogeneity 'was accomplished through the expulsion of their Muslim population'.[58] Yet it was only with the Treaty of Lausanne that these concepts of 'population transfer' and 'ethnic cleansing' became, for the first time in history, an accepted and 'institutionalized' legal solution to international conflicts: a 'pattern' that was then replicated, *mutatis mutandis*, in Palestine (through the Peel Commission of 1937) and India/Pakistan (with the partition of 1947).[59]

More specifically, the Treaty of Lausanne sanctioned the simultaneous expulsion of about 1.3 million orthodox Christians (mainly from Asia Minor, eastern Thrace and Pontus), many of them Turkish speakers, from Turkey to Greece, and of around 400,000 Muslims, plenty of whom were Greek speakers, from Greece to Turkey.[60] Quoting the first article of the Convention, that in many ways borrowed from the British way of understanding the 'millet system': 'As from 1st May, 1923, there shall take place a compulsory exchange of Turkish nationals of the Greek Orthodox Religion established in Turkish territory, and of Greek nationals of the Moslem

Figure 6.2   Burnt buildings near the quay of İzmir/Smyrna, 1922.
(Source: American Colony Photo Dept photographers. G. Eric and Edith
Matson Photograph Collection, Library of Congress, Washington DC)

religion established in Greek territory'.[61] The atrocities that accompanied the expulsions, carried out by all parties involved,[62] played a major part in speeding up the processes of homogenisation. It is enough to mention that a city like İzmir – the ancient Greek city of Smyrna, where the Ottomans carried out expulsions as early as Spring 1913 – was populated by a large Greek Orthodox majority, composed of about 75,000 Greeks and 40,000 Muslim Turks in 1860.[63] Thirty years earlier (1830) – a few years before the massive immigration of Greeks arrived in Anatolia from the Aegean Islands during the favourable economic atmosphere offered by the Tanzimāt – there were about 20,000 Greek Orthodox in İzmir, out of a total of 100,000 dwellers.[64] Despite being the third most populous city in Turkey, today it only hosts a few hundred Greek Orthodox Christians (mainly of Turkish ethnicity). This aspect, as well as the permanent scars of the years preceding the First World War, mirrors a more general trend, particularly visible in Turkey. The country still hosts fewer Christians, as a percentage of its population, than any of its neighbouring states, including Syria, Iraq and Iran.

Notwithstanding the example provided by the microcosm of İzmir and other similar cases, a wealth of primary sources, many of them held at the Centre for Asia Minor Studies in Athens, shows a rich and long history of coexistence between different communities in most areas affected by expulsions and violence. This is confirmed, and was further strengthened, by people's joint participation in religious festivals and weddings, as well as by ancient daily practices. 'Turks and Greeks', noted Basilis Paulidis, an inhabitant of Kayseri (Cappadocia), referring to the period prior to the expulsions, 'used to go to the [natural spring] together to drink the water because they believed that it would help them to have children'.[65] In an interview of 1935 about the pre-First World War period, another inhabitant of the same area, Xr. Boridis, pointed out that 'the Turkish were respectful of the priests and the church'.[66] An anonymous interviewee added that 'if a Turk was sharing a coffee with you, he could never forget it. He would always be by your side, even if this means that he would dissatisfy his own people.'[67] Many interviewees of the time ascribed the changes in the situation among local communities to the Zeitgeist that preceded and followed 'the European war' (the First World War),[68] as well as to its most direct and practical repercussions.[69]

Another aspect that clearly stands out in many testimonies is that most violence witnessed in these areas during 'simultaneous expulsions' was done by outsiders (including Muslim refugees from the Balkans and the Kemalist army). As noted by Nicholas Doumanis, atrocities were, in fact, 'rarely carried out *between* communities', and so they should not be considered as 'communal violence'.[70] This is further confirmed by the fact that on a number of occasions members of local communities continued to support each other during the most acute phases of the crisis.[71]

Figure 6.3 A family in Erbil, early twentieth century. (Source: American Colony Photo Dept photographers. G. Eric and Edith Matson Photograph Collection, Library of Congress, Washington DC)

Figure 6.4 Typical tea stand in Iraq, on the railway to the ancient city of Ur, early twentieth century. (Source: American Colony Photo Dept photographers. G. Eric and Edith Matson Photograph Collection, Library of Congress, Washington DC)

Notes

1. N. Doumanis, *Before the Nation* (Oxford: Oxford University Press, 2013), p. 18.
2. TNA CAB 21/58, Ormsby-Gore to Maurice Hankey, 19 April 1918.
3. During the war years, a series of proposals was made in the United States, as well as in South Africa and England. In the latter, in December 1916, Robert Cecil – 'a sound friend of Zionism and an idealist to the end' (N. Rose, *Chaim Weizmann: A Biography* [New York: Penguin, 1989], p. 162) – proposed to create a special committee with the task of drafting a charter for an international league. The proposal, in the terms put forth by Cecil, was set aside a little over a year later, primarily due to the scepticism shown by Wilson.
4. J. C. Smuts, *Jan Christiaan Smuts: A Biography* (New York: Morrow, 1952), p. 201.

5. In the words of the US Secretary of State Robert Lansing (1864–1928): 'When the President [Wilson] talks of "self-determination" what unit has he in mind? Does he mean a race, a territorial area, or a community? Without a definite unit which is practical, application of this principle is dangerous to peace and stability'. R. Lansing, *The Peace Negotiation – A Personal Narrative* (New York: Houghton, 1921), p. 97.

6. Writing on this subject of the American Civil War years, Wilson noted that 'the white men of the South were aroused by the mere instinct of self-preservation to rid themselves [. . .] of the intolerable burden of governments sustained by the votes of ignorant negroes'. W. Wilson, *A History of the American People* (New York: Cosimo, 2008), vol. 5, p. 58.

7. Wilson to William M. Trotter (1872–1934). White House, 12 November 1914: 'Segregation is not humiliating but a benefit, and ought to be so regarded by you [colored] gentlemen'. In 'The Crisis', January 1915, Wilson, according to Melvin Steinfield, 'furnishes one more example of a President who has developed a reputation as a spokesman for freedom, yet who, in actual fact, was an overt racist': M. Steinfield, *Our Racist Presidents* (San Ramon CA: Consensus, 1972), p. 215.

8. J. C. Smuts, *Africa and Some World Problems: Including the Rhodes Memorial Lectures Delivered in Michaelmas Term* (Oxford: The Clarendon Press, 1930), p. 76.

9. Wilson in *Atlantic Monthly*, 87, January 1901, p. 6. According to Wilson 'an extraordinary and very perilous state of affairs had been created in the South by the sudden and absolute emancipation of the negroes'. In his opinion, such people represented 'a danger to themselves as well as to those whom they had once served'.

10. E. Foner, *The Story of American Freedom* (New York: Norton, 1999), p. 129.

11. TNA CO 733/346/10.

12. In *Japan Times*, article entitled 'Racial Discrimination to End', 31 January 1919.

13. On 14 March 1919, Japanese ambassador Ishii Kikujirō (1866–1945) attended a dinner at the Japan Society of New York. He lingered on Japan's humiliation connected to racial discriminations. His claims were received with hostility by various American senators. According to Burkman, Wilson's attitude 'cooled after they encountered such sentiment': T. W. Burkman, *Japan and the League of Nations* (Honolulu: University of Hawai'i Press, 2008), p. 84.

14. The British Embassy in Paris noted that 'at the conference American jewry will doubtless have a very big say in the settlement especially as President Wilson is

sympathetic to Zionist aims and Jews have so much influence in the politics of the USA': TNA FO 608/98, 16 January 1919.

15. Cit. in P. Reynaud, *Mémoires* (Paris: Flammarion, 1960), vol. 1, p. 456.

16. The 'Smuts Resolution', drafted by Smuts when he served as the British representative at the Paris Conference, was adopted by the ten delegates of the five victorious powers on 30 January 1919. Article 22 of the Charter of the League of Nations is written using most of the terms adopted by Smuts. The 'Smuts Resolution' mentioned the names of six areas – including Palestine – that were to be governed according to Article 22. In the latter, on the contrary, it was deemed opportune to omit them.

17. TNA FO 371/7776, Balfour, eighteenth session of the Council of the League of Nations, 17 May 1922.

18. 'The White Man's Burden' was the title of a poem composed by Rudyard Kipling (1865–1936) in 1899. Over time it became a sort of manifesto for colonialism in virtue of the attention it gave to the need to civilise countries outside the European tradition.

19. Matthews noted that 'the concept of the mandates preserved the notions of racial hierarchy that typified the belief and practice of the era of High Imperialism': W. C. Matthews, *Confronting an Empire, Constructing a Nation* (London: I. B. Tauris, 2006), p. 20.

20. Smuts clarified that the former German colonies in Africa 'are inhabited by barbarians, who not only cannot possibly govern themselves, but to whom it would be impracticable to apply any idea of political self-determination in the European sense': J. C. Smuts, *The League of Nations: A Practical Suggestion* (London: Hodder, 1918), p. 15.

21. M. Cherif Bassiouni and S. Ben-Ami, *A Guide to Documents on the Arab-Palestinian/Israeli Conflict: 1897–2008* (Leiden: Brill, 2009), p. 16.

22. More recently, Foliard echoed the same position, arguing that the Paris Conference 'witnessed a wide array of participants', that is, the presence of some 'Kurds, Zionists, or exiled Armenians': Foliard, *Dislocating the Orient*, p. 8.

23. According to Anglo-Zionist weekly organ *Palestine*, 'the natural representative of Palestine and Mesopotamia is Great Britain as the mandatory power': ACAC, Scrapbook of articles, 1922–6. Editorial published on 29 January 1921.

24. TNA FO 371/6379, unsigned report, produced by the British Foreign Office, dated 24 March 1921.

25. In a letter written to his father on 8 July 1921, Bell complained that 'making kings' was more difficult than he could have imagined. However, seven months earlier, on 10 January 1921, Bell pointed out that 'we keep two Divisons there

[in Palestine] in order to carry out our iniquitous policy of making it a home for the Jews. If they withdrew the two Divisions from Palestine we could keep them here [Iraq] for a couple of years where they're so urgently needed. But no; there's the Jewish interest to reckon with'. Bell's letters are available at: http://www.gerty.ncl.ac.uk/.

26. Clayton to the Foreign Office, 2 March 1919: 'It will take years of wise and impartial government to allay the fears which have been aroused and to prove to the non-Jewish population that the Zionists are not pursuing a policy entirely opposed to the principles so frequently enunciated by the Allied leaders': ISA 2/155/15A.

27. In July 1922, the latest of numerous Arab delegations from Palestine published in London a declaration 'à la nation britannique', in which was highlighted that '*la tendance de la présente administration de la Palestine est de "sioniser" le pays*': BOA HR.IM 60/47.

28. Cit. in Weizmann, Litvinoff (ed.), *The Essential Chaim Weizmann*, p. 209. Clayton, the British official who made the meeting between Fayṣal and Weizmann possible, noted that 'Fayṣal sees in Zionism a force which, if enlisted on his side, may furnish him with the necessary economic support [. . .]. As regards political support, he recognizes in Zionism an "international" influence which permeates every country from which the future Syrian State may have anything to hope or fear. Finally, behind Zionism and working through it, he reckons on the British Empire on which in the last resort he places his trust': cit. in M. Sicker, *Reshaping Palestine: From Muhammad Ali to the British Mandate, 1831–1922* (Westport CT: Praeger, 1999), p. 140.

29. A. L. Tibawi, *Anglo-Arab Relations and the Question of Palestine, 1914–1921* (London: Luzac, 1978), p. 339.

30. G. Antonius, *The Arab Awakening* (London: Hamilton, 1938), p. 439. George Antonious (1891–1942), a staunch supporter of pan-Arabism, was born into an Orthodox Christian family in today's Lebanon.

31. C. L. Wilson noted that Ḥusayn 'has been allowed to remain under the impression that certain of his interpretations are correct and the serious misunderstanding which has all along existed appears likely to reach a crisis shortly': Wilson a Milne Cheetham (1869–1938): TNA FO 603/97, 21 January 1919.

32. H. Grief, *The Legal Foundation and Borders of Israel under International Law* (Jerusalem: Mazo, 2008), p. 221.

33. The lack of interest shown by the Arab-Palestinians for the 'Great Revolt' of 1916 is one of the reasons why Lawrence did not view them favourably. This hostility makes it possible to understand why Lawrence found it acceptable that

'Weizmann hopes for a completely Jewish Palestine in fifty years, and a Jewish Palestine, under a British façade, for the moment': G. S. Symes, *Tour of Duty* (London: Collins, 1946), pp. 321–2. This sentence was dictated by Lawrence to Stewart Symes (1882–1962) in the middle of June 1918.

34. A. Ismāʿīl and I. Khūrī, *al-Siyāsah al-Duwalīyah fī al-Sharq al-ʿArabī min sanah 1789 ilā sanah 1958* [The International Politics in the Arab East from the Year 1789 to the Year 1958] (Beirut: Dār al-Nashr li-al-Siyāsah wa-al-Taʾrīkh, 1964), vol. 2, p. 28. The fact that a minority of Palestinians might recognise Fayṣal as their possible representative is due to reasons of pure political opportunism. The same which in February 1919 pushed the twenty-eight Palestinian delegates of the first 'Arab-Palestinian Congress' to define Palestine as an appendix of Syria. In March 1920, Samuel himself wrote to Curzon: 'I can see no sufficient reasons for recognizing Feisal King of Palestine. I doubt whether he or his supporters expect it': TNA FO 371/5034.

35. Fayṣal was afterwards (August 1921) crowned king of Iraq. It was a sort of 'compensation' bestowed on him by the British authorities. See 'A. al-Razzāq al-Hassanī, *Taʾrīkh al-Wizārāt 'al-ʿIrāqīya* [History of Iraqi Cabinets] (Baghdād: Wizārat al-thaqāfa, 1982), vol. 1.

36. Cit. in J. Kimche, *There Could Have Been Peace* (New York: Dial Press, 1973), p. 55. Clayton at that time was serving under Allenby as first 'political officer'.

37. According to Clayton, 'the Jerusalem Jew of today is certainly not an attractive personality'. By contrast, Clayton awaited the arrival of the Weizmann's delegation with trepidation, in that it would put the Arabs in 'contact with the really good class Jews': TNA FO 371/3398, Clayton, 27 February 1918.

38. R. Courtney, *Palestine Policeman* (London: Jenkins, 1939), p. 41. Courtney reserved similar insults also for the Jews present there.

39. Ibid.

40. Hankey to Balfour, 12 August 1918: 'If these regions are not to be under the control of the Turk, under whose control are they to be? [. . .] there is only one possible answer [. . .] they will come under British control': BLMC, Cecil Papers, Add. 51071.

41. E. Monroe, *Britain's Moment in the Middle East: 1914–1956* (London: Chatto, 1963), p. 66. Toynbee noted that Palestinian and Syrian Arabs were completely against 'the proposal for the imposition on them of "mandates"': A. J. Toynbee, *Acquaintances* (Oxford: Oxford University Press, 1967), p. 211.

42. Italy, in Sykes's words, 'seems to me of very little importance. A couple of Italian officers employed in some unimportant district or on some function or other

will not make any appreciable difference'. Sykes, Paris, 25 December 1917. LPL, DP, 400, ff. 73–6.

43. 'I cannot remember', remarked Balfour, 'meeting any single Italian during these last years [. . .] who seemed to me the least bit of good. [Sidney] Sonnino was perhaps the best, no doubt because he was largely Jewish': BLMC, Cecil Papers, Add. 51071.

44. Itagazi Yuko in J. Morikawa, *Japan and Africa* (London: Hurst, 1997), pp. 46–7.

45. The charter containing the conditions of the mandate for Palestine had first been drafted as a result of the joint efforts of the Zionist Organization and the Foreign Office: 'There was no participation or consultation with any Arab body or representatives, whether in Palestine or elsewhere': Grief, *The Legal*, p. 118. For this reason, as well, Curzon noted that 'it is quite clear that this mandate has been drawn up by someone reeling under the fumes of Zionism. If we were all to submit to that intoxication, this draft is all right': TNA FO 371/5199, Curzon, 20 March 1920.

46. Available at: http://unispal.un.org/UNISPAL.NSF/0/48A7E5584EE1403485 256CD8006C3FBE.

47. In regard to the Arab-Palestinian delegation, John Shuckburgh noted that 'hardly any of them understand English': TNA CO 733/15, Shuckburgh to James Masterton-Smith (1878–1938), 7 November 1921. In the same weeks, Shuckburgh noted with surprise that 'whatever agreement we reach in London with the Moslem Christian Delegation it will not be ratified by the people of Palestine unless it suits them to do so. [. . .] in perpetually asking the Zionists to go slow we are killing the Zionist idea': CZA Z4/42436.

48. The Palestinian delegation was able, following what Christopher Sykes (1907–86) defined as 'a long siege', to obtain an audience with Balfour: it was the first and only meeting they had with him. This is more surprising when one thinks that the Zionist Organization had had continuous contact with Balfour for years and enjoyed 'direct access to high political personages outside the Colonial Office': TNA CO 733/15, Shuckburgh to Masterton-Smith, 7 November 1921.

49. TNA FO 371/7776, Mūsā Kāẓim al-Ḥusaynī to Lloyd George. London, 13 May 1922.

50. Humphrey Bowman, head of the department of education in Mandatory Palestine, explained that the dangers 'of going too far in the matter of educational devolution can hardly be exaggerated. [. . .] In Europe the virtues of honesty, of truth, of straight and honourable dealing, of clean living, are taught in the

home as well as at school. In Palestine, as in most Oriental countries, the inculcation of such virtues is left by the parent for the most part to the teacher [. . .]. We shall be false to our trust if we allow ourselves to be persuaded by specious arguments to hand over the power of appointment and dismissal of the teaching staff – a power of paramount importance – to local bodies': ISA RG 2/135, memorandum signed by Bowman, 4 May 1925.

51. Eugene Rogan noted that 'there are no war memorials in the towns and cities of the Arab world. Though nearly every modern Arab state was drawn into the Great War in one way or another, the conflict is remembered as someone else's war – a time of suffering inflicted on the Arab people by the failing Ottoman Empire and its rash Young Turk leadership. In the Arab world, the Great War left martyrs (especially Arab activists hanged in central squares of Beirut and Damascus that were subsequently renamed "Martyrs' Square" in both cities) but no heroes': E. Rogan, *The Fall of the Ottomans: The Great War in the Middle East, 1914–1920* (New York: Basic Books, 2015), pp. xvi–xvii.

52. Several scholars are still today supporting these arguments. According to Law Professor Eugene Kontorovich, for instance, 'the legality of the Mandate jurisprudence cannot be changed'. See L. Kamel, 'On the Legitimacy of the Settlements: A Legal and Historical Perspective', *Opinio Juris*, 4 December 2015. Available at: http://opiniojuris.org/2015/12/04/on-the-legitimacy-of-the-settlements-a-legal-and-historical-perspective.

53. Maronite Christian scholar Ahmad Fāris al-Shadyāq (1805–87), born in present-day Lebanon and later on converted to Protestantisms, is a case in point. See A. F. al-Shadyāq, *al-Wāsitah fī maʿrifat ahwāl Māltah: wa kasaf al-mukhabbaʾ ʿan funūn Ūrubbā 1834–1857* [The Means to Know the Conditions of Malta and Uncover the Hidden about the Arts of Europe 1834–1857] (Abū Dhabi: Dār al-Suwaydī, 2004).

54. H. Al-Rustom, 'Rethinking the "Post-Ottoman": Anatolian Armenians as an Ethnographic Perspective', in Altorki (ed.), *A Companion*, p. 472.

55. Plenty of Turkish and Greek refugees accused their states of adopting a selective use of the Treaty. On 4 October 1925, for instance, Mahmed Khalis, a Turkish refugee who moved to Nicosia, wrote a petition in Turkish to the British Secretary of Foreign Affairs in London pointing out that the states that signed the Treaty of Lausanne 'care and execute only the parts of the treaty which they are interested in and they disregard the others': Cyprus State Archives (CSA) SA1 1205/22/619.

56. Ibid., pp. 467–8. On the topic see also D. Bloxham, *The Great Game of Genocide* (Oxford: Oxford University Press, 2005).

57. M. Pinson, 'Demographic Warfare – an Aspect of Ottoman and Russian Policy, 1854–1866', unpublished doctoral dissertation (Cambridge MA: Harvard University Press, 1970).

58. J. McCarthy, *Death and Exile: The Ethnic Cleansing of Ottoman Muslims 1821–1922* (Princeton NJ: Darwin Press, 1995), p. 1.

59. The Peel Commission, appointed in 1936 to investigate the causes of unrest in Mandatory Palestine, proposed to implement the ethno-religious homogenisation of the area through the forced transfer of about 225,000 Arab-Palestinians and 1,250 Jews. The partition of 'British India' in 1947 displaced between 10 and 12 million people along religious lines.

60. Refugees, including those trying to reach countries other than Greece or Turkey, were further discriminated on the base of their 'class' and citizenship. British High Commissioner in Nicosia C. D. Fenn pointed out that 'I can arrange to accommodate at the Quarantine Station at Larcana 1350 third class, 100 second class and 50 first class refugees': CSA SA1 1051/1922/5. On 4 October 1922, Allenby notified Fenn of not granting any visas to refugees from Asia Minor 'other than British, French, Italian, American and Egyptian subjects': CSA SA1 1051/1922/41. On 17 October 1922, the British Consul in Athens was informed that 'emergency passes for Cyprus should be issued only to refugees who can produce certificates of British nationality': CSA SA1 1051/1922/48.

61. Exempted from the transfer were Turks of Western Thrace and the Greek orthodox community in Istanbul and the Aegean islands of Imbros and Tenedos.

62. Michael M. Gunter contended that 'even though Lausanne dashed the Kurds' hope for independence for the rest of the twentieth century, it saved them from the ethnic cleansing that had been openly planned and partly implemented by the Armenians [Kurds played a central role in the massacres of Armenians that occurred during the First World War] in large portions of the Kurdish territories scheduled by the Treaty of Sevres for inclusion in an independent Armenia': M. M. Gunter, 'Kurds', in T. M. Leonard (ed.), *Encyclopedia of the Developing World* (London: Routledge, 2006), vol. 1, p. 923. It should be mentioned that in October 1918, Kurdish nationalist Şerif Pasha (1865–1951) warned London that the Turkish authorities were aiming at fostering clashes between Kurds and Armenians with the purpose of undermining their political ambitions: TNA FO 371/3384. On the crucial role of 'Turkish patriot' Ali İhsan Pasha (1882–1957)

in stirring up religious resentment among Kurds against Christian Armenians, as well as on details regarding the massive killings of Christians ordered by İhsan Pasha in Urmia in July 1918, see the reports written by Egidio Lari, apostolic delegate in Persia, in: ASV, Arch. Nunz. Iran, b. 9 fasc. 24 n. 14, f. 355.

63. As noted by Feryal Tansuğ, people with different professions and religious affiliation shared common districts in İzmir: the communities in the city lived in unity, rather than as separate units: F. Tansuğ, *İzmir/Smyrna 1826–1864* (Peter Lang: Berlin, 2018), p. 96.

64. Massive waves of migration were of course hardly a feature only of 'Orthodox Christianity': the *Hijrah* itself, through which the Prophet Muhammad and his followers moved from Mecca to Yathrib/Medina in 622, is just one powerful example of how much local peoples' movements have shaped the region throughout much of its history. Yet, the magnitude of the demographic movements registered in the second half of the nineteenth century had little if any precedent. Within twenty years, between 1875 and 1895, the Ottoman population grew, in fact, from 19.8 to 27.2 million people. As a consequence of this, noted Yücel Terzibaşoğlu, 'the proportion of Muslims to Christians increased considerably': Y. Terzibaşoğlu, 'Land Disputes and Ethno-politics: Northwestern Anatolia, 1877–1912', in S. L. Engerman and J. Metzer (eds), *Land Rights, Ethno-Nationality, and Sovereignty in History* (London: Routledge, 2004), p. 160.

65. CAMS, KP 93, p. 42. Paulidis lived in Kayseri until the age of twenty and then moved to Istanbul.

66. CAMS, KP 328B, p. 19. Interview with Xr. Boridis, registered in 1935.

67. CAMS, KP 328B, p. 17.

68. Local populations were often perceived as useful tools to balance the equilibrium among different religious or ethnic groups. Writing about the Greek troops sent to İzmir in 1919 (the city was initially assigned to Greece by the Treaty of Sèvres; the latter was replaced by the Treaty of Lausanne in 1923), Robert Vansittart, private secretary to the Foreign Secretary, wrote about the Greek forces in the following terms: 'We put them there as a policy of Mediterranean counterpoise': TNA 608/104, Vansittart, 9 June 1919.

69. CAMS, KP 350, p. 94. Ioanna Palaxtsis, Farasa (Cappadocia), undated.

70. Doumanis, *Before the Nation*, p. 162 (emphasis in original).

71. It is a pattern witnessesed in the different ways and forms in a number of other contexts in the region. It is, for instance, the case in Hebron, where Arabs and Jews – that in the diaries and autobiographies of Khalīl Sakānīnī and Wasif Jawharīyeh (1897–1972) were referred to as *abnā al-balad* ('Sons of the

nation'), or *Yahūd awlād 'Arab* ('Jews, sons of the Arabs') – had lived together for centuries without particular tensions and often speaking the same language (S. Tamarī and I. Nassar [eds], *Al Quds al 'Uthmānīyeh* [Ottoman Jerusalem] [Jerusalem: Institute for Jerusalem Studies, 2003], vol. 1, p. 20). Sixty-seven Jews from Hebron, including several students at the newly established (1925) Yéchivah Slobodka (its large number of Ashkenite students expressed the will to live in complete separation from the local Arab population as well as from the old *Yishuv*), were massacred by Arabs in 1929. Yet more than 450 Jewish lives were then saved thanks to local Arab families who gave them refuge.

7

Beyond 'Artificiality': Borders, States, Nations

Haughty as a Persian, tender as a Syrian / elegant as an Iraqi, eloquent as a Hijazi.[1]

Twelfth-century Syrian poet Ibn Munīr al-Ṭarābulsī
writing about his male beloved

Before nationalist doctrines were imported from Europe, 'patriotic' identities had already taken shape in many parts of the world.[2]

Jurgen Osterhammel

What is the 'Syria' for which the French received a mandate at San Remo?[3]

Lord Hardinge

Unlike medieval societies, characterised by a sum of particularisms, the era of the nation-states tended towards the homogenisation of diversities. What in modern Europe was often indicated as a 'nation' (from the latin *natus*, 'to be born') in fact presupposed a feeling of belonging to a defined community that differed, as a result of 'mutual contact' between distinct groups, at a linguistic, cultural and territorial level. It presumed, in other words, a cleavage between 'us' and 'them'.[4] This was echoed in the university system developed in medieval Italy, and later in the rest of Europe, where students were divided into *nationes* ('nations'), that is, communities separated according to homogeneous linguistic-geographical criteria.[5]

Any such 'border' was much more nuanced in the Eastern Mediterranean. As we have seen, religious affiliation, as well as having one's origin in a certain village, the *ḥamūla* of belonging and local customs were all factors that marked a certain distinction between the protonations present in the region. As Johann L. Burckhardt (1818–97) noted in 1822, 'it would be an interesting subject for an artist to portray accurately the different character of features of the Syrian nations [. . .] a slight acquaintance with them enables one to determine the native district of a Syrian, with almost as much certainty as an Englishman may be distinguished at first sight from an Italian or an inhabitant of the South of France'.[6]

And yet external dangers, which are very often the basis of the need of a people to define itself in a clear-cut way, were largely missing until the growing Western enchroachment on the region. Even in the European context, *mutatis mutandis*, it was, for instance, the anti-Napoleonic mass mobilisation that contributed to transform Russia into a nation that was no longer identifiable merely with the Tsar's rule. In Germany, in the year of the French Siege of Mainz (1793), Goethe (1749–1832) turned to the German *Volk* and no longer to the Holy Roman Empire.[7] The nation-state of the modern era should thus be considered as a phenomenon that had its origin and destination mainly, but of course not only, in 'the defence of the community from potential external aggression'.[8]

Until relatively recently, Iraqis and Syrians, just as two examples, were not in need of borders that would divide their *Heimat*. Nonetheless, this should not suggest that the various fluid local regional and religious identities lacked peculiar, if not 'protonational', characteristics, or that they and their respective states are simply 'Western artificial creations'. The history of the region is very much one of variegation, multiplicity and localisms: many of the modern states in the Middle East are rooted in peculiar historical legacies. This is not to downplay the processes of standardisation that have occurred in the region in modern times: indeed, the first section of this chapter focuses on some of its most long-lasting visual expressions. Yet the common attitude of overlooking or denying the inward dimension of these themes might result in new misrepresentations.

Maps' Spatial Agenda

The imposition of borders – 'blurred, imprecise, fuzzy'[9] – and the divide-and-rule policies carried out by European powers in the Eastern Mediterranean fomented sectarian tensions and triggered some of the most amenable conditions for the perpetual 'condition of colonisation' registered in the area following the First World War.[10]

Two set of maps have been especially influential in this process, and in crystallising the fragmentation of the region within the area encompassed by present-day Syria, Lebanon, Israel and the Palestinian territories.

The first is the 'Carte du Liban', a map produced in 1862 by the French Corps Expéditionnaire de Syrie, which arrived in Mount Lebanon in order to find a solution for the civil war between Maronites and Druzes: a bloody struggle that the European powers' strategies in the area helped to ignite.[11]

As had already happened six decades earlier in Egypt – when Napoleon involved a large number of cartographers and scholars in his expedition – in the 1860s, the French brought with them several renowned scholars. These were headed by Ernest Renan (1823–92), who surveyed the region and drew the first modern map of the area. This map stretched from Nahr el Kabīr in the North to a line in the South that runs from al-Nāqūra to the Lake Hula. It was reprinted twice during the First World War and, besides being used by Lebanese nationalists such as Henri Lammens (1862–1937), was brought by the Maronite patriarch Iliyas al-Huwayik (1843–1931) to the 1919 Paris Conference in order to persuade the French to accept the idea of 'le Grand Liban', which meant, in the patriarch's words, '*la restitution au Liban de ses limites naturelles et historiques, telles qu'elles ont été tracées par l'état-major français dans le carte de 1860*'.[12]

Following the Paris Conference, the French High Commission preferred to ignore a more detailed map of the area produced by the Ottomans in 1911, opting instead, once again, for the 'Carte du Liban'. In fact, it was the 1862 map that would be used during the Paulet–Newcombe Agreement, the Franco-British Boundary Agreements signed between Paris and London 1920–3 with the aim to determine the final tri-border area between Palestine, Syria and Lebanon, as well as the regional tri-border junction. The final lines drawn in February 1923 on the map produced by Ernest Renan sixty-one years earlier created tensions that, in many cases, still affect daily life in the region. In Asher Kaufman's words:

> According to this map [of 1923], the tri-border meeting place is in the village of Ghajar, whereas Jisr al-Ghajar, the ancient Roman bridge that was in fact the tri-border meeting point until 1967 and is still regarded as such according to international law, lies about 3 kilometers south of the tri-border point, inside Syrian territory. Indeed, the village of Ghajar itself is located within

Syrian territory because the wide borderline runs on the western or right bank of the Hasbani River. The 'bend' is clearly marked on the map but it is drawn some 5 kilometers north of the village of Ghajar along the Hasbani River. The map has been somewhat prophetic, given that since its foundation Lebanon has evolved into unstable political entity.[13]

Arif Dirlik argued that 'to define, as to name, is to conquer',[14] while James C. Scott emphasised that maps 'are designed to summarise precisely those aspects of a complex world that are of immediate interest to the map-maker and to ignore the rest'.[15] Thus, maps are rarely, if ever, neutral; they almost always express a particular spatial agenda: the 'Carte du Liban' represents the geo-body on which the regional spatial agenda was framed.

But perhaps more than from the 'Carte du Liban', the development of the regional 'spatial agenda' has been shaped by the maps produced by the Palestine Exploration Fund (PEF). When, in the second half of the 1860s, Charles William Wilson (1836–1905) and other members of the PEF arrived in Palestine to conduct the first modern archaeological and topographical investigations,[16] their purpose was to provide 'the most definite and solid aid obtainable for the elucidation of the most prominent of the material features of the Bible'.[17] More specifically, they were not interested in the sites connected to the New Testament but rather in those cited in the Old Testament. This choice was due to the fact that the places mentioned in the New Testament – more precisely, the ones discovered before that time – were already under direct control of the Orthodox Christians, as well as of the Catholics and other non-Protestant denominations. More importantly, these efforts were traceable to the desire to connect Anglican Protestantism to the ancient Israelites and thus to the concept of 'chosen people'. As had already happened thirteen centuries before with the Welsh cleric Gildas (c. 500–70),[18] the purpose was clear: to create a parallel to show that the ancient 'chosen people', the Israelites, had been replaced by the new 'chosen people' – in the present case, the English.[19]

Beside these aspects, what is particularly noteworthy in the frame of the current analysis is that the maps produced by the PEF were tools that in an initial period (1871–84), through the geo-theology of the PEF, interpreted the mythical past of Biblical Palestine to apply it to that present reality. Subsequently, beginning with the First World War and due to a selective cartographic choice of colours, dimensions and names, the PEF imposed a mental framework destined to shape the future of the region.

The PEF's insistence on identifying symbols in addition to well-defined borders, using for this a plethora of terms on their maps (such as the international boundary, village boundary, district boundary, subdistrict boundary, fiscal block boundary, municipal boundary, triangulation point boundary, quarter boundary, *qita'* boundary), did not respond to any of the needs of the local populations. The latter were mostly ignored,[20] which showed what Beshara Doumani defined as 'the amazing ability to discover the land without discovering the people'.[21]

Israeli antropologist Efrat Ben Ze'ev and other scholars went a step further in assessing the consequences of the PEF's maps, claiming that the fact that the PEF only mapped the area to the West of the Jordan river represented 'the first unintended step toward the emergence of separate entity in Western Palestine'.[22] For its local majority, and more generally for most of the Islamic believers, the awareness and the perception that *Filastīn*, described in many classical sources as *Al 'Ard al Muqaddasa* (the Holy Land),[23] was a special area and therefore distinct from Syria, Jordan and Lebanon, can be considered a 'first unintended step' that predated the actions of the PEF by many centuries.[24] It is undeniable, however, that maps such as the 'Carte du Liban' and those of the PEF played a crucial role in shaping the post-First World War Middle East. Those same maps were also used in 1917/18 during the conquest of Palestine by General Edmund Allenby (1861–1936) and his troops.[25]

Iraq, Syria and the Sykes–Picot Narrative

Maps, borders, toponyms: each of these topics played a significant role in the 'process of simplification' suffered not only, but particularly, by this region over the last few centuries. If not considered in depth, however, these claims can themselves trigger some simplistic assumptions.

'Gertrude of Arabia, the Woman who Invented Iraq'.[26] This, for instance, is the title of an article published in June 2014 by Clive Irving in the *Daily Beast*. It is one of a long series of journalistic and academic works in recent years that have linked the ongoing civil war in the country to the invention of an Iraqi nation at the hands of Gertrude Bell (1868–1926) and a small group of British adventurers. Similar analyses have recently also appeared in relation to Palestine, Syria and several other areas in the region. The impression that is often conveyed through such publications is that the West 'created artificial nations' and that the Islamic State (IS) is now trying,[27] as claimed by its leaders, to erase what British Secretary of State Lord Curzon once defined as 'the sinister shade of the Sykes–Picot agreement'.[28]

The modern states in the region were far from representing well-defined and uniform geographic, social, political or cultural entities. Yet, the cultural and political evolution of countries such as Iraq (possibly derived from Sumerian 'Uruk') and Syria (*al-Sham* ['the left'] in Arabic sources; Syria was coined by the Greeks from 'Assyria' in the sixth century BCE) shows a much more complex historical development than what the Sykes–Picot narrative would suggest.[29] Societal attitudes towards the state have developed through several stages.[30] In other words, and contrary to a common misunderstanding, Palestine, Iraq and Syria are not simply artificial creations and while it is necessary to reject any 'primordialist temptation' – or the existence of communities that have been defining themselves on a territorial basis for a long time – it is equally important to pay attention to the 'traces of awareness of territorial consciousness' and thus to avoid the danger that old maps could be used, once again, crudely to simplify a complex local reality.[31]

Scholars are increasingly focused on the thesis of the 'end of the Sykes–Picot order'. If this claim has any significance it is mainly because the Sykes–Picot system postponed the rise of a new order shaped from within the region. Rather than linking what is happening in the Middle East to the end of the Sykes–Picot order it would, therefore, be more accurate to refer to it as the final stage of a historical impasse that lasted for almost a century.

The main representatives of the 'Islamic State' (IS) – formerly 'Islamic State of Iraq and the Levant' (it was renamed in order to downplay the existence of regional divisions and differences) – have pointed out on several occasions that they aim to erase the Sykes–Picot divisions, and several Western media outlets seem largely to accept this narrative. In truth, by the end of the First World War, the Sykes–Picot Agreement was already a dead letter and virtually all the measures (including the internationalisation of Jerusalem) discussed in 1915–16 have not been implemented, or have not been relevant for many decades. Sykes–Picot, for instance, aimed to divide present-day

Figure 7.1   A pile of watermelons in the fruit market of Mosul, early twentieth century. (Source: American Colony Photo Dept photographers. G. Eric and Edith Matson Photograph Collection, Library of Congress, Washington DC)

Syria and Iraq into three or four states, while the San Remo conference of 1920 explicitly postponed the determination of any such borders. A closer look at the issue suggests that the IS approach and the Sykes–Picot order represent two faces of the same coin: both base/based their approaches on an ahistorical and falsely constructed vision of the past and both reflect their own interests more than the realities of the region.

Contrary to the IS narrative, modern-day Syria and Iraq both had several antecedents in the pre-Islamic world. Focusing, for instance, on the thesis of a 'divided and artificial Iraq', what nowadays would be referred to as a non-sectarian patriotism has more complex roots in the Iraqi context than is often claimed. For a long time, such feelings proved tendentially stronger and more rooted than sectarianism. A study conducted by a group of Iraqi intellectuals for a Norwegian think tank clarified this aspect, pointing out, for example, that the claim that Iraq is an artificial creation concocted by the British after the First World War overlooks the fact that 'the separation between the three Ottoman provinces that was in place in 1914 dated back only 30 years, to 1884'.[32] For much of the eighteenth and nineteenth centuries, those same three Ottoman provinces – Basra, Baghdād, Mosul – were governed as a single entity with Baghdād as their centre of gravity. Each of these (and other) areas were inhabited by people characterised by hybrid identities; for example, Mosulis, noted Maya Wahrman, 'were not simply Kurds, Assyrian and Chaldean Christians, Yazidis, Jews, Arabs or Turks'.[33] Yet since before the sixth century as well as in early Ottoman times, local intellectuals already referred to the area as 'al-'Irāq', a name possibly derived from the Sumerian city of *Uruk*. Expressions such as 'the region of Iraq' (*al-iqlīm-i al-'Irāq*) can be found in a plethora of sources, including in the writings of tenth-century Persian intellectual Abū Hayyān al-Tawhīdī (c. 930–1023) – who described Mosul as '*bāb al-'Irāq*' (the 'gate to Iraq')[34] – as well as in eighteenth-century Ottoman chronicles such as *Gulshan-i khulafa* (1730).[35] It is certainly true that a clear-cut border between the two countries was outlined only in 1918–20 – mainly as a result of the efforts made by a group of Iraqi officers enlisted in the Syrian army[36] – but the claim that 'the only person who ever really believed Iraq existed was Saddam Hussein'[37] is a common yet misleading simplification that implictly suggests the need to impose new borders based on sectarian lines. This option, increasingly brought up in the public debates that are taking place particularly in Europe and the USA, would represent another external imposition destined to trigger more violence.

In July 2014, Abū Bakr al-Baghdadī, the leader of IS, delivered his first speech from Mosul's Great Mosque of Nūr al-Dīn (1118–74), a prominent figure who fought against the Crusaders and established a brief kingdom in several areas encompassed within modern-day Iraq and Syria. This particular location was chosen to further strenghten one of the main messages of IS: 'This blessed advance will not stop', clarified al-Baghdadī, 'until we hit the last nail in the coffin of the Sykes–Picot conspiracy'.[38] In other words, the entire area, in the eyes of al-Baghdadī and his followers, represents a monolithic Islamic state in which spatial divisions are deprived of any legitimacy.

However, and despite the supposed unification of the Islamic world under the caliphs, for a large part if not most of their histories, Iraq and Syria have been ruled by distinct regimes. The Lakhmids (300–600) once ruled broad swathes of contemporary Iraq, while the sixth-century Ghassanid Kingdom was located in much of modern Syria. Under the Umayyad Caliphate (661–750), that had Damascus as capital, Iraq was a centre of dissent, and when in 750 the Abbassids succeeded to overthrow the Umayyads, they moved their capital from Damascus to the newly built Baghdād. In the centuries to follow, the two areas were often ruled separately, or through distinct administrative units. According to medieval sources, the approximate borders of Syria and Iraq 'overlap significantly with the modern ones'.[39] This means that IS's aim to 'erase Sykes–Picot' is largely 'rooted in fiction, not history'.[40]

What has been claimed up to now is not meant to suggest that the various local ethnic groups were in need of well-defined borders, nor does it intend to downplay London's historical role regarding the problems that are still affecting the region.[41] It aims instead to emphasise that the modern and contemporary Iraqi identity has been 'imagined' and 'constructed' just like any other identity in history, and that it is towards this complex and shared identity – often stronger than sectarian divisions – that a considerable majority of the population is looking (70 per cent, according to a survey conducted in 2008 by the Iraq Centre for Research and Strategic Studies).[42]

It is the very idea of an Iraq divided along sectarian or ethnic lines that appears problematic. The local reality, as the one in most of the rest of the region, is not characterised by homogeneous communities. Indeed, many ethnicities in Iraq have Sunni and Shi'a branches that exist parallel to sectarian identity, and can hardly be treated as unchangeable and rigid categories. This further contributes to explain the reason why intermarriage has been a common practice for centuries. Iraqi Prime Minister Abd al-Karīm Qāsim (1914–63), just to give a 'prominent' example, was the son of an Iraqi Sunni man of Arab descent and of a Shi'ite woman of Kurdish origin.

All these factors appear even more pertinent if considering that, with some analogies to the history of the last decade, only following three invasions from areas external to modern Iraq – the Safavids in 1508 and 1623, and the Wahhabi sack of Karbalā' in 1801 – did bloody sectarian clashes

Figure 7.2   People belonging to variety of religions, confessions and ethnic groups passing over Tigris River, on the Katah Bridge, Baghdād, early twentieth century. (Source: American Colony Photo Dept photographers. G. Eric and Edith Matson Photograph Collection, Library of Congress, Washington DC)

occur in 'the Mesopotamian context'. It is certainly true that in early medieval Baghdād some sectarian clashes occurred, but that, as noted by Fanar Haddād, 'is extremely different from what you have in the age of the nation state'.[43] Despite the relatively modern process of ethnicisation of religious identities and the ongoing attempts to impose univocal narratives – the memory of Erbil's multifaceted past, for instance, is today hardly evident – Baghdād still hosts about a million Kurds who have never suffered from ethnic or sectarian violence. Meanwhile, a large percentage of the population of Basra is Sunni. Samarra, a city with a Sunni majority, hosts two of the most important Shi'ite ruins. The provinces of Diyāla and Salah al-Dīn, not dissimilarly from the millenary Assyrian city of Kirkūk, the Niniveh Plain and a number of other areas, have for centuries been the image of a multifaceted Iraq in which the splitting of one or more of its component parts cannot but trigger more violence.[44] This might result, in the worst case but not unlikely scenario, in ethnic cleansing *à la* former Yugoslavia (in 1999), where the (mis)use of the principle of self-determination through the imposition of ethnic homogeneity resulted in genocide.[45] This is not a way of suggesting the necessity of framing Iraq's past and present in terms of a-sectarian nationalism but aims instead to highlight that specificities of time and place should be returned to their inclusive original dimension. The awareness of this – an antidote to the rise of IS, to the policies of former Prime Minister Nouri al-Maliki and the sectarian-based quotas introduced following the US invasion of 2003 – represents the cornerstone on which to start the process of reconstruction of the Iraqi nation.[46]

The Palestinian Context as a Case Study

Every country and every ethnic group has a different history, but the tendency to deny or downplay local identities and geographical specifities can also be detected in many other parts of the Eastern Mediterranean region. This is particularly true for the Palestinian context.[47]

Despite being firmly rooted in the history of the broader region, in some respects the Holy Land represents an *unicum* which eludes frames that are valid in other contexts. There is no other place in the world where the histories of a land and of its peoples have been instrumentalised to such an extent; William Blake (1757–1827), for instance, referred to Jerusalem as a 'lovely Emanation of Albion',[48] wondering if Britain was 'the primitive seat of the patriarchal religion'.[49] Nowhere has the merging of religion, imperialism, colonialism and Orientalism been more intense. Ultimately, it is difficult to find anywhere in the world where the emergence of an alternative and inclusive local history has been so suffocated.[50]

It is perhaps 'Biblical Orientalism' – a *sui generis* and under-researched variant of Orientalism, to which Edward Said (1935–2003) did not devote the attention one might have expected – that offers one of the most effective tools for shedding light on the peculiar way in which the process of 'simplification of the other' was applied in the specific Palestinian context.[51]

Biblical Orientalism can be defined as a phenomenon based on the combination of a selective use of religion (the Bible) and a simplistic approach to its natural habitat – the Holy Land. It acted on various levels, with lasting consequences. A plethora of books, private diaries and maps, in addition to later phenomena such as the 'evangelical tourism' inaugurated by Thomas Cook (1808–92), instilled in Britain and beyond what Meron Benvenisti defined as 'the imaginary perception of Palestine based on the Bible'.[52]

Often focused on the links between biblical events and the physical characteristics of Palestine, such ideas favoured the affirmation of a historical chronology that tended to focus almost exclusively on biblical times and the Crusades, largely ignoring millennia of pre-biblical history and centuries of Islamic domination. This contributed to fixing in the Western collective memory toponyms that have, in various forms, covered up the original 'non-biblical' geography, and spread the perception that the names used by the majority of locals to refer to the millenarian cities of the region were nothing but awkward attempts to distort – through 'Arabising' and 'bastardising' – the names of ancient Israelite settlements. Although largely unfounded, this way of thinking has had repercussions which are visible up to the present day.[53]

In the sixteenth century, maps produced by Dutch cartographer Abraham Ortelius (1527–98) instilled the idea of a 'meta-Palestine' devoid of any history except that of biblical glory.[54] It was, however, only in the second half of the nineteenth century that this approach found its ideal ground and was transformed into imperialist politics. It was then that both the 'shadowing' process, with regard to the local populations, and the impression that the major towns and cities in the region had their point zero in biblical times, gained their most influential formulations.[55]

Today, this complex past is very often downplayed or ignored, and the idea of both Palestine and Palestinians are presented as if they were, and in some cases still are, abstract concepts. Bernard Lewis, for instance, argued in his *From Babel to Dragomans* that 'the word Palestine survived briefly in the early Arab Empire and then disappeared'.[56] Israeli tourism minister Uzi Landau recently asserted that Palestinians 'never existed as a nation [but] suddenly everyone talks about a state'.[57] In a recent paper published by the Jerusalem Center for Public Affairs (JCPA), anthropologist Gideon M. Kressel and historian Reuven Aharoni contend that 'a significant portion of the Palestinian Arabs came from Egypt',[58] while archaeologist Randall Price argues that 'there was no national "Palestine" nor were there "Palestinians" who had a distinct identity or private ownership of "Palestinian" land'.[59] The impression conveyed by this and other similar claims is that the West created artificial nations in the Middle East. This once again brings our minds back to the solipsistic attitudes that were common in the post-First World War days, when Mark Sykes pointed out that 'there is one Palestine for the Jews, that is the home of the Jewish nation. But there is a Palestine for the Armenians, it is Armenia. There is a Palestine for the Arabians, it is Arabia.'[60]

Palestinian poet Mahmud Darwīsh (1941–2008) used seven words to indirectly clarify most of the 'misunderstandings' mentioned up to this point. 'Who are they?', he asked in his *Une rime pour les Mu'allaqat*, in regard to the local populations under Ottoman rule: 'That's someone else's problem'.[61] In many respects, this was indeed a problem of 'others', of people external to the region. What made the difference for the 'insiders' was linked to more 'local' concerns and habits, including a way of dressing, a religious festival, or a dance (*dabkeh*).[62] For instance, the annual Nabi Musa festival,

Figure 7.3   Open court of the Nebi Mousa's shrine, 1918. (Source: Visual materials from the papers of John D. Whiting Library of Congress, Washington DC)

which gathered thousands of people, primarily from areas in present-day Israel and the Palestinian territories was the expression of a clearly emerging 'proto-national cohesion'.[63]

Before the imposition of the nationalist ideologies and the emergence of exclusivist approaches, it was these factors, not primarily political identity, that defined 'Palestinianness'.[64] Among the local majority, different senses of identity (connected to religious, local, transnational and family allegiances) coexisted, without any contradiction between them.[65] They were identities both distinguishable and overlapping. As Barnett and Telhami remark, one of the ways in which the entire region differs from others 'is that the national identity has had a transnational character'.[66]

This transnational character and the overlapping identities found in the region were not at odds with a strong attachment to the land. Elizabeth Finn (1825–1921), wife of the second British consul in Jerusalem, witnessed that the local *fellahin* were attached to their land 'with the tenacity of aboriginal inhabitants'.[67] Most of the Arab-Palestinians that a number of scholars still define as 'foreigners', or 'former invaders', were thus people deeply rooted in the land described by Jerusalemite geographer al-Muqaddasī (946–1000)[68] – who perceived himself as a 'Palestinian'[69] – and in what Khayr al-Dīn al-Ramlī (1585–1671), an influential Islamic lawyer from Ramla, defined in the seventeenth century as '*Filastīn biladuna*' ('Palestine our country').[70] This is not a way to suggest that a fully defined territorial identity existed – there was no need of this at the time – but the fact that it was not a separate political and administrative entity did not make al-Ramlī's '*Filastīn*' less real.

As for most of those who had origins in other areas, they lived in the context of a borderless region. In the JCPA paper mentioned above, Kressel and Aharoni clarify that on the southern coastal plain, in Wadi ‘Ara, Palestinian families 'called Tantawi (or Tamtawi) hailed from the area of the city of Tanta in the Nile Delta'.[71] Similar claims can be made for other family names such as Masrī, Dumyātī, Sa‘īdī and Jabalī. However, such evidence has little meaning if evaluated outside of its regional context. In Damascus, as well as in several other cities in the region, it is still possible to encounter plenty of local families with names that show clear links to areas in present-day Israel and the Palestinian territories. This further proves that considering the movements within the broader region as migratory processes among reciprocally 'foreign' populations is a simplistic way to define a situation that was far more complex. The Palestinian context, in other words, was/is an integral part of the Arab world without this erasing its peculiarities. In 'Ādil Mannā's words:

> A Palestinian who moved to south Lebanon or a Lebanese who moved to Palestine – or a Syrian or a Jordanian, for that matter – is surely not a foreigner because he is part of the culture of the society of Bilad-al-Sham, or Greater Syria, where there were no borders between countries. [. . .] It was common and natural for a Palestinian to go study in Al Azhar for instance, and remain there; or for a Hebronite merchant to go to Cairo and live there; or go to Damascus or other places, whether to study or to live [. . .] This was a natural phenomenon.[72]

Breaking the Standardisation Process: Getting *Back* into History

Following a complex process, in these last few years, large sectors of Palestinian society have demonstrated a willingness to reappraise and regain possession of their shared past, as well as a readiness to concretise what Michael Ignatieff would have defined their 'desire to master time's losses'.[73] The ongoing process that since the beginning of this century has been leading to the creation of the first Palestinian archive and to the development of techniques and methods for analysing oral history can be seen as an attempt by the Palestinians themselves to break the vicious circle triggered by the 'process of standardisation', bringing their own experiences back into a history written from 'below' by means of their voices and life experiences.[74] As argued by Beshara Doumani, this process is far from being circumscribed by the Palestinian context:

> Archive fever is spreading among Palestinians everywhere. Whether in Ramallah or London, Haifa or San Francisco, Beirut or Riyad, someone or some group is busy interviewing old people and compiling genealogies, searching for photographs and letters, collecting textiles and folksongs, visiting and renovating graveyards, scanning and repairing manuscripts, and compiling information on old houses and destroyed villages, and this is but the tip of an iceberg whose full dimensions can hardly be imagined.[75]

Today we are witnessing the convergent efforts that broad sections of Palestinian society, as well as other populations in the region, are making so that it will not be the case that only 'external archives' (British, Israeli, Turkish, Russian and American, as well as those of the United Nations) or the political agendas of Arab countries are in a position to speak or act on their behalf.[76] Furthermore, they are working towards a scenario where it will no longer only be museums such as the Palestine Archaeology Museum (today the Rockefeller Museum) – one of the main archaeological museums from colonial times – or archaeological excavations that are almost always conducted by Western and/ or Israeli researchers that are able to explain the history of their land.[77]

In line with these considerations, Rāmī Ḥamdallāh, serving at the time of interview as rector at al-Najāḥ University in Nāblus, underlined that in certain contexts such as Palestine, education, archives and libraries are 'the basis of everything. They are the instruments of survival'.[78] The director of the Department of Antiquities and Cultural Heritage (DACH) of the Palestinian National Authority (PNA), Ḥamdān Ṭāhā,[79] who has taken part in several excavations in the Nāblus area, explained that archaeology gives Palestinians 'the opportunity to participate in writing or rewriting the history of Palestine from its primary sources'.[80] Nazmi Jubeh, director of the History and Archaeology Department at Birzeit University, stated that 'the creation, maintenance and accessibility of archives are meaningful aspects in the struggle for self-determination'.[81] Mustafā Barghūti, leader of al-Mubādara ('The Initiative') party, complained that many people outside the Palestinian territories believe that his people are 'incapable of taking their own past and future into their own hands, that is unable to establish state institutions, archives and research centres worthy of the name, or of appreciating full democracy'.[82] 'Adlī Ya'īsh, mayor of Nāblus since 2005, argued that 'there will be no hypothetical reconciliation between us and the Israelis as long as it is exclusively the "others" who speak of our present and our past'.[83] Commenting on the imminent establishment of a national library, Palestinian Minister of Culture Ehāb Bseīso contended that 'we want the national Palestinian library to be our link to national libraries around the world. We want to restitute our looted heritage [by retrieving Palestinian documents from elsewhere] through agreements that protect cultural heritage and traditions and laws defending our cultural existence'.[84] These excerpts, mainly part of a survey conducted by the author in Israel and Palestine, confirm the existence of a common drive – and a related growing effort by the Palestinian authorities to gain control of the 'archive fever'[85] – to focus on these issues. Such ideas were also analysed at an unprecedented international conference, of 24–5 March 2014, at Birzeit University. During the conference, entitled 'Globalizing Palestine: Birzeit University's Archive in an International Perspective – Towards a Chaotic Order', several presentations shed light on the process of getting *back* into history that Palestinian society in particular, and much of the broader region in general, is currently experiencing.

All this calls to mind Hamid Dabashi's words regarding the fact that the 'post-colonial did not overcome the colonial; it exacerbated it by negation'.[86] This statement fits very well the history of large parts of the Middle East, as viewed from the present moment. Each of the peoples in the region is in fact struggling to break the vicious circle triggered by the double 'process of simplification' imposed on them by Sykes–Picot and the orders and narratives propounded by IS. They seek their own particular ways to get *back* into history, sustaining shared notions of belonging and rediscovering the permeabilities and specificities that, for millennia, characterised daily life in the Middle East.

Notes

1. Cit. in E. Muhanna, 'Iraq and Syria's Poetic Borders', *New Yorker*, 13 August 2014. Available at: http://www.newyorker.com/books/page-turner/iraq-syria-poetic-imagination.
2. Osterhammel, *The Transformation of the World*, p. xix.
3. TNA FO 371/5245, Permanent undersecretary at the Foreign Office Charles Hardinge, 27 July 1920.
4. Said argued that 'the development and conservation of every culture requires the existence of an *alter ego* different and in competition with it. The construction of identity [. . .] implies the construction of opposites and of "others", whose present is always subject to continuous interpretation and reinterpretation of that which differentiates them from us': E. Said, *Orientalism* (New York: Vintage, 1994), pp. 331–2.
5. Italy hosts about half of the world's twenty oldest universities. The first woman in the world to graduate from a university was Italian (Padua, 1678). At the University of Bologna, the oldest university in Europe, students were divided according to two *nationes*: *intramontani* (from 'this side of the

Alps', meaning from Italy) and *ultramontani* (from 'the other side'), that is people coming from France, Germany, Spain and other external areas. On the 'nationalisation of economics' witnessed roughly in the same historical period, particularly within the context of the French and British empires, see C. Zwierlein, *Imperial Unknowns* (Cambridge: Cambridge University Press, 2016), p. 20.

6. J. L. Burckhardt, *Travels in Syria and the Holy Land* (London: John Murray, 1822), pp. 340–1.

7. See C. Bayly, *The Birth of the Modern World, 1780–1914* (Oxford: Blackwell, 2004).

8. D. Archibugi and F. Voltaggio, *Filosofi per la pace* [Philosophers for Peace] (Rome: Editori Riuniti, 1999), p. xvi.

9. S. Ferabolli, *Arab Regionalism* (London: Routledge, 2015), p. 60.

10. Tamim al-Barghūti noted that when the colonial powers were strained during the two world wars, 'their Middle Eastern colonies got their formal independence and, because of the way they were structured and the elites that governed them, continued to behave as colonies': Al-Barghūti, *The Umma*, p. 4.

11. C. Hakim, *The Origins of the Lebanese National Idea, 1840–1920* (Berkeley: University of California Press, 2013), p. 8.

12. Cit. in K. Firro, *Inventing Lebanon: Nationalism and the State Under the Mandate* (London: I. B. Tauris, 2003), p. 18.

13. A. Kaufman, *Contested Frontiers in the Syria-Lebanon-Israel Region: Cartography, Sovereignty, and Conflict* (Washington DC: Woodrow Wilson Center Press, 2014), p. 27.

14. A. Dilrik, *What Is in a Rim?: Critical Perspectives on the Pacific Region Idea* (Lanham MD: Rowman, 1998), p. 5.

15. J. C. Scott, *Seeing Like a State* (New Haven CT: Yale University Press, 1998), p. 87.

16. On 25 September 1865, the president of the PEF (E. Ebor) asked to Secretary of State for War, Marquis of Ripon (1827–1909), for permission to give Wilson the task of investigating 'the Holy Land in a more accurate and systematic manner than has yet been done': The National Archive (TNA) OS (Ordnance Survey) 1/17/1. The year before (1864), Wilson was in Jerusalem working on a project to improve the water system of the city. He took this opportunity to produce some remarkable maps. Regarding Muslims in Jerusalem, Wilson wrote that they 'belong for the most part to the same race as the peasantry of Palestine, representatives it may be, though with a large

intermixture of foreign blood, of the Jebusite that dwelt in the land': Charles W. Wilson, *Picturesque Palestine, Sinai, and Egypt* (New York: Appleton, 1881), p. 118.

17. *Quarterly Statement of the Palestine Exploration Fund* (London: Palestine Exploration Fund, 1871), p. 3.

18. *De Excidio et Conquestu Britanniae* is the title of the most ancient surviving manuscript written by a British author. It is about the story of Albion and was composed around 564 CE by the forty-four-year-old Welsh cleric, Gildas. Although it did not host any Jewish communities at the time, Great Britain is referred to as 'the new Israel' and the battles of this 'holy nation' (*goy kadosh*: Exodus 19:6) against 'barbarian invaders' are compared to the battles of ancient Israel against Babylonians and Philistines: BLMC, HP, MS, 522, *Gildas' Chronicle 1525*, p. 76. Two centuries later, in 731, the Venerable Bede (c. 672–735) wrote the *Historia ecclesiastica gentis Anglorum*. Here some themes in Gildas's work were repeated, such as the perception of being 'God's chosen people' and 'the new Israel'. See Bede, *The Ecclesiastical History of the English Nation* (New York: Cosimo, 2007 [1474]).

19. See L. J. Moscrop, *Measuring Jerusalem: The Palestine Exploration Fund and British Interests in the Holy Land* (New York: Leicester University Press, 2000), p. 2.

20. To a large extent, this applies also to the approach adopted by Theodor Herzl and other later Zionist leaders towards the Arabs of Palestine. Already at the end of nineteenth century, the latter were largely ignored in the correspondence between the founder of political Zionism and the Ottoman authorities. Herzl unsuccessfully made potential economic assistance conditional on two prerogatives: Ottoman recognition of Jews' right to settle in Palestine and the chance to buy unlimited quantities of land: BOA Y.PRK.TöF 6/72, report produced by the Ottoman authorities in 1902. Herzl met the sultan five times in Istanbul between 1896 and 1902. He proposed to the Ottoman authorities to supply capital to save the Empire from the interference of European powers: 'We wish', wrote Herzl to Izzedin Pasha in 1899, 'to bind our futures to your future': BOA Y.HRK.HR 27/30.

21. B. Doumani, 'Rediscovering Ottoman Palestine: Writing Palestinians into History', *Journal of Palestine Studies* 21(2) (1992): 8.

22. E. Ben Ze'ev, *Remembering Palestine in 1948* (New York: Cambridge University Press, 2011), p. 29. Rogan noted that 'the modern state was introduced in Transjordan by the Ottomans in the nineteenth century, not the British or

Hashemites after the First World War [. . .] it was a state which was marked by strong continuities from its recent Ottoman past': E. Rogan, *Frontiers of the State in the Late Ottoman Empire: Transjordan, 1850–1921* (Cambridge: Cambridge University Press, 1999), pp. 1 and 241.

23. See for instance the *tafsir* (exegesis) of the Qur'an written by Tabari (838–923): Tabari (2001) *Jami' al-Bayan 'an Ta'wil al-Quran* [The Clear Collection Regarding the Interpretation of the Qur'an], 15 vols (Beirut: ed. Sidqi Jamil al-'Attar, 2001 [883]). For a later source see M. Al-Dīn, *Al-Uns al-Jalil bi-Tarikh al-Quds wa al-Khalīl* [The Glorious History of Jerusalem and Hebron] Najaf, al-Haydariya, 1968 [1595], vol. 1, pp. 65, 66, 71, 94, 101. The subject is dealt with also in Fahim Gabr, *Al-Ard al-Muqaddasa* [The Holy Land] (Nablus: Al-Najah University, 1983).

24. An Islamic text from the eighth century, attributed to the medieval scholar Abu Khalid Thawr Ibn Yazīd al-Kala'i (764–854), argued that 'the holiest place [*al-quds*] on Earth is Syria; the holiest place in Syria is Palestine; the holiest place in Palestine is Jerusalem [*Bayt al-maqdis*]': cited in J. Van Ess, *Abd al-Malik and the Dome of the Rock: An Analysis of Some Texts*, in J. Raby and J. Johns (eds), *Bayt Al-Maqdis* (Oxford: Oxford University Press, 1992), vol. 1, pp. 89–90. Detailed references to Palestine, not necessarily of a strictly religious nature, can be found in the *Kitab al-Buldan* (Book of Countries) by the Shi'i historian al-Ya'qubi (?–897) and in *Kitab al-masalik wa al-mamalik* (The Book of the Routes and Realms) by the Persian geographer al-Iṣṭakhrī (?–957). 'Filastīn', al-Istakhri wrote, 'is the most fertile among the Syrian provinces [. . .] In the province of Filastīn, despite its narrowness, there are around twenty Mosques [. . .] At its maximum extension [Filastīn goes] from Rafh [Rafah] to the edge of al-Lajjun [Legio], a traveler would need two days to travel across its entire length; and [this is also] the time [necessary] to cross the province across its breadth from Yafa [Jaffa] to Riha [Jericho]': cit. in and trans. by Guy Le Strange, *Palestine under the Moslems: A Description of Syria and the Holy Land from A.D. 650 to 1500* (London: Watt, 1890), p. 28.

25. During his campaign, Allenby relied on a number of maps and sources, including the intelligence provided by Nili, a Jewish spying organisation which assisted London in Ottoman Palestine during the First World War. See E. Linveh, *Nili: Toldoteha shel He'azah Medinit* [Nili: The History of a Political Daring] (Jerusalem: Shoken, 1961). The PEF's maps, despite having been produced several years earlier, nonetheless had a significant practical role in supporting British efforts.

26. C. Irving, 'Gertrude of Arabia, the Woman Who Invented Iraq', *Daily Beast*, 17 June 2014. Available at: http://www.thedailybeast.com/articles/2014/06/17/gertrude-of-arabia-the-woman-who-invented-iraq.html

27. M. Polner, T. E. Woods, *We Who Dared to Say No to War: American Antiwar Writing from 1812 to Now* (New York: Basic Books, 2008), p. 118.

28. TNA FO 371/5034, Lord Curzon, 30 March 1920.

29. See on this also S. Pursley, 'Lines Drawn on an Empty Map: Iraq's Borders and the Legend of the Artificial State', *Jadaliyya*, 2 June 2015. Available at: http://www.jadaliyya.com/pages/index/21759/lines-drawn-on-an-empty-map_iraq's-borders-and-the.

30. T. Dodge, 'Can Iraq Be Saved?', *Survival: Global Politics and Strategy* 56(5) (2014): 10.

31. H. Gerber, '"Palestine" and Other Territorial Concepts in the 17th Century', *International Journal of Middle East Studies* 30(4) (1998): 563.

32. See 'More than "Shiites" and "Sunnis" – How a Post-Sectarian Strategy Can Change the Logic and Facilitate Sustainable Political Reform in Iraq', in *Norwegian Institute of International Affairs Report*, February 2009. Available at: http://english.nupi.no/content/download/8891/91333/file/Iraq%20Report%20%284%29.pdf.

33. M. Wahrman, 'Blame the West for ISIS? Yes – but Go Back to 1925', in *Ha'aretz*, 5 September 2016. Available at: http://www.haaretz.com/misc/haaretzcomsmartphoneapp/.premium-1.740350. On the fallacious approach adopted by the British authorities to conduct surveys and plebiscites in Mosul after the First World War, see F. Dundar, '"Statisquo". British Use of Statistics in the Iraqi Kurdish Question (1912–1939)', *Crown Paper 7* (Boston MA: Brandeis University's Crown Center for Middle East Studies, 2012), pp. 1–67. Dundar noted that 'population statistics are inseparable from their political context [. . .] Christians, while constituting only eight percent of Mosul according to British 1921 statistics, accounted for seventy-three percent of the plebiscite results – whereas a plebiscite intended to ascertain a given population's desire for self-determination should surely have reflected its correct ethnic and religious make-up' (p. 16).

34. See A. H. Al-Tawhīdī, *Al-Imtā' wa al-Mu'ānasa* [Enjoyment and Conviviality], A. Amīn and A. al-Zayn (eds) (Beirut: Dār al-Arqam, 1953), vol. 1, p. 86. Al-Tawhīdī's perceptions were also echoed in the writings of twelfth-century Arab geographer Yāqūt al-Hamawī (1179–1229).

35. See R. Visser, 'Historical Myths of a Divided Iraq', *Survival* 50(2) (2008): 103.

36. Q. A. Al-Tala'farī, *Thawrat Tall 'Afar 1920* [Telfar's Revolution in 1920] (Baghdād: Matba'at al-Azhar, 1969), p. 418.

37. P. J. Rich, *Iraq and Gertrude Bell's The Arab of Mesopotamia* (Lanham MD: Lexington Books, 2008), p. xxix.

38. A. B. Al-Baghdadī, *Great Mosque of Nūr al-Dīn*, 5 July 2014. Video available at: https://www.youtube.com/watch?v=q1uLIcCwsn0#t=1m7s.

39. E. Muhanna, 'Iraq and Syria's Poetic Borders', *New Yorker*, 13 August 2014. Available at: http://www.newyorker.com/books/page-turner/iraq-syria-poetic-imagination.

40. J. T. Gordon, 'ISIS' Desire to Erase Sykes-Picot Is Rooted in Fiction, Not History', *National Interest*, 17 September 2014. Available at: http://nationalinterest.org/feature/isis'-desire-erase-sykes-picot-rooted-fiction-not-history-11293.

41. It is enough to mention that Fayṣal, chosen as king of Iraq by the British authorities in August 1921, never set foot in Mesopotamia before that moment, and spoke a different dialect than the local Arabs. It is true that some of the most persistent advocates of Fayṣal's kingship were the Shi'i tribes of the mid-Euphrates region who were in full-scale rebellion in 1920, but the fact remains that a 'large proportion' of Fayṣal's subjects 'did not recognize his authority' and that the new king politicised 'sectarianism to obfuscate the state's failures': Z. Al-Ali, *The Struggle for Iraq's Future* (New Haven CT: Yale University Press, 2014), pp. 19–21.

42. In 1939, Richard Hartshorne (1899–1992) argued that 'any attempt to divide the world involves subjective judgement, not in the determination of the limit of individual factors, but in deciding which of several factors is to be regarded as most important': R. Hartshorne, *The Nature of Geography*, pp. 296–7.

43. F. Haddād, *Sectarianism in Iraq: Antagonist Visions of Unity* (Oxford: Oxford University Press, 2011).

44. According to the Iraqi census of 1957 – meaning two decades before the Ba'athist Arabisation campaigns promoted by Saddām Ḥussein (1937–2006) in North Iraq – the city of Kirkūk, that stands on the site of the ancient Assyrian capital of Arrapha, was inhabited by 37 per cent Iraqi Turkmen, 33 per cent Kurds, with Assyrians and Arabs making up less than 23 per cent of its population.

45. 'The Real Roots of Iraq's Sunni–Shia Conflict', *Vox*, 20 June 2014. Available at: http://www.vox.com/2014/6/20/5827046/who-are-sunnis-who-are-shias.

46. L. Kamel, 'Despite the Popular Narrative, Iraq is not Simply an Artificial Creation', *The National*, 12 October 2014. Available at: http://www.thenational.ae/opinion/despite-the-popular-narrative-iraq-is-not-simply-an-artificial-creation.

47. This section is partially derived from L. Kamel, *Imperial Perceptions of Palestine: British Influence and Power in Late Ottoman Times* (London: I. B. Tauris, 2015). For one of the most recent attempts to downplay any source showing local awareness see Z. Foster, 'The Invention of Palestine', PhD thesis (Department of Near Eastern Studies, Princeton University, November 2017).

48. W. Blake, *Jerusalem: The Emanation of Giant Albion* (London: Blake, 1804), p. 146.

49. Ibid., p. 171.

50. L. Kamel, 'The Impact of "Biblical Orientalism" in Late 19th and Early 20th Century Palestine', *New Middle Eastern Studies* 4 (2014): 1–15.

51. As noted by Bar-Yosef, the 'Holy Land is rather marginalized in Orientalism [. . .] [Edward] Said very rarely stops to think about the distinct nature of Western interests in the Holy Land, which might distinguish it from other Orientalist encounters': E. Bar-Yosef, *The Holy Land in English Culture, 1799–1917* (Oxford: Oxford University Press, 2005), p. 6.

52. M. Benvenisti in a roundtable transcribed in Scham, Salem and Pogrund (eds), *Shared Histories*, p. 85.

53. O'Connor clarified that 'the wedge script records an inventory of sounds that is closer to that found in Classical Arabic (ca. 28 sounds) than to that found in Biblical Hebrew (ca. 22 sounds)': M. O'Connor, 'Epigraphic Semitic Scripts', in P. Daniels and W. Bright (eds), *The World's Writing System* (Oxford: Oxford University Press, 1996), p. 92.

54. Plenty of works exist on Ortelius's maps and his approach. See, for instance, Judy Hayden and Nabil Matar (eds), *Through the Eyes of the Beholder: The Holy Land, 1517–1713* (Leiden: Brill, 2013).

55. The local inhabitants – Arab-Palestinian majority, Jewish minority and other sections of the population – were often portrayed as a simple appendix to the ancient biblical scenery. 'Every object', commented London painter William Henry Bartlett (1809–54) about the Jaffa area, 'is novel and Oriental in character, and independent of its picturesque beauty, is linked by a delicious association with our earliest dreams of Biblical scenery and incident': William Henry Bartlett, *Walks about the City and Environs of Jerusalem* (London: Virtue, 1844), p. 9.

56. B. Lewis, *From Babel to Dragomans* (London: Phoenix, 2005), p. 191. Assaf Likhovski noted that prior to 1917 Palestine 'was merely a geographical term':

A. Likhovski, *Law and Identity in Mandate Palestine* (Chapel Hill: University of North Carolina Press, 2006), p. 10.

57. M. Mualem, 'Israeli Minister: "A Palestinian State Is not the Solution"', *al-Monitor*, 29 May 2013. Available at: http://www.al-monitor.com/pulse/originals/2013/05/israeli-minister-two-states-for-two-people-will-not-bring-p.html.

58. G. M. Kressel and R. Aharoni, *Egyptian Émigrés in the Levant of the 19th and 20th Centuries* (Jerusalem: Jerusalem Center for Public Affairs, 2013), p. 3. Available at: http://jcpa.org/wp-content/uploads/2013/03/Egypt2.pdf.

59. R. Price, *Fast Facts on the Middle East Conflict* (Eugene OR: Harvest, 2003), p. 23.

60. Cit. in M. Nisan, *Minorities in the Middle East: A History of Struggle and Self-Expression* (Jefferson NC: McFarland, 2002), p. 7.

61. M. Darwīsh (transl. by E. Sanbar), *La terre nous est étroite et autres poèmes* [The earth is close to us and other poems], 1966–99 (Paris: Gallimard, 2000).

62. In late Ottoman Palestine, *Dabkeh* and other characteristic dances were more than simple celebrations. They also represented a genuine expression of a 'collectivization of trauma': N. Rowe, *Raising Dust: A Cultural History of Dance in Palestine* (London: I. B. Tauris, 2010), p. 53. George Ibrahim, director of the Al-Kasaba theatre in Ramallah, believes that dancing and acting are also and above all useful tools to express the 'collective malaise of a nation': George Ibrahim, interview with the author. Ramallah, 13 February 2010.

63. The Nabi Musa festival was designed to commemorate the traumatic events related to the Crusades. See K. al-Asali, *Mawsim al-Nabi Musa fi Filastin: Tarikh al-Mawsim wa 'l-Maqam* [The Nabi Musa Festival in Palestine: the History of the Festival and of the Shrine] ('Amman: Dar al-Karmil, 1990), and U. S. Barghūti, *Al-Marahil* [Turning Points] (Beirut: al-Mu'assasat al-Arabīyya, 2001), pp. 76–7. Just after the First World War, it became a political tool used by Arab leaders to test the degree of Arab resentment as a political manifestation. See R. Mazza, *Jerusalem from the Ottomans to the British* (London: I. B. Tauris, 2009), pp. 165–78.

64. Some aspects connected to this have been analysed by L. Fishman, C. Gratien and E. Safa Gürkan, *Palestinianism and Zionism during the Late-Ottoman period*, 'Ottoman History Podcast' 84, 16 December 2012. Available at: http://www.ottomanhistorypodcast.com/2012/12/palestine-zionism-settlement-nationalism.html.

65. R. Khālidī, *Palestinian Identity* (New York: Columbia University Press, 1997), p. 19.

66. S. Telhami and M. Barnett (eds), *Identity and Foreign Policy in the Middle East* (New York: Cornell University Press, 2002), p. 19.

67. E. Finn, *The Fellaheen of Palestine*, in The Committee of the PEF, *The Surveys of Western Palestine: Special Papers on Topography, Archaeology, Manners and Customs* (London: PEF, 1881), p. 333. Finn highlighted the lack of 'national cohesion' among the peasants. However, he added that 'no clan has for a long time overpassed the boundaries of its own district, and they show no disposition to do so [. . .] Nothing but the strong arm of government can ever induce a Fellah to quit his native village'.

68. 'The Fellahin', argued CMS missionary C. T. Wilson in 1905, 'have a great love for their native place and think it is a real hardship to have to settle elsewhere': C. T. Wilson, *Peasant Life in the Holy Land* (London: John Murray, 1906), p. 85. This explains why Palestinian surnames often include the village of origin: Nabulsi, Ramli, Rantissi and so on.

69. al-Muqaddasī, *Ahsan al-taqāsīm fī maʿrifat al-aqālīm* [The best division for the knowledge of the provinces] (Beirut 2003), p. 362. The full passage by al-Muqaddasī: 'I mentioned to them [workers in Shiraz] about the construction in Palestine and I discussed with them these matters. The master stonecutter asked me: Are you Egyptian? I replied: No, I am Palestinian.'

70. al-Ramli, *Al-fatawa al-Khayriyya li-naf al-bariyya* [Consolatory Legal Response in favour of the Creation] (Cairo: Dar al-Maʿrifa, n.a.), vol. 2, pp. 151–60. 'Biladuna' was for that matter also the expression used three centuries later by ʿĪsā al-ʿĪsā (1878–1950) on his editorials on Filastīn, the bi-weekly that he founded in 1911. See MDC, 'Filastīn', 29 July 1911, p. 2. Similar expression appeared in a number of Palestinian newspapers of the time: 'How much longer will the vulture [the Zionist organisations] eat at the heart of our country? If we lose our country what are we living for?' MDC—'al-Karmil', 27 November 1912.

71 Kressel, Aharoni, *Egyptian Émigrés*, p. 25.

72. 'Ā. Mannāʿ', in Scham, Salem and Pogrund (eds), *Shared Histories*, p. 34.

73. M. Ignatieff, *The Russian Album* (New York: Picador, 2001), p. 5.

74. According to Sherna Gluck, when publishing online oral testimonials, an oral historian becomes an 'unwitting archivist': S. Gluck, excerpt from a presentation entitled 'Reflections on the Promises and Perils of Online Archiving', delivered at Birzeit University, 25 March 2014.

75. B. Doumani, 'Archiving Palestine and the Palestinians: the Patrimony of Ihsan Nimr', *Jerusalem Quarterly* 36 (2009): 3. On Palestinian archives see also the

works of Vincent Lemire, including V. Lemire, *Jérusalem 1900: La ville sainte à l'âge des possibles* [Jerusalem 1900: The holy city in the age of possibilities] (Paris: Armand Colin, 2013).

76. The United Nations Archives (UNA) in New York and the UNRWA offices in 'Amman, Gaza and Jerusalem are principally repositories of documents, videos and photos about post-1948 and post-1967 Palestinian refugees. An additional group of documents focuses on the administrative and legal aspects of the UN programmes, as well as on children's living conditions after 1948. According to a UN report of 19 August 1948, based on data supplied by A. W. Cordier (executive assistant to the UN Secretary), 300,000–400,000 children became refugees that year: UNA S-0158-0005-05.

77. The Palestine Archaeological Museum was opened in 1938 as a result of the efforts of J. H. Breasted (1865–1935), the support of J. D. Rockefeller (1874–1960) and the encouragement of the British High Commissioner in Palestine Lord Plumer (1857–1932). As the documentation in the museum reports, it was set up 'to host the Department of Antiquities, a vast archaeological library and the archives'.

78. Rami Hamdallah. Interview with the author. Al-Najah University, Nāblus, 19 May 2010.

79. DACH, funded mainly by European donors, was established in 2002 following the merging of two departments set up in 1994 by the PNA as part of the Oslo process; according to Taha, 'it is considered an official comeback to history after several attempts of historical banishment': H. Taha. *Managing Cultural Heritage in Palestine*, 'UNDP Focus', 1 (2004): 31.

80. O. Kessler, 'Excavations done at former Israelite capital Shechem', *Jerusalem Post*, 25 July 2011. Available at: http://www.jpost.com/National-News/Excava-tions-done-at-former-Israelite-capital-Shechem.

81. Nazmi Jubeh. Interview with the author. Birzeit University, Ramallah, 12 January 2012.

82. Mustafā Barghūti. Interview with the author, Palestinian Medical Relief Society, Ramallah, 24 November 2009.

83. 'Adlī Ya'īsh. Interview with the author. The Mayor's Office, Nāblus, 20 May 2010.

84. Ehāb Bseīso quoted in A. Nofa, 'Why Palestine Needs National Library more than Presidential Palace', in *Al-Monitor*, 9 October 2017. Available at: http://www.al-monitor.com/pulse/originals/2017/10/palestines-national-library-first-step-to-gathering-archive.html#ixzz4vBUvW3gv.

85. The Palestinian Digital Archive at Birzeit University is a case in point. The latter, opened in June 2011, holds several thousand documents (documents, photos,

videos), all digitalised and online at awraq.birzeit.edu. Soon after its inauguration, five representatives of the Palestinian National Authority went to Professor Roger Heacock's office intimating him to block the project, which they saw as contrasting with the previously announced creation of a 'Palestinian national archive'. Roger Heacock, interview with the author, Birzeit University, Ramallah, 12 January 2012. An exhibition, entitled 'Sea of Stories: Voyages of the Palestinian Archives', presented at Beirut's Dar El-Nimer for Arts and Culture on November 2016, aimed at shedding light on the ongoing attempts made by the Palestinian authorities to control any narrative produced through Palestinian archival materials.

86. H. Dabashi, *The Arab Spring: The End of Postcolonialism* (New York: Zed Books, 2012), p. xvii.

Conclusion: The Present's Past

It was assumed that the peoples had no 'history', except one following the imposition of rule by modern outsiders which had resulted in 'culture contact' and therefore some cultural change.[1]

Immanuel Wallerstein

They keep trying to establish power by making us [inhabitants of the Middle East] separate, isolated peoples. We are interdependent, interconnected and overlapping people.

Answer provided via Twitter to the author by an
anonymous profile on 26 September 2017.

'People adapt their memories to suit their sufferings.'[2] Since the time the Athenian historian Thucydides (*c*.460–*c*.395 BCE) wrote these words, the world has witnessed enormous changes. Nonetheless, they remain as powerful as ever. People continue to focus on some specific aspects of their past, while neglecting others, in order to cope with the daily challenges of life.

The validity of Thucydides' statement is especially relevant if applied with the purpose of understanding how the history of the last two centuries has been instrumental in establishing clearer notions of the 'self' and 'other'. Throughout this long and often dramatic historical juncture, 'sealed identities' have increasingly been projected into the ancient past through a plethora of myths and memories. The first victim of this process has been the original inclusive dimension of communal interactions.

The permeabilities that for millennia characterised the daily life of the Middle East seem today largely to have vanished in favour of an ongoing process of homogenisation of diversities. It is a phenomenon that bears some resemblance to the historical period between the end of the nineteenth and the early twentieth centuries, when the 'demographic fabric' of large parts of the region was homogeneised through the expulsion of millions of people from Anatolia, Bulgaria, Thrace, Macedonia and a number of other areas. Yet the extent and the potential long-term repercussions of the current processes might trigger unprecedented and more complex consequences for much of the Eurasian space.

A few examples might help to better explain how these demographic shifts are affecting the Middle East. The war in Syria is forcing hundreds of thousands of Sunnis to leave the areas under the regime for Jordan and Lebanon. With the aim of strengthening the local Alawite and Shi'ite dominance, President Bashār al-'Assad, supported by Tehran, has stripped thousands of their citizenship, not renewing their ID cards and making possession of updated biometric documents compulsory. While the partnership between a pan-Arab secular state (Syria) and an Islamic republic (Iran) can hardly be explained simply by their common Shi'a roots and interests, it cannot be denied that the Syrian regime has also carried out the systematic demolition of Sunni mosques, used harsh repression in Palestinian refugee camps, such as Yarmouk, and granted citizenship to thousands of Shi'a immigrants from Iraq.[3]

Lebanon, on the other hand, now hosts over 1 million new Sunni refugees: this new demographic reality poses 'a potential existential threat to an already fragile country' and is reducing, for the first time since the beginning of this century, the influence of Hezbollah, the Shi'a Islamist political, military and social welfare organisation.[4] Jordan has received 1.4 million Syrian refugees (more than 50 per cent of Syrian refugees in Jordan are unregistered), putting a strain on the country's infrastructure and lowering, possibly for the first time, the total percentage of the Palestinian population in the country.[5]

As for Iraq, IS has forced a large number of non-Sunnis to emigrate. The aim of this was to create a largely homogenous Sunni demographic reality – a goal that some analysts have linked to a few external actors, including Saudi Arabia, identified in US embassy cables as 'the most significant source of funding to Sunni terrorist groups worldwide'[6] – as a means to counterbalance the Iranian ascendency in the region.

The simplified ethnic demographies triggered by these epochal shifts is fostering an opinion that is gaining force: the wars that are plaguing large parts of the Middle East – so goes the claim – are generating a process of 'ethnocentric stabilisation'. Some scholars, for instance, have pointed out that 'we are witnessing the rearrangement of populations in the region to better fit the nation-states that were fixed after WWI'.[7] Others have gone a step further, contending that amid tragedy and horror, Syria, Iraq, Lebanon and Jordan 'are becoming a bit more stable',[8] and that a 'Shiitestan' in Iraq's south,[9] as well as the 'partition' of Syria, might represent stabilising solutions.[10] Similar impressions, such as the idea that 'Iraq is the fault line between the Shia and the Sunni world', or 'the main issue [in Yemen] is the 7th century struggle over who is the rightful heir to the Prophet Muhammad – Shiites or Sunnis',[11] and solutions, such as 'to defeat ISIS, create a Sunni state',[12] have been expressed by dozens of public figures, diplomats and journalists in the mainstream media.[13]

'Orders', 'Categories', 'Systems'

There is indeed much debate among scholars about the 'rearrangements of populations' and the shifts in identity and power that are currently taking place across the Middle East. In an interview with Adam Shatz, the director of the Center for Middle East Studies at the University of Oklahoma, Joshua Landis, argues that the Middle East is witnessing the 'return' of the twelfth century, when Shi'ite lords, supported by Persia, dominated much of the Northern Syria and the rest of the region. The Mamluks and then the Ottomans, Landis contends, changed that: 'they pushed out the Shi'ites, marginalised them – they became very impotent'.[14]

This 'narrative' has a long historical antecedence. For example, in a letter to her father on 23 August 1920, Gertrude Bell referred to Shi'a clerics in a strongly Shi'a region of Iraq in the following terms: 'It's as though you had a number of alien popes permanently settled at Canterbury and issuing edicts which take precedence of the law of the land. The Turks were always at loggerheads with them and the Arab govt of the future will find itself in the same case.'[15] These sorts of approach, aimed at branding local Shi'ites as 'alien', have had repercussions that are visible up to the present day and are once again rooted in the necessity of reading local realities in terms more suitable and useful for external observers. Fostering imaginary 'orders' (including the rising 'Shi'a order'), 'categories' (for instance the one of the *Mizrahim*) and 'systems' (millets, castes, and so on) is, in this sense, necessary to systematise and stabilise complex local contexts.[16]

Popular 'narratives' such as the one of the 'rising Shi'a order' of the Middle East not only ignore the fact that today Shi'ites represent about 40 per cent of the total Muslim population in the Middle East and that, from a theological perspective, there are fewer differences between Sunnis and Shi'ites than there are between Catholics and Protestants, but also overlook the historical context surrounding the dynamics of 'Shi'ite marginalisation'.

Shi'ite communities – characterised by a diversity of beliefs and purposes[17] – have at times been viewed with suspicion by and faced discrimination from Sunni rulers, Mamluks and Ottomans first and foremost. Yet their process of marginalisation historically has had much less to do with, say, Mamluks' violence and discrimination (twelfth century), and more to do with practical interests connected, among other things, to the exploitation of the Silk Road during the times (early seventeenth century) of Ma'nī Prince Fakhr-al-Dīn II, when the growth of commercial ties with the West went hand in hand with dramatic changes in the demographic composition of much of Greater Syria.

Maronite peasants were then prompted to settle in southern Druze areas to cultivate the land, to the disadvantage of the Shi'a components, who were forcibly dispossessed. In the long term, this made Christians a majority population in southern Lebanon and ignited a long-lasting asymmetry that, in Fawwaz Traboulsi's words, 'served as the matrix upon which the sectarian system and sectarian mobilization were built'.[18] The new demographic composition had a destabilising effect, particularly from a social and economic perspective, on all local communities.

In this context, it should be noted that Shi'ite lords, as Landis reminded us, were long supported by Persia. Equally relevant, however, is that Persia's population (like that of neighbouring Azerbaijan) was at that time still largely Sunni (Shafi'i and Hanafi schools): the massive and forced conversion of Persia – from 'marginalized' Sunnis to newly 'empowered' Shi'ites – in fact took place, at the hands of the Safavids, between the sixteenth and the eighteenth centuries.

Too much emphasis on the narrative of the return of the 'historically marginalized Shi'a communities', however, risks overshadowing once again the

Figure C.1   The vegetable market of Beirut, early twentieth century.
(Source: American Colony Photo Dept photographers G. Eric and Edith
Matson Photograph Collection, Library of Congress, Washington DC)

lived experience of a region in which religious boundaries were, for most of its
history, shifting, blurred and ambiguous. Paraphrasing Peter Sluglett, 'Christians, Jews and Muslims were largely indistinguishable from one another in
most of the cities of the [Ottoman] Empire'.[19]

Speaking in a public square in Beirut in the Spring of 1909, Jewish lawyer
Shlomo Yellin (1874–1912) stated that 'it is not lawful to divide according to
race; the Turkish, Arab, Armenian, and Jewish elements have mixed one with
other, and all of them are connected together'.[20] In the same period, in a religious city par excellence such as Jerusalem, almost 80 per cent of the inhabitants lived in mixed neighbourhoods and quarters.[21] In Yaacov Yehoshua's

memoir, *Yaldut be-Yerushalayim ha-yashena*, the author recalled that in the city 'there were joint compounds of Jews and Muslims. We were like one family [. . .] Our children played with their [Muslim] children in the yard, and if children from the neighborhood hurt us the Muslim children who lived in our compound protected us. They were our allies'.[22]

All this should not suggest that inter-religious and/or confessional conflicts were unknown. As this book also confirms, instances of Sunni–Shi'a violence, for instance, were documented as early as the Middle Ages. Yet their nature and scope are hardly comparable to those of more recent times. More importantly, they do not reflect the actual history of most of the region's past.

Multifaceted Pasts

Commenting on the massacres that occurred during the 1860 Civil War in Syria, and which culminated in the slaughter at Damascus, a number of British and French newspapers provided the image of a 'civilised' world (Europe) witnessing the actions of an ancient, fanatic and inherently violent Islamic East: 'the more disreputable Moslems of Damascus began to be exceedingly insolent to the Christians', noted the Beirut correspondent of the *London Post*, 'these low Moslems are a numerous, a very troublesome, and an exceedingly bigoted race'.[23] Just like in present-day Middle East, such clashes had little to do with any 'ancestral cleavage' between Islam and Christianity but were instead largely rooted in a number of practical aspects (including the rise of ethno-religious nationalism, the 'partition' of Lebanon, the long-lasting effects of 'humanitarian imperialism' and the 'homogenising' effects of the Tanzimāt) without which it is still difficult to comprehend the genesis – but also the consequences – of such phenomena. Not only did most acts of murder and looting that occurred at the time involve mainly Druzes and Maronites, but, as witnessed by the British commissioner for Syria, Alexander John Fraser (1821–66), 'great numbers of Christians had found refuge in the Moslems' houses in the streets near the Christian quarter'.[24]

Today, as also happened, *mutatis mutandis*, at that time, all the different peoples in the Middle East are struggling to find their peculiar place in a new and largely destabilised region. Many of them – in the Baghdād belt, in the provinces of Diyāla, Lātakīa, Tartūs, Bāniyās and many more areas in Iraq,

Syria and elsewhere – are also experiencing the increasing need to rediscover the 'confusion of races',[25] with their various permeabilities and specificities, that for millennia characterised much of the daily life in the region. Shedding light on these still incomplete yet significant efforts is a way of supporting their attempts to 'regain possession' of those multifaceted pasts. More importantly, it is a powerful antidote to geopolitical reductionism, so popular in our times.

To be sure, the cleavages and sectarian strife that are increasingly brewing in the region have once again less to do with ethnic tensions and religious differences than with economics and identity politics,[26] largely related to the 1979 Iranian Revolution, the 2003 US invasion of Iraq and the Arab uprisings, when, deprived more and more of social security networks by their states, local communities turned increasingly inward (towards their families, communities, confessions), looking for protection.[27]

It may be argued that the economic and political causes of many of the conflicts that are occurring now were nonetheless partially produced by sectarian constraints on the state dictated by a given regime's need to retain power (the largely Alawite leadership in Syria is a case in point). Yet this standpoint requires a further, deeper and more practical understanding of local dynamics. Very briefly, the Syrian uprising of 2011 broke out, as in the Tunisian case, in an agricultural area, the province of Darʿā, where reportedly more than 100,000 people attended an anti-government demonstration on 25 March 2011.[28] Despite having been a stronghold of the Syrian regime for decades, Darʿā was one of the areas that suffered the most from the neoliberal economic reforms implemented by Bashār al-ʾAssad soon after he succeeded his father in 2000. In addition to cutting economic support for agricultural areas, these reforms reached their climax in March 2009 with the launching of the Damascus Stock Exchange. Syrian markets were opened to cheaper agricultural imports and, as a result, farming communities, also affected by the devastating droughts in the country in recent years, were increasingly unable to rely on agriculture as a source of stable livelihood.[29] The exclusion, marginalisation and peripheralisation of these and other areas and sectors of the local population triggered some of the main conditions for the 'revolutionary moment' and the 'epistemological break' that we are currently witnessing.[30]

If the religious differences and ethnic tensions can only explain the current historical dynamics to a limited degree, the same doubts can be expressed about the explanatory powers of the regional stabilisation thesis. Particularly in consideration of the Middle East's peculiar history, the process of homogenisation that is taking place in the region appears to be a detrimental and ahistorical phenomenon destined only to deepen tensions. As noted by Elias Muhanna, 'the violence in Syria is not some messy centrifugal separation of an artificial state into its primordial ethnic or sectarian ingredients. Under the right economic and political conditions, there should not be anything inevitable about such affiliations.'[31]

Nevertheless, a few academic works that have appeared in recent years in Western countries would seem to contradict what has just been argued. For example, the study entitled 'Good Fences: The Importance of Setting Boundaries for Peaceful Coexistence' posits that peace 'does not depend on integrated coexistence, but rather on well defined topographical and political boundaries separating groups'.[32] Taking Switzerland as a case study (the Belgian case might have provided different but equally significant insights), the authors argue that 'mountains and lakes are an important part of the boundaries between sharply defined linguistic areas'.[33]

However, focusing on findings that are based on theories and methods that deliberately avoid properly considering the historical context can lead to misleading conclusions. The considerations just described, for instance, fail to take into account the peculiar historical effects that the secular antagonism between Papal authority and monarchical states for the guidance of religious practice have had on most of the West's 'good fences'. Moreover, such considerations make even less sense if applied to the specific context of the Eastern Mediterranean, an area of the world still largely devoid of homogeneous communities and with linguistic characteristics that can hardly be equated with those of the European context.

'Fibonacci's Paradigm':[34] How Quickly Human Beings Tend to Forget

The Palazzo Colonna in Rome houses some of the most celebrated paintings of 1571's Battle of Lepanto, when the Muslim fleets of the Ottoman Empire faced the vessels of the Christian Holy League. Since European

Figure C.2   A Jew and a Muslim playing chess in thirteenth-century al-Andalus. In *El Libro de los Juegos* (commissioned by Alphonse X of Castile), Biblioteca del Monasterios de San Lorenzo Escorial, 1283, fol. 63.

Christians considered the crucifix to be an evocative symbol of their religion, the crescent moon (as with, *mutatis mutandis*, the Star of David for Jews) was automatically read by European artists using the same criteria. Hence, the Christian fleets were depicted – as is sumptuously shown in the frescoes in the Galleria Colonna itself – with crossed sails and the Turkish ones with the crescent moon. The latter symbol, however, pre-dated Islam by several thousand years (dating back to early Sumerian civilisation) and did not hold such significance within the cultural universe that it was meant to represent. It was utilised exclusively for decorative purposes and not only in the *dār al-Islām* (house of Islam). In fact, there are no emblems in Islam and early Muslim communities did not really have a symbol to identify themselves (no mention of such a symbol occurs in the Quran). Over the centuries, as has happened for many other things, the dominant perception on both shores of the Atlantic led a significant percentage of Muslims to accept and, later on, to use a symbol largely pinned on them from the outside.[35] Attempts to interpret and simplify the 'other' are thus rooted deep in the past.[36]

Figure C.3   The Battle of Lepanto, oil on canvas (1270 mm x 2324 mm), by an unidentified artist, in the collection of the National Maritime Museum in Greenwich, London.

Yet, despite its largely 'solipsistic background', the crescent moon can also be perceived as the symbol of the empathetic interactions that for millennia characterised much of the life in the Mediterranean basin and beyond. One example of this might be found in the statues erected along the banks of the River Liffey in Dublin in 1997, in remembrance of the event that, more than anything else, marked the history of modern Ireland. A series of petrified silhouettes commemorate the Great Famine that killed about a million Irish people between 1845 and 1849; over a million more were forced to emigrate, mainly to the United States.

Despite it being a distant country, and of the Christian faith, Ottoman Sultan Abdülmecid I (1823–61), who acquired the title of *Ghāzī* ('Warrior for the Faith') at the outbreak of the Crimean War (1853–6),[37] was struck by this catastrophe and expressed the will to send £10,000 (around 10 million euros today) to support the Irish peasants. The offer was declined by Queen Victoria (1819–1901), who had committed herself to donate only £2,000. The sultan was forced to accept the 'diktat', and sent £1,000 only. Secretly, however, he also dispatched three ships loaded with grain and food that arrived a few weeks later in the harbour of Drogheda (56km north of Dublin). In the decades and centuries that followed, this generous gesture

Figure C.4   The Famine statues in Dublin.

has been acknowledged in a number of publications, including James Joyce's (1882–41) *Ulysses*.[38] Moreover, a number of sources claim that, with the purpose of commemorating the humanitarian spirit of this act, the city of Drogheda inserted a star and a crescent into its coat of arms.[39] Both are still visible in the logos of both the Drogheda United (the local football team) and the Turkish football team of Trabzonspor: the two teams still share the same colours on their kits.

This reminds us of how quickly human beings tend to forget things. The humanitarian and cultural intersections that have shaped the daily lives of 'pagan peoples', religious groups and confessions for millennia are often hidden and 'covered' by dense layers of history, mainly linked to the homogenising effects of nationalism and the racialisation of religious belonging. Yet a wide range of documents and oral sources confirm this deeply rooted history of interactions – that includes also the rich contacts between the Vikings and the 'Arab world' between the ninth and the eleventh centuries[40] – and the problems connected to the modern and contemporary processes (for instance, see the Lebanese civil war, or the ongoing Greek–Turkish clashes over Cyprus) of what Lord Curzon defined the 'ethnic unmixing of peoples'.[41]

As witnessed by many Ottoman observers quoted in this work, and in reference to a wide range of different areas, 'different denominations lived like a family'.[42] As we have seen, similar situations were visible in areas where ethno-sectarian drives have contributed to generating extreme expressions of violence. 'Turks were like brothers [*adelfia*] for us', remarked Greek housewife Maria Xatziheodorou in reference to pre-First World War Potamia (central Greece); 'we used to go to their [meeting] places and they used to come in our houses [. . .] When İzmir was destroyed [1919–22] a radical change occurred'.[43] Shedding light on such realities and perceptions as these should not be viewed as an attempt to promote the image of an interfaith or interracial utopia, of a 'golden age' in which Muslims, Christians, Jews and other religious or ethnic groups worked together in full equality and harmony. Instead, it is a way of examining history in its complexity, providing a deeper intra-regional understanding of the (past and ongoing) politicisation of ethno-religious differences.[44] In this sense, to examine the transition from shared spaces to sealed identities is, to a large extent, and from an Eastern Mediterranean perspective, a way of revealing the passage from an 'internal' history to an 'external' one. Indeed, those observing the region from the outside often have the tendency, paraphrasing Amílcar Cabral's words at the Conference of Dār es-Salām in 1963, to believe 'that it was they who brought us into history: today we show that this is not so. They made us leave history, our history, to follow them, right at the back, to follow the progress of their history'.[45] Millions of people in the areas covered in this volume are acting or speaking while driven by this very same spirit. It is time to pay more attention to their voices, sustaining and supporting their growing efforts to get back into their own histories.

Notes

1. I. Wallerstein, *World-Systems Analysis* (Durham NC: Duke University Press, 2004), p. 7.
2. Thucydides, *History of the Peloponnesian War* (New York: Penguin Books, 1954 [first English trans. 1550]), p. 127.

3. See M. Ataie, 'The Iran-Syria Alliance: Sectarianism or Realpolitik?', *Syria Comment*, 14 June 2015. Available at: http://www.joshualandis.com/blog/the-iran-syria-alliance-sectarianism-or-realpolitik-by-mohammad-ataie/

4. Al-Qashawi, 'Lebanon's Syrian-Refugee Time Bomb', *Al Ahram Weekly*, 13 January 2015. Available at: http://weekly.ahram.org.eg/News/10166.aspx.

5. 'Population Stands at around 9.5 million, Including 2.9 Million Guests', *Jordan Times*, 30 January 2016. Available at: http://www.jordantimes.com/news/local/population-stands-around-95-million-including-29-million-guests.

6. 'US Embassy Cables: Hillary Clinton Says Saudi Arabia "a Critical Source of Terrorist Funding"', *The Guardian*, 30 December 2010. Available at: http://www.theguardian.com/world/us-embassy-cables-documents/242073.

7. J. Landis, 'The Great Sorting Out: Ethnicity & the Future of the Levant', *Qifa Naqbi*, 18 December 2013. Available at: http://qifanabki.com/2013/12/18/landis-ethnicity.

8. D. Pipes, 'Like-to-Like Ethnic Migration in the Middle East', *Washington Times*, 25 February 2015. Available at: http://www.washingtontimes.com/news/2015/feb/25/daniel-pipes-like-to-like-ethnic-migrationin-the-.

9. R. Wright, 'Imagining a Remapped Middle East', *New York Times*, 28 September 2013. Available at: http://www.nytimes.com/2013/09/29/opinion/sunday/imagining-a-remapped-middle-east.html?pagewanted=all&_r=0.

10. J. Stavridis, 'It's Time to Seriously Consider the Partition of Syria', *Foreign Policy*, 9 March 2016. Available at: (http://foreignpolicy.com/2016/03/09/its-time-to-seriously-consider-partitioning-syria.

11. T. Friedman, 'Tell Me How This Ends Well', *New York Times*, 1 April 2015. Available at: http://www.nytimes.com/2015/04/01/opinion/thomas-friedman-tell-me-how-this-ends-well.html?_r=0.

12. J. Bolton, 'To Defeat ISIS, Create a Sunni State', *New York Times*, 24 November 2015. Available at: http://www.nytimes.com/2015/11/25/opinion/john-bolton-to-defeat-isis-create-a-sunni-state.html?_r=0.

13. See for instance the UN Special envoy Martin Kobler cited in Associated Press, 'UN Envoy: Iraq and Syrian Conflicts are Merging', *Dunya News*, 16 July 2013. Available at: http://dunyanews.tv/en/World/183617.

14. A. Shatz, 'The Syrian War: Adam Shatz Talks to Joshua Landis', *London Review of Books*, 21 April 2017. Available at: https://www.lrb.co.uk/2017/04/21/adam-shatz/the-syrian-war.

15. Gertrude Bell to her father, Sir Hugh Bell, 23 August 1920. The Gertrude Bell Collection is available at http://www.gerty.ncl.ac.uk/letter_details.php?letter_id=411.

16. The single miscellaneous category of *Mizrahim* (literally, 'the Easteners', meaning Jews from Arab/Muslim countries) was coined after the creation of the State of Israel and became particularly popular in the 1990s. Ella Shohat, whose family is of 'Mizrahi' origins, noted that it was a 'Zionist invention' and that 'Zionism obliged Arab-Jews to redefine themselves in relation to new ideological polarities [. . .] Mizrahi idendity marks a departure from previous concepts of Jewishness': E. Shohat, 'The Invention of the Mizrahim', in Altorki (ed.), *A Companion*, pp. 322–3. In this sense, the category of 'Mizrahi' fosters a homogenising interpretation of Jewish history, lumping together a number of ancient 'hybrid identities' and their peculiar histories.

17. Such diversity is also mirrored in the very critical approach of a number of Shi'a clerics in Iraq and Iran toward Khomeini's theory of *velāyat-e faqīh* (Persian: 'governance of the jurist').

18. F. Traboulsi, *A History of Modern Lebanon* (London: Pluto Press, 2007), p. 16.

19. P. Sluglett, 'From Millet to Minority: Another Look at the Non-Muslim Communities in the Late Nineteenth and Early Twentieth Centuries', in Robson (ed.), *Minorities and the Modern Arab World*, p. 21.

20. Cit. in Campos, *Ottoman Brothers*, p. 2.

21. The same applies to a number of other cities in the region. For instance, there were about 50,000 Jews in Baghdād in the 1920s and many of them lived in mixed areas. In the early 1930s, just before the rising of Rashīd 'Ālī al-Kaylānī (1892–1965) to power, about 1,500 Jews still lived in a relatively 'mixed' Kirkūk. There were by then about 15,000 Jews in Iraqi Kurdistan. On Jewish community in Iraq in the first decades of the century see TNA AIR 23/806, 'The Jews of Iraq' (Memo 82B), January–December 1934. According to Efron, Weitzman and Lehmann, 'When the British arrived in 1917, Baghdad was a noticeably "Jewish city." Jews were the single largest ethnic group in the capital. Of a total population of 202,000, 80,000 or 40 percent were Jews. Sunnis, Shi'ites, and Turks totaled 101,000; Christians, 12,000; Kurds, 8,000; and Persians, 800': J. Efron, S. Weitzman, M. Lehmann, *The Jews: A History* (New York: Routledge, 2016), p. 404.

22. J. Yehoshua, *Yaldut be-Yerushalayim ha-yashena* [Childhood in Old Jerusalem] (Jerusalem: Rubin Mass, 1965), vol. 2, p. 215. The fate of Muslims and Jews had been intertwined for most of history. A meaningful example is provided by Juan Rodriguez Bermejo (1469–1535), the first of Columbus's crew to sight the 'Americas'. Bermejo, a Jew, was forced to convert to Christianity ('Marrano'). Ultimately, in the latter part of his life, he decided to convert to Islam.

23. *London Post*, Beirut, 15 July 1860. Reproduced in *The Examiner*, 4 August 1860, p. 487.

24. BLMC, John Fraser Papers, 1853–61, Add. 44912. Fraser, 9 July 1860. For a differentiation of the social meaning and character of Druze-Maronite clashes in 1841, 1845 and 1860 see C. P. Issawī, *The Fertile Crescent, 1800–1914: A Documentary Economic History* (New York: Oxford University Press, 1988). Issawī noted that 'religious antagonism accentuated the deepening social contradictions and allowed the separate political and social groups to use it in their political interests', p. 50. Largely overlooking the historical causes of the civil wars of 1840 and 1860, Mark Farha implied instead that communal clashes were inherently part of the region, and that the subsequent French 'confessional concessions were a strategy to stave off communal strife': M. Farha, 'Secularism in a Sectarian Society? The Divisive Drafting of the 1926 Lebanese Constitution', in A. Ü. Bâli and H. Lerner (eds), *Constitution Writing, Religion and Democracy* (Cambridge: Cambridge University Press, 2017), p. 102.

25. Hybrid identities were expressed in terms of 'confusion of races' by the commission entrusted (1925) by the League of Nations to define Iraq's borders. See League of Nations, *Question of Frontier between Turkey and Iraq*, Geneva 1924. Available at: http://biblio-archive.unog.ch/Dateien/CouncilMSD/C-400-M-147-1925-VII_BI.pdf. The report clarifies that 'So great is the confusion of races in the disputed territory that in fixing the frontier purely racial considerations cannot be taken into account', p. 87.

26. B. N. Ghalioun, *al-Tā'ifiya min al-Dawla ila al-Qabīla* [The Sectarian System from the State to the Tribe] (Beirut: al-Markaz al-Taqāfi al-Arabī, 1990), pp. 27–8.

27. D. Byman, 'Sectarianism Afflicts the New Middle East', *Survival: Global Politics and Strategy* 56(1) (2014): 84. The divisive policies adopted, particularly in the 1990s, by long-lasting regimes such as the one led by Saddām Ḥuseīn played a role in shaping a sect-centric political culture, but they can provide only a limited explanation. On the reasons why religious considerations are currently gaining the upper hand over secular aspects, see S. Hashim, *Al-Intifadhat al-'Arabīya 'ala Dhaou Falsafit al-Tarīkh* [The Arab Uprising in Light of the Philosophy of History] (Beirut: Dār al-Saqī, 2013).

28. The Tunisian uprisings started among marginalised groups in rural areas such as Sidi Bouzid. Yet, the first signs of a potential major shift in the local societal and political equilibrium could already be seen two years earlier, when the small town of Redeyef, situated 350km south of Tunis, witnessed months of bloody

protests at the Gafsa Phosphate Company. The turmoil was triggered by a phenomenon that was anything but new: the open call for manpower organised by the state-run enterprise was rigged and the available jobs were given to supporters of then-president Zine El Abidine Ben Ali.

29. R. Zurayk and A. Gough, 'Bread and Olive Oil: The Agrarian Roots of the Arab Uprising', in F. Gerges (ed.), *The New Middle East: Protest and Revolution in the Arab World* (Cambridge: Cambridge University Press, 2014), p. 112.

30. Ibid., p. 2. Due to the lack of transparency of the Syrian regime, the revenues of these neoliberal policies have essentially gone to the Assad clan and its associates: G. Achcar, *The People Want: A Radical Exploration of the Arab Uprisings* (Berkeley: University of California Press, 2013), p. 275.

31. E. Muhanna, 'Iraq and Syria's Poetic Borders', *New Yorker*, 13 August 2014.

32. A. Rutherford, *The Geography of Ethnic Violence*, in P. Vos Fellman, Y. Bar-Yam and A. A. Minai (eds), *Conflict and Complexity* (New York: Springer, 2015).

33. Ibid.

34. The life of Italian mathematician Fibonacci (c. 1175–c. 1250) is a further powerful reminder of Mediterranean interactions. Fibonacci, educated in Bougie (Algeria) and fluent in Arabic, introduced the decimal system and the concept of 'zephyrus' – from Arabic '*sifr*' (that in pre-Islamic times had the meaning 'empty'), that is, zero – in Europe.

35. Euben focuses on how Western travel produced the 'colonized other', noting the importance of also 'shifting the theoretical perspective': R. L. Euben, *Journeys to the Other Shore* (Princeton NJ: Princeton University Press, 2006), p. 2.

36. Emile Bustani (1907–63) notes that 'even Arabs in the early years of their history were among the most ardent imperialists that the world has encountered': E. Bustani, *Doubts and Dynamite* (London: Allan Wingate, 1958), p. 28. However, a sea change regarding what we refer to as 'imperialism' took place in the second half of the nineteenth century. See E. Kedourie, *Nationalism in Asia and Africa* (London: Weidenfeld, 1971), p. 3. On the perception of Europe in the Medieval Arabic literature, see N. F. Hermes, *The [European] Other in Medieval Arabic Literature and Culture* (New York: Palgrave, 2012).

37. BOA HR.MKT 68/4, 6 December 1918.

38. James Joyce on the Ottoman contribution during the Irish famine: 'Even the Grand Turk sent us his piastres. But the Sassenach [Saxons] tried to starve the nation at home while the land was full of crops that the British hyenas bought and sold in Rio de Janeiro': J. Joyce, *Ulysses* (Oxford: Oxford University Press, 2008 [1922]), p. 316.

39. See A. Kelly, 'New Evidence Shows Turkey Delivered Food to Ireland during the Famine', *IrishCentral*, 2 June 2012. Available at: https://www.irishcentral.com/news/new-evidence-shows-turkey-delivered-food-to-ireland-during-the-famine-156681255-237507681.

40. On these interactions and the first-ever written description of Viking customs and practices – often described in negative terms – see the work of Arab traveller Aḥmad ibn Faḍlān (877–960) in S. al-Dahhān (ed.), *Risālat Ibn Faḍlān* [Ibn Faḍlān's Account] (Damascus: al-Majma' al-'Ilmī al-'Arabī, 1959), ch. 1.

41. Cit. in M. R. Marrus, *The Unwanted: European Refugees in the Twentieth Century* (New York: Oxford University Press, 1985), p. 41. Brubaker defined the 'ethnic unmixing' as the process by which formerly heterogeneous populations were 'sifted, sorted and recomposed into relatively homogeneous blocks corresponding to state frontiers': R. Brubaker, *Nationalism Reframed* (Cambridge: Cambridge University Press, 1996), p. 153.

42. W. Jawhariyyeh, 'My Last Days as an Ottoman Subject: Selections from Wasif Jawhariyyeh's Memoirs', *Jerusalem Quarterly* 9 (Summer 2000): 28–34.

43. CAMS—KP 328B, p. 13. Maria Xatziheodorou, housewife from Potamia (island of Thasos, Greece), writing about the late nineteenth century.

44. Roy Porter (1946–2002) noted that 'Today's history comes deodorized'. See Porter's foreword to A. Corbin, *The Foul and the Fragrant: Odour and the French Social Imagination* (Basingstoke: Macmillan, 1996), p. v.

45. A. Cabral and R. Handyside (eds), *Revolution in Guinea* (New York: Monthly Review Press, 1969), p. 78.

Bibliography

Archives

ACAC	American Colony Archive Collections, Jerusalem
ASDMAE	Archivio Storico-Diplomatico del Ministero degli Affari Esteri, Rome
ASV	Archivio Segreto Vaticano, Rome
BLMC	British Library Manuscript Collection, London
BOA	Başbakanlık Osmanli Arşivi, Istanbul
BOL	Bodleian Library, Oxford
CAMS	Centre for Asia Minor Studies, Athens
CDM	Centre for Documents and Manuscripts, 'Amman
CHIR	Centre for Heritage and Islamic Research, Abu Dis
CSA	Cyprus State Archives, Nicosia
CZA	Central Zionist Archive, Jerusalem
DKAW	Egyptian National Library and Archives, Cairo
ISA	Israel State Archives, Jerusalem
ITAC	Archives of the Israeli Trust of the Anglican Church, Jerusalem
JIA	Jabotinsky Institute Archive, Tel Aviv
JNUL	Jewish National and University Library, Jerusalem
LANT	Les Archives Nationales Tunisiennes, Tunis
LPL	Lambeth Palace Library, London
MDC	Moshe Dayan Center, Tel Aviv
MECA	Middle East Centre Archives, St Antony's College, Oxford
NARA	National Archives and Records Administration, Washington DC
PEF	Palestine Exploration Fund, London
TNA	The National Archives, London
UNA	United Nations Archives, New York

Oral Sources

Mustafā Barghūti. Interview with the author, Palestinian Medical Relief Society, Ramallah, 24 November 2009.

George Ibrahim. Interview with the author, Ramallah, 13 February 2010.

Rami Hamdallah. Interview with the author, Al-Najah University, Nablus, 19 May 2010.

'Adlī Ya'īsh. Interview with the author. The Mayor's Office, Nablus, 20 May 2010.

Sam Bahūr. Interview with the author, al-Manāra, Rāmallāh, 12 October 2011.

Nazmi Jubeh. Interview with the author. Birzeit University, Ramallah, 12 January 2012.

Ussama Makdisi. Conversation with the author, European University Institute, Florence, 5 June 2015.

Majeda Omar, Director of the Royal Institute for Interfaith Studies in Jordan. Conversation with the author, 'Amman, 18 July 2016.

Prince Hassan bin Talal. Conversation with the author held at the prince's private residence, 18 July 2016.

Avraham Sela. Conversation with the author, The Mandel School for Advanced Studies, Jerusalem, 19 July 2017.

Journals

Associated Press, 'UN Envoy: Iraq and Syrian Conflicts are Merging', *Dunya News*, 16 July 2013. Available at: http://dunyanews.tv/en/World/183617.

Ataie, M., 'The Iran–Syria Alliance: Sectarianism or Realpolitik?', *Syria Comment*, 14 June 2015. Available at: http://www.joshualandis.com/blog/the-iran-syria-alliance-sectarianism-or-realpolitik-by-mohammad-ataie.

Avnery, A., 'Günter the Terrible', *Uri Avnery's Column*, 14 April 2012. Available at: http://zope.gush-shalom.org/home/en/channels/avnery/1334242715.

Beauchamp, Z., 'The Real Roots of Iraq's Sunni-Shia Conflict', *Vox*, 20 June 2014. Available at: http://www.vox.com/2014/6/20/5827046/who-are-sunnis-who-are-shias.

Bolton, J., 'To Defeat ISIS, Create a Sunni State', *The New York Times*, 24 November 2015. Available at: http://www.nytimes.com/2015/11/25/opinion/john-bolton-to-defeat-isis-create-a-sunni-state.html?_r=0.

Byman, D. 'Sectarianism Afflicts the New Middle East', *Survival: Global Politics and Strategy*, 56(1) (2014): 84.

Carmichael, J., 'Islam and Arab Nationalism. The Role of Religion in Middle Eastern Politics', *Commentary*, 1 July 1957. Available at: https://www.commentarymagazine.com/articles/islam-and-arab-nationalismthe-role-of-religion-in-middle-eastern-politics.

Clark, J. C. D., 'Protestantism, Nationalism, and National Identity, 1660–1832', *The Historical Journal*, 43(1) (2000): 249–76.

al-Dagher, M., 'A Striking Positive Shift in Sunni Opinion in Iraq is Underway. Here's What it Means', *The Washington Post*, 14 September 2017. Available at: https://www.washingtonpost.com/news/monkey-cage/wp/2017/09/14/iraqi-sunnis-are-impressed-by-the-defeat-of-isis-heres-what-that-could-mean/?utm_term=.7fadc3aabe5c.

Danforth, N., 'Forget Sykes–Picot. It's the Treaty of Sèvres That Explains the Modern Middle East', *Foreign Policy*, 10 August 2015. Available at: http://foreignpolicy.com/2015/08/10/sykes-picot-treaty-ofsevres-modern-turkey-middle-east-borders-turkey.

Dodge, T., 'Can Iraq Be Saved?', *Survival: Global Politics and Strategy*, 56(5) (2014): 10.

Doumani, B. 'Rediscovering Ottoman Palestine: Writing Palestinians into History', *Journal of Palestine Studies*, 21(2) (1992): 8.

Doumani, B., 'Archiving Palestine and the Palestinians: The Patrimony of Ihsan Nimr', *Jerusalem Quarterly*, 36 (2009): 3.

Epstein, Y., 'A Hidden Question', *Ha-Shilo'ah*, 17 (July–December 1907): 193–206.

Fishman, L., Gratien, C., and Gürkan, E. S., 'Palestinianism and Zionism during the late-Ottoman Period', *Ottoman History Podcast*, 84, 16 December 2012. Available at: http://www.ottomanhistorypodcast.com/2012/12/palestine-zionism-settlement-nationalism.html.

Friedman, T., 'Tell Me How This Ends Well', *The New York Times*, 1 April 2015. Available at: http://www.nytimes.com/2015/04/01/opinion/thomas-friedman-tell-me-how-this-ends-well.html?_r=0.

Gerber, H., '"Palestine" and Other Territorial Concepts in the 17th Century', *International Journal of Middle East Studies*, 30(4) (1998): 563.

Ghazal, M., 'Population Stands at around 9.5 million, Including 2.9 Million Guests', *The Jordan Times*, 30 January 2016. Available at: http://www.jordantimes.com/news/local/population-stands-around-95-million-including-29-million-guests.

Gilley, B., 'The Case for Colonialism', *Third World Quarterly*, e-version, September 2017: 1–17.

Gordon, J. T., 'ISIS' Desire to Erase Sykes–Picot Is Rooted in Fiction, Not History', *The National Interest*, 17 September 2014. Available at: http://nationalinterest.org/feature/isis'-desire-erase-sykes-picot-rooted-fiction-not-history-11293.

The Guardian, 'US Embassy Cables: Hillary Clinton Says Saudi Arabia "a critical source of terrorist funding"', *The Guardian*, 30 December 2010. Available at: http://www.theguardian.com/world/us-embassy-cables-documents/242073.

Gula-Ndebele, E., '"Tribalism": A Scar Today, a Wound Tomorrow', *Conversation Zimbabwe*, 30 November 2014. Available at: https://conversationzimbabwe. com/2014/11/30/tribalism-a-scar-today-a-wound-tomorrow.

Haddād, F., '"Sectarianism" and Its Discontents in the Study of the Middle East', *Middle East Journal*, 71(3), Summer 2017: 362–83.

Hanssen, J., '"Malhamé–Malfamé": Levantine Elites and Transimperial Networks on the Eve of the Young Turk Revolution', *International Journal of Middle East Studies*, 43(1) (2011): 25–48.

Hayden, R. M. and Naumović, S., 'Imagined Commonalities: The Invention of a Late Ottoman "tradition" of Coexistence', *American Anthropologist*, 115(2) (June 2013): 324–34.

Hobsbawm, E., 'Identity Politics and the Left', *New Left Review*, May–June 1996, 217(1): 38–47.

Irving, C., 'Gertrude of Arabia, the Woman Who Invented Iraq', *The Daily Beast*, 17 June 2014. Available at: http://www.thedailybeast.com/articles/2014/06/17/ gertrude-of-arabia-the-woman-who-invented-iraq.html.

Ismael, M., 'Kurdish Independence and the Unheard Yazidi Voice', *Al-Arabiya*, 22 September 2017. Available at: https://english.alarabiya.net/en/views/news/middle-east/2017/09/22/Kurdish-Independence-and-the-unheard-Yazidi-voice.html.

Jawhariyyeh, W., '"My Last Days as an Ottoman Subject": Selections from Wasif Jawhariyyeh's Memoirs', *Jerusalem Quarterly*, 9 (Summer 2000): 28–34.

Kamel, L., 'Despite the Popular Narrative, Iraq is Not Simply an Artificial Creation', *The National*, 12 October 2014. Available at: http://www.thenational.ae/opin-ion/despite-the-popular-narrative-iraq-is-not-simply-an-artificial-creation.

Kamel, L., 'The Impact of "Biblical Orientalism" in Late 19th and Early 20th Century Palestine', *New Middle Eastern Studies*, 4 (2014): 1–15.

Kamel, L., 'Artificial Nations? The Sykes–Picot and the Islamic State's Narratives in a Historical Perspective', *Diacronie Studi di Storia Contemporanea*, 25(1) (2016): 1–20.

Kelly, A., 'New Evidence Shows Turkey Delivered Food to Ireland during the Famine', *Irish Central*, 2 June 2012. Available at: https://www.irishcentral. com/news/new-evidence-shows-turkey-delivered-food-to-ireland-during-the-famine-156681255-237507681.

Kemal Oke, M., 'Jews and the Question of Zionism in the Ottoman Empire, 1908–1913', *Studies in Zionism*, 7(2) (Autumn 1986): 199–203.

Kessler, O., 'Excavations Done at Former Israelite Capital Shechem', *The Jerusalem Post*, 25 July 2011. Available at: http://www.jpost.com/National-News/Excava-tions-done-at-former-Israelite-capital-Shechem.

Landis, J., 'The Great Sorting Out: Ethnicity and the Future of the Levant', *Qifa Naqbi*, 18 December 2013. Available at: http://qifanabki.com/2013/12/18/landis-ethnicity/.

Lewis, B., 'Some Reflections of the Decline of the Ottoman Empire', *Studia Islamica*, 9 (1958): 111–27.

Lewis, B., 'Rethinking the Middle East', *Foreign Affairs*, 71(4) (Autumn 1992): 117.

Lewis, B., 'The New Anti-Semitism', *The American Scholar*, LXXV(1) (Winter 2006): 25–36.

Lowe, C., 'The Trouble with Tribe', *Teaching Tolerance*, 19, Spring 2001. Available at: https://www.tolerance.org/magazine/spring-2001/the-trouble-with-tribe.

Maxse, L., 'The Second Treaty of Versailles', *National Review*, 73 (1919): 819.

Miles, J. 'How Will the Mideast War End? Christian History May Provide a Clue', *New Perspectives Quarterly*, 32(2), April 2015: 52–8.

Molinari, M., 'Da dove viene il branco di Colonia', *La Stampa*, 10 January 2016. Available at: http://www.lastampa.it/2016/01/10/cultura/opinioni/editoriali/difendere-leuropa-dal-ritorno-delle-trib-fl3u3Wh0fpyzgEdDi81ycN/pagina.html.

Monitor's Editorial Board, 'Iraq's Opportunity in the Battle for Mosul', *The Christian Science Monitor*, 30 August 2017. Available at: https://www.csmonitor.com/Commentary/the-monitors-view/2016/0830/Iraq-s-opportunity-in-the-battle-for-Mosul.

Mualem, M., 'Israeli Minister: "A Palestinian State Is not the Solution"', *al-Monitor*, 29 May 2013. Available at: http://www.al-monitor.com/pulse/originals/2013/05/israeli-minister-two-states-for-two-people-will-not-bring-p.html.

Muhanna, E., 'Iraq and Syria's Poetic Borders', *The New Yorker*, 13 August 2014. Available at: http://www.newyorker.com/books/page-turner/iraq-syria-poetic-imagination.

Nofa, A., 'Why Palestine Needs National Library More than Presidential Palace', in *Al-Monitor*, 9 October 2017. Available at: http://www.al-monitor.com/pulse/originals/2017/10/palestines-national-library-first-step-to-gathering-archive.html#ixzz4vBUvW3gv.

NUPI, 'More than "Shiites" and "Sunnis" – How a Post-Sectarian Strategy Can Change the Logic and Facilitate Sustainable Political Reform in Iraq', Norwegian Institute of International Affairs Report, February 2009. Available at: http://english.nupi.no/content/download/8891/91333/file/Iraq%20Report%20%284%29.pdf.

Page, S., Interview with L. Panetta 'Panetta: "30-Year War" and a Leadership Test for Obama', *USA Today*, 6 October 2014. Available at: https://www.usatoday.com/story/news/politics/2014/10/06/leon-panetta-memoir-worthy-fights/16737615/.

Pipes, D., 'Like-to-Like Ethnic Migration in the Middle East', *The Washington Times*, 25 February 2015. Available at: http://www.washingtontimes.com/news/2015/feb/25/daniel-pipes-like-to-like-ethnic-migrationin-the-/.

Preville, J., 'Interview with Mark Cohen on Muslim-Jewish Relations: History and Relevance Today', *ISLAMICommentary*, 26 January 2015. Available at: http://www.worldreligionnews.com/religion-news/islam/interview-mark-cohen-muslim-jewish-relations-history-relevance-today.

Pursley, S., '"Lines Drawn on an Empty Map": Iraq's Borders and the Legend of the Artificial State', *Jadaliyya*, 2 June 2015. Available at: http://www.jadaliyya.com/pages/index/21759/lines-drawn-on-an-empty-map_iraq's-borders-and-the.

Rodrigue, A., 'Difference and Tolerance in the Ottoman Empire: Interview by Nancy Reynolds', *Stanford Humanities Review*, 5(1) (Spring 1996): 81–92.

Rothkopf, D., 'A Time of Unprecedented Instability?', *Foreign Affairs*, 21 July 2014. Available at: http://foreignpolicy.com/2014/07/21/a-time-of-unprecedented-instability/.

Salzman, P. C., 'The Middle East's Tribal DNA', *The Middle East Quarterly*, 15(1) (Winter 2008): 23–33. Available at: http://www.meforum.org/1813/the-middle-easts-tribal-dna.

Sarç, Ö. C., 'Tanẓīmāt ve Sanayimiz' [The Tanẓīmāt and our Industry], in *Tanẓīmāt*, vol. 1 (Istanbul: Maarif Vekâleti, 1941), pp. 423–40.

Shatz, A., 'The Syrian War: Adam Shatz Talks to Joshua Landis', *London Review of Books*, 21 April 2017. Available at: https://www.lrb.co.uk/2017/04/21/adam-shatz/the-syrian-war.

Simms, B., 'Ending the Thirty Years War', *New Statesman*, 26 January 2016. Available at: http://www.newstatesman.com/politics/uk/2016/01/ending-new-thirty-years-war.

Stavridis, J., 'It's Time to Seriously Consider the Partition of Syria', *Foreign Policy*, 9 March 2016. Available at: http://foreignpolicy.com/2016/03/09/its-time-to-seriously-consider-partitioning-syria.

Sullivan, A., 'The Thirty Years' War Brewing in the Middle East', *The Sunday Times*, 16 December 2006.

Taha, H., 'Managing Cultural Heritage in Palestine', *UNDP Focus*, 1 (2004): 31–2.

Tas, L., 'The Myth of the Ottoman Millet System', *International Journal on Minority and Group Rights*, 21 (2014): 497–526.

The Select Committee, 'The Aborigines of British Settlements', *The Asiatic Journal and Monthly Miscellany*, 24 (1837): 89.

Ülker, E., 'Contextualising "Turkification": Nation-building in the Late Ottoman Empire, 1908–18', *Nations and Nationalism*, 11(4) (2005): 623.

Urban, S., *The Gentleman's Magazine*, vol. 31, January–June 1840, Nichols, London (1849): 81.

Vennekens, J., 'The Influence of Tribalism in the Middle East', *International Perspective*, 22 September 2015. Available at: http://www.internationalperspective.be/insight/2015/09/the-influence-of-tribalism.

Visser, R., 'Historical Myths of a Divided Iraq', *Survival*, 50(2) (2008): 103.

Wahrman, M., 'Blame the West for ISIS? Yes – But Go Back to 1925', *Ha'aretz*, 5 September 2016. Available at: http://www.haaretz.com/misc/haaretzcomsmartphoneapp/.premium-1.740350.

Wright, R., 'Imagining a Remapped Middle East', *The New York Times*, 28 September 2013. Available at: http://www.nytimes.com/2013/09/29/opinion/sunday/imagining-a-remapped-middle-east.html?pagewanted=all&_r=0.

Books in Non-Western Languages

n.a., *Kitāb Tawārīkh Mokhtasar Yunbī Mamalek wa Bilad 'Edīdah wa mā Hadatha fiha men Qadīm al-Zamān 'ela 'Asrenā Hathā* [A Brief History Book Tells about Kingdoms and Many Countries and What Happened in them from Ancient Times until Today] (Malta, 1833).

'Abduh, M. and 'Imarāh, M. (eds), *al-A'māl al-kāmila lil-Imam Muḥammad 'Abduh* [The Full Works of the Imam Muḥammad 'Abduh], vol. 3 (Beirut: al-Mu'assasat al-Arabīyya, 1972).

'Abduh, M. and 'Imarāh, M. (eds), *Al-Islam wa al-Mar'ah fi Ra'i al-Imam Muḥammad 'Abduh* [Islam and the Woman in the Opinion of the Imam Muḥammad 'Abduh] (Cairo: Al-Qāirah li al-Thaqāfa al-'Arabīyya, 1975).

Abū-'Izzedīn, S., *Ibrahīm Pasha fi Sūrīya* [Ibrahīm Pasha in Syria] (Beirut: al-Matba'ah al-'Ilmīya, 1929).

al-'Āref, Ā., *Tārīkh al-Quds* [The History of Jerusalem] (Cairo: Dār al- Ma'ārif, 1951).

al-Asali, K., *Mawṣim al-Nabi Musa Filastīn: tā'rīkh al-Mawṣim wa 'l-Maqam* [The Nabi Musa Festival in Palestine: the History of the Festival and of the Shrine] ('Amman: Dar al-Karmil, 1990).

al-Dīn, M., *Al-Uns al-Jalil bi-Tarikh al-Quds wa al-Khalīl* [The Glorious History of Jerusalem and Hebron], vol. 1 (Najaf: al-Haydariya, 1968 [1595]).

al-Husri, S., *Al-Bilād al-'Arabiyya wa al-Dawla al-'Utmāniyya* [The Arab Countries and the Ottoman State] (Beirut: Dār al-'Ilm li-al-Malāyīn, 1960).

al-Mubarrad, *Al-Kāmil* [The Perfect One] (Cairo: Dār Nahdat Misr, 1956).

al-Muhibbī, M., *Khulāṣat al-Athār fi A'yān al-Qarn al-hādī 'Ashar* [Compendium of the Notables of the Eleventh Century], vol. 4 (Cairo: al-Matba'a al-Wahbīya, 1867).

al-Muqaddasī, S., *Ahsan al-taqāsīm fi ma'rifat al-aqālīm* [The Best Division for the Knowledge of the Provinces] (Beirut: Dār al-Kutub al-'Ilmiyya, 2003).

al-Qaradāwī, Y., *Al-Hulūl al-Mustawrada wa Kayfa Janat 'ala Ummatinā* [The Imported Solutions and how they are Rooted in our Community], vol. 1 (Cairo: Maktabat Wahba, 1977).

al-Raf'i, A., *'Asr Muhammad 'Ali* [The Age of Muhammad 'Ali] (Cairo: Dār al-Ma'ārif, 1989).

al-Ramli, K., *Al-fatawa al-Khayriyya li-naf al-bariyya* [Consolatory Legal Response in Favour of the Creation], vol. 2 (Cairo: Dar al-Ma'rifa, 1974).

al-Razzāq al-Hassanī, 'A., *Tā'rikh al-Wizārāt 'al-'Irāqīya* [History of Iraqi Cabinets], vol. 1 (Baghdād: Wizārat al-thaqāfa, 1982).

al-Sayyid, R., *Min al- shu'ūb wa al-qaba'il ila al-umma. Dirāsa fi takawwn mafhm al-umma fi al-Islam* [From Peoples and Tribes to the Nation. A Study about the Concept of the Nation in Islam] (Beirut: n.p., 1984).

al-Shadyāq, A. F., *al-Wāsitah fi ma'rifat ahwāl Māltah: wa kasaf al-mukhabbā' 'an funūn Ūrubbā 1834–1857* [The Means to Know the Conditions of Malta and Uncover the Hidden about the Arts of Europe 1857–1834] (Abū Dhabi: Dār al-Suwaydī, 2004).

al-Shihābī, M., *Al-Qawmīya al-'Arabīya* [Arab Nationalism] (Cairo: Muhādarāt, 1961).

al-Tahtāwī, R., *Kitab Takhlīs al-Ibrīz fi Talkhīs Bārīs* [The Book of the Extraction of Pure Gold in the Compendium of Paris] (Cairo: al-Haya al-Misrīya al-'Amma li al-Kitāb, 1993 [1834]).

al-Tahtāwī, R., *al-Murshid al-Amīn li al-Banāt wa al-Banīn* [The Trustworthy Guide for the Education of Guys and Girls] (Cairo: al-Majlis al-A'lā lil-Thaqāfah, 2002).

al-Tahtāwī, R. and 'Imarāh, M. (eds), *al-'Amāl al-Kāmilah li al-Tahtāwī* [The Full Works of al-Tahtāwī] (Beirut: al-Mu'assasat al-Arabīyya, 1973).

al-Tala'farī, Q. A., *Thawrat Tall 'Afar 1920* [Telfar's revolution in 1920] (Baghdād: Matba'at al-Azhar, 1969).

al-Tawhīdī, A. H., '*Al-Imtāʿ wa al-Muʾānasa*' [Enjoyment and Conviviality], in A. Amīn and A. al-Zayn (eds), *Dār al-Arqam*, vol. 1 (Beirut: Dār al-Maktaba bi-al-Hayyāh, 1953).

Barghūti, U. S., *Al-Marahil* [Turning Points] (Beirut: al-Muʿassasat al-Arabīyya, 2001).

Biger, G., *Erets rabat gvulot* [The Land of Many Borders] (Sde Boker: ha-Merkaz le-moreshet Ben-Gurion, 2001).

Fahim Gabr, A., *Al-Ard al-Muqaddasa* [The Holy Land] (Nablus: Al-Najah University, 1983).

Ghalioun, B. N., *al-Tāʾifīya min al-Dawla ila al-Qabīla* [The Sectarian System from the State to the Tribe] (Beirut: al-Markaz al-Taqāfi al-Arabī, 1990).

Hashim, S., *Al-Intifadhat al-ʾArabīya ʿala Dhaou Falsafīt al-Tarīkh* [The Arab Uprising in Light of the Philosophy of History] (Beirut: Dār al-Saqī, 2013).

Ismāʿīl, A. and Khūrī, I., *al-Siyāsah al-Duwalīyah fī al-Sharq al-ʾArabī min sanah 1789 ilā sanah 1958* [The International Politics in the Arab East from the Year 1789 to the Year 1958], vol. 2 (Beirut: Dār al-Nashr li-al-Siyāsah wa-al-Taʾrīkh, 1964).

Khuri, Y., *Al-Sahāfa al-ʾArabyya fī Filastīn* [The Arabic Press in Palestine] (Beirut: Institute for Palestine Studies, 1976).

Livneh, E., *Nili: Toldoteha shel Heʿazah Medinit* [Nili: The History of a Political Daring] (Jerusalem: Shoken, 1961).

Meroz, T., *Tel Aviv-Yafo: Sipur HaʾIr* [Tel Aviv-Jaffa: History of a City] (Tel Aviv: Ben-Zion, 1978).

Mukhlīs, A., *Al-Muslimūn wa al-Naṣāra* [Muslims and Christians] (Ḥaifā: n.p., 1929).

Nadvi, S. H. H., *Filasṭīn Aur Bain Al-Aqvaīmiī Siyaīsiyaīt* [Palestine and International Politics] (Karachi: Academia, 1976) (in Urdu).

Radwān, A., *Tarīkh Matbaʿah Būlāq* [History of the Būlāq Press] (Cairo: Al-Amīriya/Būlāq, 1953).

Rustum, A. J. *Hurūb Ibrāhīm Pāshā fī Sūriyah waʾl-Anādūl* [The Wars of Ibrāhīm Pāshā in Syria and Anatolia], 2 vols (Beirut: Al-Maktaba al-Bulusiyya, 1986).

Rustum, A. J., *al-Mahfūzāt al-Malikīya al-Misrīya* [A Record of State Papers from the Egyptian Royal Archives], vol. 2 (Beirut: Al-Maktaba al-Bulusiyya, 1986–7).

Rustum, A. J. (ed.), *Al-Usūl al-ʾArabīyya li-Tāʾrikh Sūriyah fī ʾAhd Muhammad ʾAli Pāshā* [Materials for a Corpus of Arabic Documents Concerning the History of Syria under Muhammad ʾAli Pāshā] (Beirut: Al-Maktaba al-Bulusiyya, 1987).

Shur, N., *Toldot Sfat* [History of Safed] (Jerusalem: Ariel, 1983).

Tabari, *Jami' al-Bayan 'an Ta'wil al-Quran* [The Clear Collection Regarding the Interpretation of the Qur'an], 15 vols (Beirut: ed. Sidqi Jamil al-'Attar, 2001 [883]).

Tamarī, S. and Nassar, I. (eds), *Al Quds al 'Uthmanīyeh* [Ottoman Jerusalem], vol. 1 (Jerusalem: Institute for Jerusalem Studies, 2003).

Tarbīn, A., *Lubnān Mundhu 'Ahd al-Muteṣarrīfīyah ilá Bedāyat al-Intidāb, 1860-1920* [Lebanon from the Time of the Muteṣarrīfiyah to the Beginning Mandate, 1860–1920] (Cairo: Ma'had al-Buhūth wa al-Dirasāt al-'Arabiyya, 1968).

Yehoshua, A. B., *Bizkhut ha-normaliut* [In Defence of Normality] (Tel Aviv: Schocken, 1980).

Yehoshua, J., *Yaldut be-Yerushalayim ha-yashena* [Childhood in Old Jerusalem], vol. 2 (Jerusalem: Rubin Mass, 1965).

Yehoshua, J., *Tārīkh al-Ṣaḥāfa al-'Arabīya fī Filasṭīn fi al-'Ahd al-'Uthmānī, 1909–1918* [The History of the Arabic Press in Palestine during the Ottoman Era] (Jerusalem: Maṭba'at al-Ma'ārif, 1974).

Selected Secondary Sources in French, English, Italian, German, Latin

Abdo, G., *The New Sectarianism* (Oxford: Oxford University Press, 2016).

Abu-'Uksa, W., *Freedom in the Arab World* (Cambridge: Cambridge University Press, 2016).

Achcar, G., *The People Want: A Radical Exploration of the Arab Uprisings* (Berkeley: University of California Press, 2013).

Adelson, R., *Mark Sykes: Portrait of an Amateur* (London: Cape, 1975).

Adib-Moghaddam A., *Psycho-nationalism* (Cambridge: Cambridge University Press, 2018).

al-Ali, Z., *The Struggle for Iraq's Future* (New Haven CT: Yale University Press, 2014).

al-Barghūti, T., *The Umma and the Dawla* (London: Pluto Press, 2008).

al-Naqeeb, K. H., *Society and State in the Gulf and the Arabian Peninsula* (London: Routledge, 1990).

Al-Rustom, H., 'Rethinking the "Post-Ottoman": Anatolian Armenians as an Ethnographic Perspective', in S. Altorki (ed.), *A Companion to the Anthropology of the Middle East* (Hoboken NJ: Wiley Blackwell, 2015).

Amery, L., 'Introduction' in P. Goodman (ed.), *Chaim Weizmann: A Tribute on his Seventieth Birthday* (London: Gollancz, 1945).

Amery, L., *My Political Life*, vol. 2 (London: Hutchinson, 1953).

Anderson, B., *Imagined Communities* (New York: Verso, 1991).

Antonius, G., *The Arab Awakening: The Story of the Arab National Movement* (London: Hamish Hamilton, 1938).

Archibugi, D. and Voltaggio, F., *Filosofi per la pace* [Philosophers for Peace] (Rome: Editori Riuniti, 1999).

Arnold, T. W., *The Preaching of Islam* (Lahore: Ashraf, 1961).

Asquith, H. H., *Memories and Reflections, 1852–1927*, vol. 2 (Boston MA: Little, 1928).

Atasoy, Y., *Turkey, Islamists and Democracy* (London: I. B. Tauris, 2005).

'Athāmina, K., *Le premier siècle de l'Islam: Jérusalem, capitale de la Palestine* [The First Century of Islam: Jerusalem, Capital of Palestine], in F. Mardam-Bey and E. Sanbar (eds), *Jérusalem: le sacré et le politique* [Jerusalem: The Holy and the Political] (Arles: Sindbad, 2002).

Auron, Y., *The Banality of Indifference* (New Brunswick NJ: Transaction, 2009).

Ayalon, A., *Language and Change in the Arab Middle East: The Evolution of Modern Arabic Political Discourse* (Oxford: Oxford University Press, 1987).

Balanche, F., 'The Levant: Fragmentation and Remapping', in A. J. Tabler (ed.), *100 Years of Sykes–Picot* (Washington DC: The Washington Institute for Near East Policy, 2016).

Balfour, A., *Henry Sidgwick Memorial Lecture* (Cambridge: Cambridge University Press, 1908).

Bâli, A. Ü. and Lerner, H. (eds), *Constitution Writing, Religion and Democracy* (Cambridge: Cambridge University Press, 2017).

Bartlett, W. H., *Walks about the City and Environs of Jerusalem* (London: Virtue, 1844).

Bar-Yosef, E., *The Holy Land in English Culture, 1799–1917* (Oxford: Oxford University Press, 2005).

Bayly, C., *The Birth of the Modern World, 1780–1914* (Oxford: Blackwell, 2004).

Bechev, D. and Nicolaïdis, K., *Mediterranean Frontiers: Borders, Conflict and Memory in a Transnational World* (London: I. B. Tauris, 2010).

Bede, The Venerable, *The Ecclesiastical History of the English Nation* (New York: Cosimo, 2007).

Bell, D. P., *Jews in the Early Modern World* (Lanham MD: Rowman & Littlefield, 2008).

Belliard, A. D. and Douin, G. (eds), *Une mission militaire Française auprès de Mohamed Aly* [A French Military Mission to Mohamed Aly] (Cairo: Institut français d'archéologie orientale pour la Société royale de géographie d'Égypte, 1923).

Belloc, H., *The Jews* (London: Constable, 1922).

Beloff, M. (ed.), *Britain's Liberal Empire 1897–1921*. vol. 1 (London: Palgrave, 1987).

Ben-Arieh, Y., *The Rediscovery of the Holy Land in the Nineteenth Century* (Jerusalem: Magnes Press, 1979).

Ben-Arieh, Y., *Jerusalem in the 19th Century. The Old City* (Jerusalem: St. Martin's, 1984).

Ben-Arieh, Y., Davis M. (eds), *Jerusalem in the Mind of the Western World, 1800–1948* (Westport: Praeger, 1997).

Benvenisti, M., *Son of the Cypresses* (Berkeley: University of California Press, 2007).

Ben Ze'ev, E., *Remembering Palestine in 1948* (New York: Cambridge University Press, 2011).

Berggren, J., *Guide français-arabe vulgaire des voyageurs et des francs en Syrie et en Égypte: avec carte physique et géographique de la Syrie et plan géométrique de Jérusalem ancien et moderne, comme supplément aux voyages en orient* (Uppsala: Leffer et Sebell, 1844).

Berlin, I., *Personal Impressions* (Oxford: Oxford University Press, 1982).

Berque, J., 'Introduction', in W. Polk and R. Chambers (eds), *Beginnings of Modernization in the Middle East* (Chicago: University of Chicago Press, 1969).

Bertie, F., *The Diary of Lord Bertie of Thame, 1914–1918*, vol. 2 (New York: Hodder, 1924).

Beshara, A. (ed.), *The Origins of Syrian Nationhood: Histories, Pioneers and Identity* (London: Routledge, 2011).

Bicheno, J., *The Restoration of the Jews* (London: Barfield, 1807).

Black, C. E. and Brown, L. C., *Modernization in the Middle East* (Princeton NJ: Darwin Press, 1992).

Blake, W., *Jerusalem: The Emanation of Giant Albion* (London, William Blake, 1804).

Bloxham, D., *The Great Game of Genocide* (Oxford: Oxford Univerity Press, 2005).

Blumi, I., *Foundations of Modernity: Human Agency and the Imperial State* (New York: Routledge, 2012).

Bovet, F., *Viaggio in Terra Santa* [A Voyage to the Holy Land] (Florence: Tipografia Claudiana, 1867).

Bowle, J., *Viscount Samuel, A Biography* (London: Gollancz, 1957).

Boyle, S. S., *Betrayal of Palestine* (Boulder CO: Westview, 2001).

Braudel, F., *Civilization and Capitalism, 15th–18th Century: The Structure of Everyday Life* (Berkeley: University of California Press, 1992).

Brenner, M., *A Short History of the Jews* (Princeton NJ: Princeton University Press, 2010).

British Foreign Office, *Documents on British Foreign Policy, 1919–1939* (London: HMSO, 1952).

Broch, M. and Broch, E. (eds), *H. H. Asquith, Letters to Venetia Stanley* (Oxford: Oxford University Press, 1982).

Brubaker, R., *Nationalism Reframed* (Cambridge: Cambridge University Press, 1996)

Brustein, W., *Roots of Hate* (Cambridge: Cambridge University Press, 2003).

Bryant, R. (ed.), *Post-Ottoman Coexistence: Sharing Space in the Shadow of Conflict* (New York: Berghahn, 2016).

Buchan, J., *The Thirty-Nine Steps* (New York: Doran, 1915).

Burckhardt, J. L. *Travels in Syria and the Holy Land* (London: John Murray, 1822).

Burkman, T. W., *Japan and the League of Nations* (Honolulu HI: University of Hawai'i Press, 2008).

Bustani, E., *Doubts and Dynamite* (London: Allan Wingate, 1958).

Cabral, A. and Handyside, R. (eds), *Revolution in Guinea* (New York: Monthly Review Press, 1969).

Campos, M. U. *Ottoman Brothers* (Stanford CA: Stanford University Press, 2011).

Caplan, G., *The Betrayal of Africa* (Toronto: Groundwood Books, 2008).

Catlos, B. A., *Infidel Kings and Unholy Warriors* (New York: Farrar, Straus and Giroux, 2015).

Chalcraft, J., *Popular Politics in the Making of the Modern Middle East* (Cambridge: Cambridge University Press, 2016).

Chan, S., *Grasping Africa: A Tale of Tragedy and Achievement* (London and New York: I. B. Tauris, 2007).

Cherif Bassiouni, M. and Ben-Ami, S., *A Guide to Documents on the Arab-Palestinian/ Israeli Conflict: 1897–2008* (Leiden: Brill, 2009).

Chesterton, G. K., *The New Jerusalem* (London: Hodder, 1920).

Chevallier, D., *La société du mont Liban à l'époque de la révolution industrielle en Europe* (Paris: Geuthner, 1971).

Clayton, A., *The British Empire as a Superpower, 1919–39* (Athens GA: University of Georgia Press, 1986).

Cohen, A., *Israel and the Arab World* (New York: Funk, 1970).

Cohen, A., *A World Within: Jewish Life as Reflected in Muslim Court Documents from the Sijill of Jerusalem (XVIth Century)*, vol. 1 (Philadelphia PA: Center for Judaic Studies, University of Pennsylvania, 1994).

Cohen, M. J., *Britain's Moment in Palestine: Retrospect and Perspectives, 1917–1948* (London: Routledge, 2014).

Conder, C. R., *Palestine* (London: Dodd, 1889).

Corbin, A., *The Foul and the Fragrant: Odour and the French Social Imagination* (Basingstoke: Macmillan, 1996).

Couroucli, M., 'Introduction', in D. Albera and M. Couroucli (eds), *Sharing Sacred Spaces in the Mediterranean* (Bloomington IN: Indiana University Press, 2012).

Courtney, R., *Palestine Policeman* (London: Jenkins, 1939).

Dabashi, H., *The Arab Spring* (New York: Zed Books, 2012).

Darwin, J., *The Empire Project: The Rise and Fall of the British World-System, 1830–1970* (Cambridge: Cambridge University Press, 2009).

Darwīsh, M. (trans. by Elias Sanbar), *La terre nous est étroite et autres poèmes* [The Earth is Close to Us and Other Poems], 1966–99 (Paris: Gallimard, 2000).

Davidov, V. and Andersen, B., 'Mimetic Kinship: Theorizing Online "Tribalism"', in T. L. Adams and S. A. Smith (eds), *Electronic Tribes* (Austin TX: University of Texas Press, 2009).

Davies, G. (ed.), *The Chosen People: Wales and the Jews* (Bridgend: Seren, 2002).

Dawn, E., *From Ottomanism to Arabism* (Urbana IL: University of Illinois Press, 1973).

Dawn, E., 'Ottomanism to Arabism: The Origin of an Ideology', in A. Hourani, P. Khoury, and M. Wilson (eds), *Modern Middle East: A Reader* (Berkeley: University of California Press, 1993).

De Benoist, A., *Identità e comunità* (Naples: Guida, 2005).

De Haas, J., *History of Palestine – The Last Two Thousand Years* (New York: Macmillan, 1934).

De Madariaga, S. and Brailsford, H. N., *Can the League Cope with Imperialism?* (New York: The Foreign Policy Association, 1928).

De Roover, J., 'A Nation of Tribes and Priests', in M Fárek, D. Jalki, S. Pathan and P. Shah (eds), *Western Foundations of the Caste System* (London: Palgrave, 2017).

Dirks, N., *Castes of Mind: Colonialism and the Making of Modern India* (Princeton: Princeton University Press, 2011).

Dirlik, A., *What is in a Rim?: Critical Perspectives on the Pacific Region Idea* (Lanham MD: Rowman, 1998).

Divine, D. R., *Politics and Society in Ottoman Palestine* (London: Rienner, 1994).

Dodge, T., 'State Collapse and the Rise of Identity Politics in Iraq', in G. Montserrat and J. Rex (eds), *The Ethnicity Reader* (Cambridge: Polity Press, 2010).

Doumani, B., *Rediscovering Palestine: Merchants and Peasants in Jabal Nablus, 1700–1900* (Berkeley: University of California Press, 1995).

Doumanis, N., *Before the Nation* (Oxford: Oxford University Press, 2013).

Doyle, M. W. *Empires* (Ithaca NY: Cornell University Press, 1986).

Duncan Hall, H., *Mandates, Dependencies and Trusteeship* (Washington DC: Carnegie Endowment for International Peace, 1948).

Dundar, F., '"Statisquo". British Use of Statistics in the Iraqi Kurdish Question (1912–1939)', *Crown Paper* 7 (Boston MA: Brandeis University's Crown Center for Middle East Studies, 2012).

Efron J., Weitzman, S. and Lehmann, M., *The Jews: A History* (New York: Routledge, 2016).

Endelman, T. M., *The Jews of Britain, 1656 to 2000* (Berkeley: University of California Press, 2002).

Erskine, S., *Palestine of the Arabs* (London: Harrap, 1935).

Euben, R. L., *Journeys to the Other Shore* (Princeton NJ: Princeton University Press, 2006).

Fagan, B., *The Little Ice Age: How Climate Made History, 1300–1845* (New York: Basic Books, 2000).

Fawaz, L., *Merchants and Migrants in Nineteenth-Century Beirut* (Cambridge MA: Harvard University Press, 1983).

Ferabolli, S., *Arab Regionalism* (London: Routledge, 2015).

Ferenczi, I., *International Migrations*, vol. 2 (New York and London: Gordon and Breach, 1969).

Ferguson, N., *Empire: The Rise and Demise of the British World Order and the Lessons for Global Power* (New York: Basic Books, 2002).

Finn, E., 'The Fellaheen of Palestine', in The Committee of the PEF, *The Surveys of Western Palestine: Special Papers on Topography, Archaeology, Manners and Customs* (London: PEF, 1881).

Firro, K., *Inventing Lebanon: Nationalism and the State under the Mandate* (London: I. B. Tauris, 2003).

Foliard, D., *Dislocating the Orient: British Maps and the Making of the Middle East, 1854–1921* (Chicago: University of Chicago Press, 2017).

Foner, E., *The Story of American Freedom* (New York: Norton, 1999).

Frey, J. S., *Judah and Israel* (New York: Fanshaw, 1812).

Fried, M. H., 'The Notion of "Tribe" and "Tribal Society"', in J. Helm et al. (eds), *Proceedings of the 1967 Annual Meeting of the American Ethnological Society* (Seattle WA: University of Washington, 1968), pp. 3–20.

Friedman, I., *British Pan-Arab Policy, 1915–1922* (New Brunswick NJ: Transaction Publishers, 2011).

Fromkin, D., *A Peace to End All Peace: The Fall of the Ottoman Empire and the Creation of the Modern Middle East* (New York: Holt & Company, 1989).

Ghandour, Z. B., *A Discourse on Domination in Mandate Palestine: Imperialism, Property and Insurgency* (New York: Routledge, 2010).

Gilbert, M., *Exile and Return* (Philadelphia PA: Lippincott, 1978).

Girard, P., 'Historical Foundations of Antisemitism', in Joel E. Dimsdale (ed.), *Survivors, Victims and Perpetrators: Essays on the Nazi Holocaust* (Washington DC: Hemisphere Publishing, 1980), pp. 55–77.

Goodman, P. (ed.), *The Jewish National Home* (London: Dent, 1943).

Gran, P., *Islamic Roots of Capitalism* (Syracuse NY: Syracuse University Press, 1979).

Grief, H., *The Legal Foundation and Borders of Israel under International Law* (Jerusalem: Mazo, 2008).

Grose, P., *Israel in the Mind of America* (New York: Knopf, 1983).

Guys, H., *Beyrouth et le Liban: Relation d'un séjour de plusieurs années dans ce pays*, 2 vols (Paris: Dār Lahad Khater, 1850).

Haddād, F., *Sectarianism in Iraq: Antagonist Visions of Unity* (Oxford: Oxford University Press, 2011).

Haddād, W. W., *Nationalism in a Non-National State: The Dissolution of the Ottoman Empire* (Columbus OH: Ohio State University Press, 1977).

Haight, S. R., *Letters from the Old World*, vol. 1 (New York: Harper and Brothers, 1840).

Hajjar, J., *Le Christianisme en Orient* [Christianity in the East] (Beirut: Librairie du Liban, 1971).

Hakim, C., *The Origins of the Lebanese National Idea, 1840–1920* (Berkeley: University of California Press, 2013).

Halliday, F., *The Middle East in International Relations* (Cambridge: Cambridge University Press, 2005).

Halperin, S. and Palan, R. (eds), *Legacies of Empire* (Cambridge: Cambridge University Press, 2015).

Hartshorne, R., *The Nature of Geography: A Critical Survey of Current Thought in the Light of the Past* (Lancaster PA: Association of American Geographers, 1939).

Hashemi, N. and Postel, D. (eds), *Sectarianization* (London: Hurst, 2017).

Hayden, J. and Matar, N. (eds), *Through the Eyes of the Beholder: The Holy Land, 1517–1713* (Leiden: Brill, 2013).

Heng, G., *The Invention of Race in the European Middle Ages* (Cambridge: Cambridge University Press, 2018).

Hermes, N. F., *The [European] Other in Medieval Arabic Literature and Culture* (New York: Palgrave, 2012).

Hertz, E. E., *Reply* (New York: Myths and Facts, 2005).

Herzl, T., *The Complete Diaries of Theodor Herzl*, vol. 1 (New York: Herzl Press, 1960).

Hobsbawm, E., *The Age of Extremes* (New York: Vintage, 1996).

Hourani, A., *The Emergence of the Modern Middle East* (Berkeley: University of California Press, 1981).

Hourani, A., *A History of the Arab Peoples* (London: Faber, 1991).

House of Commons, *Accounts and Papers* (London: HMSO, 1878).

Howard, D. A., *A History of the Ottoman Empire* (Cambridge: Cambridge University Press, 2017).

Hyam, R., *Britain's Imperial Century, 1815–1914* (London: Batsford, 1976).

Hyamson, A. M., *British Projects for the Restoration of the Jews* (Leeds: Petty, 1917).

Ignatieff, M., *The Russian Album* (New York: Picador, 2001).

International Court of Justice (ICJ), *Reports of Judgments, Advisory Opinions, and Orders* (Leiden: A. W. Sijthoff, 1975).

Iordachi, C., 'The Ottoman Empire', in T. Baycroft and M. Hewitson (eds), *What Is a Nation? Europe 1789–1914* (Oxford: Oxford University Press, 2006).

Issawī, C. (ed.), *The Economic History of the Middle East 1800–1914* (Chicago: University of Chicago Press, 1966).

Issawī, C., *The Fertile Crescent, 1800–1914: A Documentary Economic History* (New York: Oxford University Press, 1988).

Jabar, F., 'Sheikhs and Ideologues: Deconstruction and Reconstruction of Tribes under Patrimonial Totalitarianism in Iraq, 1968–1998', in F. Jabar and H. Dawod (eds), *Tribes and Power: Nationalism and Ethnicity in the Middle East* (London: Saqi, 2003).

Jabārah, T., *Palestinian Leader, Hajj Amin al-Husayni, Mufti of Jerusalem* (Princeton NJ: Kingston Press, 1985).

Jowett, W. *Christian Researches in Syria and the Holy Land* (London: Church Missionary Society, 1825).

Joyce, J., *Ulysses* (Oxford: Oxford University Press, 2008 [1922]).

Judd, D., *Balfour and the British Empire* (London: Macmillan, 1968).

Kamel, L. *Imperial Perceptions of Palestine: British Influence and Power in Late Ottoman Times* (London and New York: I. B. Tauris, 2015).

Kamel, L. (ed.), *The Frailty of Authority: Borders, Non-State Actors and Power Vacuums in a Changing Middle East* (Rome: Nuova Cultura, 2017).

Kandiyoti, D. 'Enduring Concerns, Resilient Tropes, and New Departures', in S. Altorki (ed.), *A Companion to the Anthropology of the Middle East* (Hoboken NJ: Wiley Blackwell, 2015).

Karpat, K. H., *Ottoman Population, 1830–1914* (Madison WI: University of Wisconsin Press, 1985).

Karpat, K. H. 'Historical Continuity and Identity Change or How to be Modern Muslim, Ottoman, and Turk', in K. H. Karpat (ed.), *Ottoman Past and Today's Turkey* (Boston MA: Brill, 2000).

Karpat, K. H., *Studies on Ottoman Social and Political History* (Leiden: Brill, 2002).

Kattan, V., *From Coexistence to Conquest* (New York: Pluto Press, 2009).

Kaufman, A., *Contested Frontiers in the Syria-Lebanon-Israel Region: Cartography, Sovereignty, and Conflict* (Washington DC: Woodrow Wilson Center Press, 2014).

Kayalı, H., *Arabs and Young Turks: Ottomanism, Arabism and Islamism in the Ottoman Empire, 1908–1918* (Berkeley: University of California Press, 1997).

Kedourie, E., *Nationalism in Asia and Africa* (London: Weidenfeld & Nicolson, 1971).

Kennedy, A. L., *Salisbury, 1830–1903: Portrait of a Statesman* (New York: Kraus, 1971).

Khālidī, R., 'Ottomanism and Arabism in Syria Before 1914: A Reassessment', in R. Khālidī, L. Anderson, M. Muslih, and R. S. Simon (eds), *The Origins of Arab Nationalism* (New York: Columbia University Press, 1991).

Khālidī, R., *Palestinian Identity* (New York: Columbia University Press, 1997).

Khālidī, R., *Brokers of Deceit* (Boston MA: Beacon Press, 2013).

Khalīl, O., *America's Dream Palace: Middle East Expertise and the Rise of the National Security State* (Cambridge MA: Harvard University Press, 2016).

Kimche, J., *The Unromantics, the Great Powers and the Balfour Declaration* (Liverpool: Tinling, 1968).

Kimche, J., *The Second Arab Awakening* (London: Thames & Hudson, 1970).

Kimche, J., *There Could Have Been Peace* (New York: Dial Press, 1973).

König, D. G., *Arab-Islamic Views of the Latin West* (Oxford: Oxford University Press, 2015).

Korany, B., 'Analyzing Change in the Middle East: A Framework Revisited', in C. Jones (ed.), *The Politics of Change in the Middle East*, Durham Middle East Paper, No. 78, March 2017.

Kostiner, J., *The Making of Saudi Arabia, 1916–1936: From Chieftaincy to Monarchical State* (Oxford: Oxford University Press, 1993).

Kressel, G. M. and Aharoni, R., *Egyptian Émigrés in the Levant of the 19th and 20th Centuries* (Jerusalem: Jerusalem Center for Public Affairs, 2013).

Kupferschmidt, U., *The Supreme Muslim Council* (Leiden: Brill, 1987).

Kushner, D. (ed.), *Palestine in the Late Ottoman Period* (Jerusalem: Ben-Zvi, 1986).

Lansing, R., *The Peace Negotiation – A Personal Narrative* (New York: Houghton, 1921).

Lemire, V., *Jérusalem 1900: La ville sainte à l'âge des possibles* [Jerusalem 1900: The Holy City in the Age of Possibilities] (Paris: Armand Colin, 2013).

Leslie, S., *Mark Sykes: His Life and Letters* (New York: Cassell, 1923).

Le Strange, G., *Palestine under the Moslems: A Description of Syria and the Holy Land from A.D. 650 to 1500* (London: Watt, 1890).

Levine, G. M., *The Merchant of Modernism* (New York: Routledge, 2003).

LeVine, M., *Overthrowing Geography: Jaffa, Tel Aviv and Struggle for Palestine* (Berkeley: University of California Press, 2005).

Lévi-Strauss, C., *La pensée sauvage* [The Savage Mind] (Paris: Plon, 1969).

Lewis, B., *The Shaping of the Modern Middle East* (New York: Oxford University Press, 1994).

Lewis, B., *From Babel to Dragomans* (London: Phoenix, 2005).

Libbey, W. and Hoskins, F. E., *The Jordan Valley and Petra*, vol. 1 (New York: Putnam, 1905).

Likhovski, A., *Law and Identity in Mandate Palestine* (Chapel Hill NC: University of North Carolina Press, 2006).

Little, D., *American Orientalism* (London: I. B. Tauris, 2003).

Lloyd George, D., *War Memoirs of David Lloyd George* (Boston MA: Little, 1934).

Lloyd George, D., *Memoirs of the Peace Conference*, vol. 2 (New Haven CT: Yale University Press, 1939).

Lockman, Z., *Field Notes: The Making of Middle East Studies in the United States* (Stanford CA: Stanford University Press, 2016).

Longrigg, S. H., *Syria and Lebanon under French Mandate* (London and New York: Oxford University Press, 1958).

Luke, H., *The Making of Modern Turkey* (London: Macmillan, 1936).

Lynn, M., 'British Policy, Trade, and Informal Empire in the Mid-Nineteenth Century', in A. Porter, *The Oxford History of the British Empire*, vol. 3 (Oxford: Oxford University Press, 1999).

Maalouf, A., *Les identités meurtrières* (Paris: Grasset, 1998).

McCarthy, J., *Death and Exile: The Ethnic Cleansing of Ottoman Muslims 1821–1922* (Princeton NJ: Darwin Press, 1995).

McDowall, D., *A Modern History of the Kurds* (London: I. B. Tauris, 2007).

McEwen, J. M. (ed.), *The Riddell Diaries, 1908–1923* (London: Athlone, 1986).

Mackay, R. F., *Balfour, Intellectual Statesman* (Oxford: Oxford University Press, 1985).

Makdisi, U., *The Culture of Sectarianism: Community, History, and Violence in Nineteenth-Century Ottoman Lebanon* (Berkeley: University of California Press, 2000).

Makdisi, U., 'The Problem of Sectarianism in the Middle East in an Age of Western Hegemony', in N. Hashemi and D. Postel (eds), *Sectarianization* (London: Hurst, 2017).

Malcolm, J. A., *Origins of the Balfour Declaration: Dr Weizmann's Contribution* (London: British Museum, 1944).

Mamdani M., *Citizen and Subject: Contemporary Africa and the Legacy of Late Colonialism* (Princeton NJ: Princeton University Press, 1996).

Mansfield, P., *The British in Egypt* (London: Holt, 1972).

Ma'oz, M., *Muslim Attitudes to Jews and Israel* (Eastbourne: Sussex University Press, 2010).

Marrus, M. R., *The Unwanted: European Refugees in the Twentieth Century* (New York: Oxford University Press, 1985).

Martin, R. M., *Colonial Policy of the British Empire* (London: Allen & Co., 1837).

Massad, J., *Colonial Effects* (New York: Columbia University Press, 2001).

Masters, B., *Christians and Jews in the Ottoman Arab World: The Roots of Sectarianism* (Cambridge: Cambridge University Press, 2001).

Matar, N., *Turks, Moors, and Englishmen in the Age of Discovery* (New York: Columbia University Press, 1999).

Matthews, W. C., *Confronting an Empire, Constructing a Nation* (London: I. B. Tauris, 2006).

Maybury-Lewis, D., *Indigenous Peoples, Ethnic Groups, and the State* (Boston MA: Allyn and Bacon, 1997).

Mayhew, H., *London Labour and the London Poor*, vol. 2 (London: Griffin, 1864).

Mazza, R., *Jerusalem from the Ottomans to the British* (London: I. B. Tauris, 2009).

Mazza, R., 'Transforming the Holy City: From Communal Clashes to Urban Violence, the Nebi Musa Riots in 1920', in U. Freitag, N. Fuccaro, C. Ghrawi, and N. Lafi (eds), *Urban Violence in the Middle East* (New York: Berghahn, 2015).

Meinertzhagen, R., *Middle East Diary, 1917–1956* (London: Cresset, 1959).

Milner, A., *The Milner Papers*, vol. 2 (London: Cassell, 1931).

Mohs, P. A., *Military Intelligence and the Arab Revolt: The First Modern Intelligence War* (London: Routledge, 2008).

Monroe, E., *Britain's Moment in the Middle East. 1914–1956* (London: Chatto, 1963).

Moore, J. N., *The Arab-Israeli Conflict: Readings* (Princeton NJ: Princeton University Press, 1975).

Morikawa, J., *Japan and Africa* (London: Hurst, 1997).

Moscrop, L. J., *Measuring Jerusalem: the Palestine Exploration Fund and British Interests in the Holy Land* (New York: Leicester University Press, 2000).

Nash, G., 'Politics, Aesthetics and Quest in British Travel Writing on the Middle East', in T. Youngs (ed.), *Travel Writing in the Nineteenth Century* (London: Anthem Press, 2006).

Nasr, V., *The Shia Revival* (New York: Norton, 2006).

Nicolaïdis, K., Sèbe, B., and Maas, G. (eds), *Echoes of Empire: Memory, Identity and Colonial Legacies* (London: I. B. Tauris, 2015).

Nisan, M., *Minorities in the Middle East: A History of Struggle and Self-Expression* (Jefferson NC: McFarland, 2002).

Nursi, S., *Letters, 1928–1932* (Istanbul: Sözler, 1993).

O'Connor, M., 'Epigraphic Semitic Scripts', in P. Daniels and W. Bright (eds), *The World's Writing System* (Oxford: Oxford University Press, 1996).

Ohaegbulam, F. U., *Nationalism in Colonial and Post-Colonial Africa* (Washington DC: University Press of America, 1977).

Orosius, P., *Historiarum adversum paganos libri*, vol. 6 (Leipzig: Teubner, 1889).

Osterhammel, J., *The Transformation of the World* (Princeton NJ: Princeton University Press, 2014).

Ouar, L., *Le procès de l'impérialisme et du colonialisme français: l'Algérie, bastion de la résistance* (Algiers: Entreprise Nationale du Livre, 1986).

Owen, R., *The Middle East in the World Economy, 1800–1914* (London: I. B. Tauris, 2002).

Özil, A., *Orthodox Christians in the Late Ottoman Empire: A Study of Communal Relations in Anatolia* (New York: Routledge, 2013).

Palestine Royal Commission Report (London: HMSO, 1937).

Pappé, I., *The Rise and Fall of a Palestinian Dynasty: The Husaynis, 1700–1948* (Berkeley: University of California Press, 2011).

Papstein, R., 'From Ethnic Identity to Tribalism: The Upper Zambezi Region of Zambia, 1830–1981', in L. Vail (ed.), *The Creation of Tribalism in Southern Africa* (Berkeley: University of California Press, 1991).

Pearlman, E., 'The Representation of Jews on Edwardian Postcards', in B. Cheyette and N. Valman (eds), *The Image of the Jew in European Liberal Culture, 1789–1914* (London: Vallentine Mitchell, 2004).

Peirce, L., 'An Imperial Caste', in M. R. Greer, W. D. Mignolo, and M. Quilligan (eds), *Rereading the Black Legend* (Chicago: University of Chicago Press, 2007).

Philip, T., 'From Rule of Law to Constitutionalism: The Ottoman Context of Arab Political Thought', in J. Hanssen and M. Weiss (eds), *Arabic Thought Beyond the Liberal Age* (Cambridge: Cambridge University Press, 2016).

Pollard, L., *Nurturing the Nation* (Berkeley: University of California Press, 2005).

Polner, M. and Woods, T. E., *We Who Dared to Say No to War: American Antiwar Writing from 1812 to Now* (New York: Basic Books, 2008).

Porter, J. L., *A Handbook for Travellers in Syria and Palestine*, vol. 1 (London: John Murray, 1858).

Price, R., *Fast Facts on the Middle East Conflict* (Eugene OR: Harvest, 2003).

Purcell, H., *Lloyd George* (London: Haus, 2006).

Quataert, D., *The Ottoman Empire, 1700–1922* (Cambridge: Cambridge University Press, 2000).

Quigley, J., *The Statehood of Palestine* (Cambridge: Cambridge University Press, 2010).

Ra'ad, Basem L., *Hidden Histories* (London: Pluto Press, 2010).

Rabi, U. (ed.), *Tribes and States in a Changing Middle East* (London: Hurst, 2016).

Rafeq, A. K. 'A Different Balance of Power: Europe and the Middle East in the Eighteenth and Nineteenth Centuries', in Y. M. Choueiri (ed.), *A Companion to the History of the Middle East* (Oxford: Blackwell, 2005).

Ranger, T., *The Invention of Tribalism in Zimbabwe* (Gweru: Mambo Press, 1985).

Renton, J., *The Zionist Masquerade: The Birth of the Anglo-Zionist Alliance 1914–1918* (New York: Palgrave, 2007).

Reynaud, P., *Mémoires*, vol. 1 (Paris: Flammarion, 1960).

Rich, P. J., *Iraq and Gertrude Bell's The Arab of Mesopotamia* (Lanham MD: Lexington Books, 2008).

Richardson, J., *A Dictionary, Persian, Arabic, and English*, vol. 1 (London: Bulmer, 1806).

Robbins, K., *Sir Edward Grey* (London: Cassell, 1971).

Robson, L., *Colonialism and Christianity in Mandate Palestine* (Austin TX: University of Texas Press, 2011).

Robson, L. (ed.), *Minorities and the Modern Arab World* (Syracuse NY: Syracuse University Press, 2016).

Rodinson, M., *Israel and the Arabs* (London: Penguin, 1982).

Rogan, E., *Frontiers of the State in the Late Ottoman Empire: Transjordan, 1850–1921* (Cambridge: Cambridge University Press, 1999).

Rogan, E., *The Fall of the Ottomans: The Great War in the Middle East, 1914–1920* (New York: Basic Books, 2015).

Rose, N., *Chaim Weizmann: A Biography* (New York: Penguin, 1989).

Rowe, N., *Raising Dust: A Cultural History of Dance in Palestine* (London: I. B. Tauris, 2010).

Ruppin, A., *Three Decades of Palestine* (Westport CT: Greenwood, 1936).

Russell, G., *Heirs to Forgotten Kingdoms* (London: Simon & Schuster, 2014).

Russell, M. B., *The Middle East and South Asia* (Lanham MD: Rowman, 2014).

Rutherford, A., 'The Geography of Ethnic Violence', in P. Vos Fellman, Y. Bar-Yam and A. A. Minai (eds), *Conflict and Complexity* (New York: Springer, 2015).

Sabrī, M., *L'empire égyptien sous Mohamed-Ali et la question d'Orient* [The Egyptian Empire under Mohamed-Ali and the Eastern Question] (Paris: Geuthner, 1930).

Sachar, H. M., *Farewell Espana: The World of the Sephardim Remembered* (New York: Vintage Books, 1994).

Sachar, H. M., *A History of Israel: From the Rise of Zionism to Our Time* (New York: Knopf, 2006).

Said, E., *Culture and Imperialism* (London: Vintage, 1993).

Said, E., *Orientalism* (New York: Vintage, 1994).

Samuel, H., *Great Britain and Palestine* (London: The Jewish Historical Society of England, 1935).

Samuel H., *Mémoirs* (London: Cresset Press, 1945).

Sanders, R., *The High Walls of Jerusalem* (New York: Holt, 1984).

Sangambo, M. K., *The History of the Luvale People and their Chieftainship* (Zambezi: Mize Palace, 1984).

Sarshar, H. M. (ed.), *The Jews of Iran* (London: I. B. Tauris, 2014).

Scham, P., Salem, W. and Pogrund, B. (eds), *Shared Histories* (Walnut Creek CA: Left Coast Press, 2005).

Schneer, J., *The Balfour Declaration* (London: Bloomsbury, 2010).

Schölch, A. (ed.), *Palestinians over the Green Line* (London: Ithaca Press, 1983).

Schorske, C. E., *Fin-de-siècle Vienna* (New York: Vintage Books, 1981).

Scott, C. P., *The Political Diaries of C. P. Scott, 1911–1928* (London: Collins, 1970).

Scott, J. C. *Seeing Like a State* (New Haven CT: Yale University Press, 1998).

Sharkey, H. J., *A History of Muslims, Christians, and Jews in the Middle East* (Cambridge: Cambridge University Press, 2017).

Shorter, A., *East African Societies* (London: Routledge, 1974).

Sicker, M., *Reshaping Palestine: From Muhammad Ali to the British Mandate, 1831–1922* (Westport CT: Praeger, 1999).

Smith, A., *Ethno-symbolism and Nationalism* (London: Routledge, 2009).

Smuts, J. C., *The League of Nations. A Practical Suggestion* (London: Hodder, 1918).

Smuts, J. C., *Africa and Some World Problems: Including the Rhodes Memorial Lectures Delivered in Michaelmas Term* (Oxford: The Clarendon Press, 1930).

Smuts, J. C., *Jan Christian Smuts: A Biography* (New York: Morrow, 1952).

Sokolow, N., *History of Zionism*, vol. 1 (London: Longmans, Green, 1919).

Stein, L., *The Balfour Declaration* (New York: Simon & Schuster, 1961).

Steinfield, M., *Our Racist Presidents* (San Ramon CA: Consensus, 1972).

Stillman, N., 'The Jews in the Medieval Arabic-Speaking World', in A. T. Levenson (ed.), *Jews and Judaism* (Chichester: Wiley-Blackwell, 2012).

Storrs, R., *Lawrence of Arabia: Zionism and Palestine* (New York: Penguin, 1943).

Şükrü Hanioğlu, M., *A Brief History of the Late Ottoman Empire* (Princeton NJ: Princeton University Press, 2008).

Sykes, C., *Crossroads to Israel* (Bloomington IN: Indiana University Press, 1973).

Sykes, M., *Through Five Turkish Provinces* (London: Bickers, 1900).

Sykes, M., *The Caliphs' Last Heritage* (London: Macmillan, 1915).

Sykes, M., Smith J. H., and Brown, E. G., *Dar-ul-Islam* (London: Bickers, 1904).

Symes, G. S., *Tour of Duty* (London: Collins, 1946).

Szajkowski, Z., *Jews, Wars, and Communism*, vol. 2 (New York: Ktav, 1972).

Tamarī, S., *The Great War* (Oakland CA: University of California Press, 2017).

Tansuğ, F., *İzmir/Smyrna 1826–1864* (Peter Lang: Berlin, 2018).

Telhami, S. and Barnett, M. (eds), *Identity and Foreign Policy in the Middle East* (New York: Cornell University Press, 2002).

Terzibaşoğlu, Y., 'Land Disputes and Ethno-politics: Northwestern Anatolia, 1877–1912', in S. L. Engerman and J. Metzer, *Land Rights, Ethno-nationality, and Sovereignty in History* (London: Routledge, 2004).

Thucydides, *History of the Peloponnesian War* (New York: Penguin Books, 1954 [first English trans. 1550]).

Ṭībāwī, A., *A Modern History of Syria, Including Lebanon and Palestine* (New York: Macmillan, 1969).

Ṭībāwī, A. L., *Anglo-Arab Relations and the Question of Palestine, 1914–1921* (London: Luzac, 1977).

Tilley, V., *The One-State Solution* (Ann Arbor MI: University of Michigan Press, 2005).

Toynbee, A. J., *Acquaintances* (Oxford: Oxford University Press, 1967).

Traboulsi, F., *A History of Modern Lebanon* (London: Pluto Press, 2007).

Tuchman, B., *Bible and Sword* (New York: New York University Press, 1956).

Turner, J., *Britain and the First World War* (London: Unwin Hyman, 1988).

Ubicini, M. A., *Lettres sur la Turquie*, vol. II (Paris: Dumaine, 1854).

Università Commerciale Luigi Bocconi, *Annuario* (Milan: Società Tipografica Editrice Popolare, 1903).

van Dyke, H., *Out-Of-Doors in the Holy Land* (New York: Scribner, 1908).

van Ess, Josef, 'Abd al-Malik and the Dome of the Rock: An Analysis of Some Texts', in J. Raby and J. Johns (eds), *Bayt Al-Maqdis*, vol. 1 (Oxford: Oxford University Press, 1992).

Wallerstein, I., *World-Systems Analysis* (Durham NC: Duke University Press, 2004).

Warburton, E., *The Crescent and the Cross*, vol. 1 (New York: Wiley, 1845).

Weizmann, C., *Trial and Error: The Autobiography of Chaim Weizmann* (Westport CT: Greenwood, 1972).

Weizmann, C., *The Letters and Papers of Chaim Weizmann*, vol. 6 (Oxford: Oxford University Press, 1973).

Weizmann, C. (ed. B. Litvinoff), *The Essential Chaim Weizmann* (London: Weidenfeld & Nicolson, 1982).

Weizmann, C., *The Letters and Papers of Chaim Weizmann*, vol. 1 (New Brunswick NJ: Transaction Publishers, 1983).

Wells, H. G., *The War that Will End War* (London: Palmer, 1914).

Weulersse, J., *Paysans de Syrie et du Proche-Orient* [Farmers in Syria and the Middle East] (Paris: Gallimard, 1946).

White, B., *The Emergence of Minorities in the Middle East* (Edinburgh: Edinburgh University Press, 2011).

Wilson, C. T., *Peasant Life in the Holy Land* (London: John Murray, 1906)

Wilson, C. W., *Picturesque Palestine, Sinai, and Egypt* (New York: Appleton, 1881).

Wilson, W., *A History of the American People*, vol. V (New York: Cosimo, 2008).

Wishnitzer, A., *Reading Clocks, Alla Turca: Time and Society in Late Ottoman Empire* (Chicago: University of Chicago Press, 2015).

Yapp, M., *The Making of the Modern Near East 1792–1923* (London: Routledge, 1988).

Yaqub, D., *Imperfect Strangers: Americans, Arabs, and U.S.–Middle East Relations in the 1970s* (New York: Cornell University Press, 2016).

Yazbak, M., *Haifa in the Late Ottoman Period, 1864–1914: A Muslim Town in Transition* (Leiden: Brill, 1998).

Yehoshua, A. B., *Elogio della normalità* [Praising of Normality] (Florence: Giuntina, 1991).

Yossef, A. and Cerami, J. R., *The Arab Spring and the Geopolitics of the Middle East* (London: Palgrave, 2015).

Zhang, W., *Confucianism and Modernization* (New York: Palgrave, 2000).

Zolla, E., *Uscite dal mondo* [Out of this World] (Milan: Adelphi, 1992).

Zurayk, R. and Gough, A. 'Bread and Olive Oil: The Agrarian Roots of the Arab Uprising', in F. Gerges (ed.), *The New Middle East: Protest and Revolution in the Arab World* (Cambridge: Cambridge University Press, 2014).

Zwierlein, C., *Imperial Unknowns* (Cambridge: Cambridge University Press, 2016).

Index

EU Authorised Representative:

Easy Access System Europe Mustamäe tee 50, 10621 Tallinn, Estonia

gpsr.requests@easproject.com

Printed and bound by CPI Group (UK) Ltd, Croydon, CR0 4YY

31/03/2026

02081409-0001